ON WRITING

ON WRITING

A.L. KENNEDY

JONATHAN CAPE

LONDON

Published by Jonathan Cape 2013

2 4 6 8 10 9 7 5 3 1

Copyright © A.L. Kennedy 2013

A.L. Kennedy has asserted her right under the Copyright, Designs
and Patents Act 1988 to be identified as the author of this work

First published in Great Britain in 2013 by
Jonathan Cape
Random House, 20 Vauxhall Bridge Road,
London SW1V 2SA

www.vintage-books.co.uk

Addresses for companies within The Random House Group Limited can be found at:
www.randomhouse.co.uk/offices.htm

The Random House Group Limited Reg. No. 954009

A CIP catalogue record for this book is available from the British Library

ISBN 9780224096973

The Random House Group Limited supports The Forest Stewardship Council (FSC®),
the leading international forest certification organisation. Our books carrying the
FSC label are printed on FSC® certified paper. FSC is the only forest certification
scheme endorsed by the leading environmental organisations, including Greenpeace.
Our paper procurement policy can be found at:
www.randomhouse.co.uk/environment

Typeset in Adobe Garamond by Palimpsest Book Production,
Falkirk, Stirlingshire

Printed and bound in Great Britain
by Clays Ltd, St Ives PLC

Contents

Introduction

The blogs which make up the greater part of this book were written with a number of aims in mind. I intended to write regular, brief pieces which might in some way be useful to writers. I sought to make technical suggestions, offer general support and occasionally focus on specific areas of the writing life. I am fairly certain this process has helped me more than anyone else, but newer writers have been very kind about some of the content. I also intended to provide something of interest to those who had no wish to write, but who were interested in the process of writing. And I wanted to explore the positive role that the arts in general, and reading and writing in particular, can play in any life. If the tone of some pieces seems overly light-hearted, I can only say that I also intended to cheer readers and writers along during a period in which British publishing, writing and the wider world of arts activity can seem both beleaguered and self-defeating. I am also aware that even people who love writing and are free to write may sometimes need something to smile about. I have hoped to be entertaining.

The blogs are largely unaltered from their original form, beyond small edits and some insertions to provide context. They cover something over three years – from the conclusion of a book of short stories, through the writing and publication of a novel and on to work for the next book of short stories. Although the blog continues, it seemed somehow fitting to begin with one anthology and end with another. The book runs through a period of prolonged ill health in 2011, during which my ability to write the blogs was a great comfort and some kind of proof that I was still partly functional. At the time of writing, I am well and am determined to remember that ill-governed schedules, bad working practices and minor illnesses are recurrent themes throughout the book. I should take better care of myself. I probably won't.

The blogs are followed by a short talk written for BBC radio, looking a little more personally at one aspect of my life as a writer. You will also find a lecture, 'To Save Our Lives', delivered for the London Arts in Health Forum at their London Creativity and Well-Being Week in the summer of 2012, and then three more technical pieces intended primarily for writers and which explore writing workshops, the development of character in fiction and the pursuit and support of voice.

The final piece here is a transcript of 'Words', the one-person show about writing and language which I have toured with for a number of years. The show has been performed in several countries and at a variety of festivals. This book, in fact, pretty much covers the active period of the script, which has now been retired – although I have retired it several times already and it seems unwilling to disappear completely as a performance. I hadn't fully anticipated what a positive and encouraging experience acting out my professional passions would prove to be and I am very grateful to all of the audiences who attended. Various recordings of the piece do exist and there are plans to make a definitive audio version, but there has been a certain demand for a written version to be made available. The show was designed to sound spontaneous, in as far as I could simulate spontaneity, and so it will not read as a piece of straight prose.

I am aware that certain themes and key inspirations do repeat through this material: Chekhov, Shakespeare, love, my grandfather, working with other writers, the importance of creative activity, the importance of self-maintenance, my inability to stay that far away from a train for any length of time. In my defence, I would say that I feel some points are worth repeating and that I am only glad my inspirations do run through my life and work with any kind of regularity.

In conclusion, I would thank the readers of the blog – and those who also follow me on Twitter – for their support and for the community of letters they seem to have developed over time. I would also thank the students and staff involved with the Warwick Writing Programme for the continuing inspiration they provide, and my agent Antony Harwood and my editor Robin Robertson for their continuing support. It would be impossible for me to adequately express my gratitude for the part that reading and writing have played, and continue to play, in my life.

A.L. Kennedy
August 2012, London

Blog

Blog

I

On the road again . . . Somebody – I am currently too tired to remember who – once described me as *The Littlest Hobo of Literature*. Although I save far fewer orphans (in fact, none) and lack the buoyant charm of the raggle-eared original, I can currently see what they meant. I do have a home, of course. I know that it contains furniture, tinned foodstuffs and items of clothing (probably black) that I may never have worn. I also know I don't really live there. So – less time worrying about the neighbours and more time worrying about why so many B&Bs are run by former law-enforcement personnel. On the one hand, their emergency-related skills are probably cracking and, on the other, they clearly harbour a pressing need to lock people up overnight in tiny rooms with inadequate plumbing and facilities. When I started writing no one told me it would come to this.

But I do try to tell other people what it will come to – hence my occasional visits to Warwick University and its Creative Writing students. They want to write, they have application and vigour, they've all come on since I read them last and yet . . . it would be unfair not to remind them of how horrible their futures may become. If they're unsuccessful, they'll be clattering through a global Depression with a skill no one requires, a writing demon gnawing at their spine to be expressed and a delicately nurtured sensitivity which will only make their predicaments seem worse – and all of it of minimal interest to anyone else. If they're successful, they still may not make a living, will travel more than a drug-mule, may be so emotionally preoccupied that they remain unblissfully ignorant of entire relationships, will have to deal with media demands they don't even want to understand and may wear far too much black. (Yes, it is slimming, but unisex Richard III isn't always what every occasion demands. Trust me – experience is a painful teacher.)

Naturally, I don't believe anyone will be deterred by my mad-eyed and negative rantings. Once somebody wants to write it's almost impossible to stop them without also killing them to some significant degree. Nothing beats that raging delight at three in the morning when sentence number fifteen finally agrees to do what you want, and never has banging wiggly marks on to a computer screen seemed so heroic – even if you're simply ensuring that the orthopaedic surgeon ravishing your senior nurse in the sluice room doesn't seem implausibly limber and can meanwhile reawaken echoes of that summer afternoon with her funny uncle . . . And if you think you might actually be doing some good, amusing someone other than yourself – making them less lonely, more alive, more informed – well, you're just not going to chuck that over in favour of crafting, long walks and a quiet life. Hence the number of regimes and leaders who have discovered that killing writers until they are entirely dead is the only effective way to slow their output. And may angels and ministers of grace preserve the students, and indeed myself, from any shades of that. It's quite possible we feel hard done by – writers often do – but, for individuals trapped in a society intent upon eating its own tongue, we're probably doing fairly well.

And I try not to mention the publishing industry to the students – the legions of people with names like Miffy, Muffy, Tufty: *is there anybody out there who isn't one of Santa's little helpers?* – and the fact that it's all been spiralling into recession ever since the Net Book Agreement went south. Countries that are keen on having a national literature haven't followed that path, but we have to make the best of what we've got: which is deep discounts, dump bins and more mindless staring than you'd get from a warren full of rabbits trapped at the Indy 500. Weirdly, the bleakness may even be a help to the artistically inclined. I set off on my wonky career path during the Thatcher years, when unemployment was so massive that a non-proper job didn't seem any more foolish than, say, working in a bank. Now that so many of us dream of bitch-slapping bankers up and down the high street and there are, once again, no safe havens, new writers may feel they have nothing to lose by taking the plunge into typing. I'm a creature of extremes, I'll admit, but surely it is generally better to live a life that tries to find its own edges and push them a bit, rather than simply settling for habitual numbness.

And some days those edges may involve going over other people's manuscripts (much less upsetting than going over your own) in a borrowed office all day and then trying to rewrite a play all night in an extremely secure bedroom, while living on Red Bull, Complan and iron tablets. That does cover each of the food groups, I believe. Next week it's a photographer (why I said *yes* to that, I've no idea – there's already ample evidence abroad that I'm a gurning, horse-faced muppet), more rewrites, inventing a synopsis of something that doesn't exist and may never have to, learning a one-hour show about writing and trying to forget that I need to sleep. Onwards.

II

O nce again my life is taking the road less travelled without packing enough sandwiches for the trip.

Gripe Number One: I am in Belfast. I have no problem with Belfast *per se*, it's a lovely town, but I should currently be in Glasgow. My massive fear of flying means that I'm relying on ferries to get me home – ferries which aren't sailing today because of gales.

Gripe Number Two: my left ear has taken to aching and developing obscure infections whenever I've had to go without food, sleep, light and tickling for weeks at a time. I had it syringed last year, and I feel exposure to the open air has left it feeling shy and wayward. At the start of this month I had been under the unusual and exhilarating impression that all was well with me, my skull and parts appertaining thereunto. I then scampered down to London – as you do – so that I could read an essay and play the banjo for a BBC wireless emission – as you do if you inhabit some kind of alternative, unmusical reality. The banjoing and basic literacy test went fine, but my ear was already becoming unruly and I was aware that my week was due to run, if not gallop, between London, Glasgow, Manchester, Belfast, Dublin, Waterford and Backagain. (I had high hopes of Backagain.) This meant my best option for health and safety was to find a quick and available doctor in the Central London area, lest the sinister side of my head should decompose inconveniently.

Gripe Number Three: as it turned out, there was only one 'private clinic' which could see me during the five hours I had available. Lovely though the establishment was, in a homely and vaguely unhygienic way, the place was clearly geared towards patients afflicted by ailments too embarrassing for their family doctor, rather than those seeking, say, celebrity breast adjustments – or suffering from ear infections. I therefore entered the consulting room – which cunningly doubled as a storage cupboard – and proceeded to be examined at cross-purposes.

'What's wrong?'

'I have an ear infection.'

'Well, just pop up on the examination . . . shelf there and remove your jeans and hampering underthings.'

'Um . . . Thanks for asking, but I actually have an ear infection.'

'Of course you do. You'll find there's enough space to lie down between the paper towels and those boxes of stool-softener.'

'No, I mean I have an ear infection that's in my ear.'

'If you can just remove your things.'

'And afterwards will you look at my ear?'

I left with some horse tablets and proceeded to Manchester for a workshop and a reading, which may have gone well, but mainly seemed far away and wibbly under the influence of whatever the pills were. Still, at least my ear was hurting less.

Gripe Number Four: a Manchester audience member subsequently took it upon himself to rid my Wikipedia entry of its fallacious reference to my keeping a pet luwak. I mentioned during the reading that I have never owned a luwak and have never said I do – there is simply at least one person who enjoys adding local colour to my Global Information Presence. Someone, for that matter, also submits Amazon book reviews in my name, which is rather puerile and tedious of them – but I have to say that I do miss my imaginary luwak, now he's gone. I had decided to call him Wiki and had already bought him imaginary chew-toys and taken him on imaginary outings to nearby parks.

Meanwhile, on I went to Waterford and its small, but jim-dandy Seán Dunne Literary Festival. My outward journey was accomplished without the aid of air transport – by train, ferry, cab, train, cab and train – and went off without a hitch, although the poker school in the back of the Belfast cab was slightly disconcerting, and sprinting for the last connection at Dublin, Heuston, while still on my tablets did leave me wondering whether their powerful effects had accidentally challenged my spinal column in some unhappy way. My very visible distress caused a kindly train guard to hold the service and also to nip out and gather up the many important belongings I had dropped while I ran, returning them to me softly as I curled up on the floor in a luggage storage area and twitched myself into a better frame of mind.

Gripe Number Five: although the Waterford gigs went fine and the show for Edinburgh is shaping up well, the hotel lift made the most extraordinary variety of retro-sci-fi noises I've ever encountered. All night, every night, on it would go – MWAWhhaaooooo . . . neeneeneeneeneenee . . . MWARNngngng . . . My dodgy ear prevented me from using earplugs and so I either lay awake or dreamed fitfully of being strapped inside the Tardis while the cast of *Blake's* 7 played didgeridoos at me with evil intent.

Gripe Number Six: if I'm lucky, tomorrow will see me arriving at possibly the world's most hideous ferry terminal, Stranraer. Even on a bright and balmy day, every surly inch of it suggests it was constructed in a hurry by condemned men on loan from Stalin's Russia and was intended for the transportation and/or slaughter of livestock. But off I go, in any case. Onwards.

III

From time to time I do ponder what actually inspires writers – or, indeed, anyone. We typing folk are meant – apparently – to thrive and prosper if we attend workshops. And people who provide workshops certainly make money out of selling them as a necessary thing. I myself – not being especially sociable – didn't much enjoy the few workshops I attended in my youth, other than as an opportunity to meet people I hadn't made up earlier and as a reminder that the insides of strangers' heads are occasionally much more bizarre than I might assume. As a tutor I feel that workshops are often designed to make all those involved feel they're achieving something, while taking part in an activity that is almost exactly not writing. They fill up time, if not timetables: that, and you can maybe flirt a bit in them, should you wish to embark upon something with a scribbler. Poorly balanced workshops can very easily descend into a horrible demonstration of what happens when the verbally blind lead the creatively deaf with a bit of arty bullying and random rule-invention thrown in for colour. And overly dominated ones simply offer the tutor an opportunity to do something which would more usually involve personal fluids and some DVDs in the privacy of their own lovely home.

But what does make you/me/someone else want to rush for the keyboard/notebook/back of the hand with a lumpy biro?

There is the *sitting alone in a black polo neck at the edge of a café* type of option, but outside of certain tolerant and bohemian areas this kind of behaviour may elicit derisive nostril-snorting from passers-by and perhaps murmurs of *Tosser*, accompanied by non-lethal assaults – which is fair enough, really. If you're lucky, published and better at small talk than I am, you may happen upon the offer of an empty holiday home, Tuscan villa, artists' colony or partially restored Bond-villain volcano lair in which to snuggle yourself and your muse away for some serious creating – but if you have a day job, friends, family, lovers, or value your sanity, then high levels of geographical isolation may not be for you. (Curiously, although I lack many of the elements reputedly essential to 'having a life', even I would baulk at being trapped in a picturesque setting far from conventional policing and then forcing myself to deal with the creative despair of others, tetchy sculptors, the horrors of communal dining and perhaps compulsory soirées with Lady Tabitha and her rare-breed llamas. It's bad enough trying to type in my study.)

I can't speak for anyone else, but I find more interesting avenues and areas of inspiration arise from a mental commitment to find everything inspirational. This means my environment need not change, but my mindset undoubtedly may. And it's really cheap. I'm not saying this is anything like perfect in practice, but if I can approach my life with some kind of interested enthusiasm, then it can become inspirational. (Sounds appallingly self-helpy, doesn't it? But, once again, I would emphasise – cheap and convenient.)

To fling in a practical example, the very excellent gentleman and decorator who painted my mother's bathroom is also a falconer. This made it not entirely complicated or difficult for me to arrange a small encounter with, as it happened, a dapper and highly intelligent Harris hawk this week. The hawk could not have helped being fascinating, even if it had tried by wearing an anorak, or pretending to be a mallard. I have no idea if or when I will make use of Mr Hawk, but he will have rattled something somewhere which will eventually rattle something else and meanwhile it was a blast to meet him. Please note that the *being inspired by everything* option does offer the handy and acceptable-even-to-Calvinists effect of generating treats of this kind, for purely professional reasons. *It's not really fun with Mr Hawk – it's work.* Plus, the next time I talk to any writing students I can tell them about the way a hawk's head and body are so very alert and flexible and mobile, while mentioning that their eyes have exactly the killer focus that you would expect from a focused killer. That level of focus in a writer might be no bad thing.

And, talking of good eyes and focus, I was delighted to parcel myself off on Friday and visit the new perhaps-portrait of Shakespeare. Although soaking myself in Shakespeare every summer as a nipper made me want to be a writer, I still wasn't sure what I'd get out of seeing his face (should it be his face), given that he remains dead and therefore unavailable for chats. But it was worth a whirl, just to see what would happen – and possibly to uncover what kind of a man his words had caused me to inadvertently assume he might be. As it turns out, the portrait, which is aesthetically pleasing in itself, does seem peculiarly convincing – the big and sad and clever eyes, the sexy mouth, the weak chin and exceptionally neat beard, the weirdly big hair, concealing a catastrophically retreating hairline. The overall effect chimes remarkably well with the Shakespeare I've built in my head. Whoever it is looks intelligent, interestingly risky and extremely alive. And to bring me back to our theme – in as far as we have one – being extremely alive is a real possibility for anyone intending to use, for instance, writing as an excuse for paying attention to their life.

On a train again at the moment, I am heading for home with

two small nubbins of inspiration, both of which are still settling and thumping against each other as they do so. I have an enlarged sense of Shakespeare as muscle and blood, as someone more and less than the words (whatever he looked like) and an odd little reminder of the risk in his writing, another angle on that big dark edge. I also have another angle on how grateful I am that other people wrote before me, gave me all kinds of things as a reader and allowed me to be (in a very small way) a writer – to have a profession when I was otherwise unemployable. And, thanks to the Harris hawk, *A lover's eyes will gaze an eagle blind* gets a whole new kick. Tomorrow I get to find something majestical and of use in washing and ironing a travel-week's worth of clothes. Yeah, well, if I could actually do that, I'd be a majestical and useful author. As it is, I do what I can. Onwards.

IV

Well, I know I'm still here because I can feel me breathing – other than that, it's all up for grabs. Since I last wrote I have, Dear Reader, been in Glasgow, Ullapool, Aberdeen, Oxford, London, Bakewell, Tissington and various bits of leafy Warwickshire. This is partly a continuation of my cunning plan to inspire the bejeezus out of myself with random experiences – Tissington involved well-dressing, for example. I had never seen a dressed well before and will henceforth be shocked if I meet a well in a state of undress. 'Lawks-a-mercy!' I shall cry. 'A bare-nekkid well. I must avert my eyes.'

Mainly, however, my travelling is a testament to the truly impressive number of literary festivals with which the UK now provides itself. All over the country, large and small organisations bring together appropriately sized numbers of readers and other interested parties to have, in the widest possible sense, literary experiences that are at the very least fun (if not inspiring) and which are woefully under-represented in the wider media. How long these particular gatherings will last is anybody's guess as publishers cut expenses to the bone, through the bone and out to the threadbare trousering on the other side. (I was thinking of a leg bone. If you weren't, you're just going to have to imagine someone who can't dress themselves proper, or picture a sleeve or other suitable habiliment all by yourself. I know you'll manage.) Publishers currently subsidise travel and accommodation for many festival appearances, and withdrawing this support may mean some smaller festivals fold – which would be quietly tragic, because festivals kindle, meet and encourage a range of excellent things to do and be, which might otherwise simply remain undiscovered, or make a noise like a hoop and roll away for lack of support. At the very least, festivals add to the sum of human happiness and sell books.

And, on a related topic, now *The South Bank Show*'s gone. Is this wise? I know *SBS* didn't involve yelling or tits and was therefore unsuitable for British television, but I've met so many people who sat at home like me when they were nippers and/or teenagers and had their heads tickled open and their sanity saved by that show. There we were, possibly feeling we were slightly strange compared with our surroundings, and there Melvyn was with his diddly theme tune and a weekly blast of things we'd guessed we might like and ended up loving. He also, perhaps more importantly, supplied bushels of stuff we'd never heard of, or might have avoided, and worlds and worlds of unimagined possibility – there other people were, imagining those possibilities; we could hear from them, see them. When I was young, unsure of most things, buried alive in Dundee and gave every sign of being unable to find a job that wouldn't make me crazy and then fired, *SBS* was like getting a weekly jolt of oxygen and hope. It's our loss if we let it go without at least an equivalent replacement and some kind of thank-you.

No, it's particularly the loss of the generation from whom we have already stolen an education system, a functioning and credible democracy and a variety of other things they might have found useful. It's not that I like all children indiscriminately – some of them are appalling – but I would rather they didn't grow up being more than averagely miserable and under-fulfilled.

Meanwhile, and on a not-unrelated topic, let's talk about Ullapool. It runs a great wee festival all the way up in the far(ish) North – next stop, Isle Martin and the Summer Isles – with the listeningest audiences I've ever met. It provided me with a weekend of talk and thought and a genuine sense of one long conversation/meditation being conducted over the course of consecutive events. The organisers looked after everyone extremely well with friendly attention to detail in a remarkable location. In that kind of environment writers can really get to know each other – and their audiences – and exchange ideas. (Most of us were too old or too married to exchange anything else – just think of sleeves; they'll calm you if your mind was wandering to shady places.) Everyone there got to throw ideas around and appreciate a genuinely resourceful and imaginative community. And our final conclusion as a sunny Sunday eased its way towards lunch? That none of what we do would be worth doing or would really mean much without love.

Dreadful, I know – but we'd got all relaxed and unparanoid and truthful and there it was: love. At which point I have to cough a lot and think about death to counteract any disturbing or embarrassing sensations of well-being.

Death was, of course, present up in Ullapool – as it is everywhere else. I was forcibly reminded of the Reaper presence as I made an ultimately unsuccessful attempt to rescue an unwell gannet on one of Ullapool's beaches. Gannets, it turns out, are remarkably heavy birds and can be tetchy. I ended up simply having the thing die in my arms – after forty-five minutes of carriage – as I approached the outskirts of Ullapool. I feel you may agree that it is socially uncomfortable to meet a succession of strollers and dog walkers as you carry a suddenly stiffened, wings-outstretched and madly staring dead gannet. (Yes, and I didn't know they do that when they die, either.)

And please don't write in. I was advised to try carrying it, had covered its head, had not chased it about . . . it was just a very poorly gannet. I have since received a surprisingly high number of gannet emails, gannet postcards and gannet-related items. Obviously, the idea of a gannet-bearing novelist catches the imagination, somehow. I can only say that divesting oneself of a large, very blue-eyed and rigid corpse at the edge of a small and inquisitive town is something I would not necessarily wish upon you. Onwards.

V

Ah, Dear Readers – I now know for sure and certain that, counted all together, you would add up to more than double figures. How do I know this? Because the disturbing gush of gannet-related items and communications has not abated, although I am now weeks away from the Ullapool Gannet Incident. (See previous post.) I can even identify chums out from amongst their surroundings and other faces (I am not good at facial recognition) because my pals will be the ones imitating dead gannets. That, or spasming, staring and simulated wing contortions are all side-effects of swine-flu and I have lately been chatting warmly to a number of infectious strangers. I do, after all, occasionally live in what we probably now have to call a Pandemic Hot Spot.

The decision to move the official swine-flu description from *epidemic* to *pandemic* is, of course, interesting to a wordsmith. *Epidemic* suggests bodies in the street, plague pits and disease lurking in your cupboards and breathing-air. *Pandemic* sounds much worse, but is more about geography than numbers – although it's about numbers too. So an initial response to *pandemic* which runs, 'Ooh, Nelly, you mean we're all going to die? This morning? I must laminate my children at once', rapidly declines into – 'Oh, just some people coughing in a number of different countries . . . right . . . So I can still sneeze on old ladies for a lark, then? And lick door knobs?'

Medical language tends to be *challenging* – a word currently used as a shorthand for 'If this problem doesn't kill you, we probably will.' I still remember that I missed my grandfather by half an hour because I was unable to translate *quite poorly* into *could die at any moment*. Not that I in any way lack admiration for people who spend parts of most days having to say (or obliquely hint) to other people that someone they care for very much will be leaving this earthly plane directly. See? Hard to talk about death. Hard to say – 'She's dead. He's already started decomposing. Her digestive system has begun digesting itself – as, eventually, yours will – unless you fall into a volcano, or experience some especially unusual demise. Oh, and try to avoid those big, sucky in-breaths when you pass the crematorium.'

Meanwhile, August is looming and so my director and I trotted out the one-person show about writing again for an evening at the Centre for Contemporary Arts, Glasgow. We had a very pleasant and appreciative audience, although possibly the fact that the room was hot enough to vaporise lead may mean that we'll be medically challenged in later life. This was the first time I've done 'Words' in a space roughly equivalent to the one in Edinburgh and without a mike – so lots to think about and have fun with. It's been fascinating, working on my literal voice again for a while (in order to be audible and flexible) and seeing that work slowly have an effect on the 'voice' on the page.

I've always been in favour of writers working with their voices. Although we are usually fugitive creatures, often grating (at best) in person and rambling of tongue, writers will almost inevitably end up reading their work in public for many pressing financial reasons. This will very often involve standing in a space specifically designed to make spoken-word events impossible and to irritate all parties involved. There will be noise, there will be atrocious sight-lines, there will be non-functioning mikes, there will be wild pigs in the foyer . . . you simply have to accept that nothing will run smoothly. Meanwhile, as the writer, you have to make the experience as nice as possible for the ladies and gentlemen (I never like kiddies to hear my versions of adult life, in case they become disheartened and go all *Tin Drum* and stunted) who have turned out for the event. Your audience may even have paid money for the reading to happen at them.

Trying to please your audience is not only polite – it's also deeply practical. If a writer can experience their words being enjoyed by others, can make strangers laugh, or go 'Hmmmmm . . .' or sigh, or cry, or clap, or sit – alarmingly – with eyes closed in an attitude of profound concentration, sleep, or death, then the writer can feel more confidence in his or her words and move forward with them. This short-circuits something of that 'playing alone with fake strangers for the benefit of real strangers' aspect of the typing life. Of course, a good reading style can partially conceal the fact that your writing is rubbish – but the aim would be to have your preparation perhaps lead you to reassess and improve your words, to have your desire to touch others enlarge your words and then your presentation assist your words.

And if that all sounds as if we have passed briskly into the Enthusiastically Sticky zone of the Self-Love Continuum, then let us consider the dark side of the equation – the gangly young author trembles behind an unreliable lectern, his or her hands shake, pages fall to the floor, are scrambled after and then reassembled in the wrong order. There is an excruciating pause before his or her stran-gled voice stumbles dryly through a mangling PA system and manages to make shiny, lovely words into a numbing wash of communal shame and boredom. Ten minutes are transformed into an ugly and debilitating lifetime, after which the author plods limply off to the sound of one hand clapping, vowing never to write again.

Which would be what we don't want. Onwards.

*T*he post below refers to the anthology What Becomes.

When my first novel was published there was a small and helpful burst of accompanying publicity which, nevertheless, caused me to feel suddenly exposed, examined and poised on the lip of some horrible pit of compensatory doom – *today* The Guardian *profile, tomorrow the freak case of galloping leprosy/lycanthropy/demonic possession.* In an effort to comfort me, a friend of mine remarked, 'Never mind, it'll all be back to normal soon.' I remember the evening clearly, because it also involved his pouring the contents of a box of Trill down my collar and my chasing him up the street. (We were young, he had a budgie, seed-throwing was popular, all the cool kids were doing it . . .) Of course, my life never did get back to normal, and during weeks like the last one my chum still calls and sepulchrally announces, 'Never mind, it'll all . . .' while I yowl with busyness and tiredness and all the side-effects of still having a job when many others don't, and being able to earn a living as a writer when many others also don't. It seems ungracious to complain, but there are weeks that exceed even my capacity to anticipate extreme workloads, sleep-deprivation, train travel and the naggingly persistent sense that any media exposure will inevitably lead to a hideous disaster of some especially unnameable sort.

So, although – for example – it's always lovely to do things for Radio 4 (they're very polite and kindly and remain a quite civilised part of the BBC), I do get perversely alarmed by the thought that something, somewhere *will end in tears* – if only my day, as I subside into a tepid bath while typing and eating a sandwich and wondering if a blood transfusion from a healthy child would mean I'd clear this month unscathed. Meanwhile, I have to remember what city I'm meant to be in, what I'm meant to be doing and where I put the railway tickets I bought expensively at the last minute to replace the ones I bought cheaply earlier.

Before my plans changed.

Again.

Then there's the book introduction I promised I'd write and the play to be finished and the radio play and the research for the next novel (which is alternately exhilarating and brain-melting – while always being terrifying) and all of the small but persistent requests for prose that seem to rise up with the morning and hang about my shins until I either fall over or deal with them. The danger of this inadvertent lifestyle being that I may end up too tired to be of any use to myself or others and may also fail to have any fun.

No fun for me, no fun for the reader. This isn't a rule I made up – it's a natural law. There has to be joy in the process, or the stuff just dies on the page. Naturally, the possibility of myself being found dead on the page also looms as I curl into yet another Holiday Inn bed, push in the earplugs and hunch under the covers for a nourishing whole three or four hours' kip.

Not that there haven't been bright points as I've barrelled along. At the weekend I was again a judge on the panel for the Warwick Shootout – a short (and moderately impossible) film competition for Warwick University students. All kinds of technical limitations and regulations are heaped upon the entrants, and yet hordes of disgustingly imaginative and talented young production teams still come up with lovely little movies every year. And then we get to give them Perspex award-thingies in recognition of their mad skills in variously designated areas. All this and I get to be on a panel with – among others – the fine man and fine writer, Barrie Keefe.

And the following day involved me running 'Words' at Warwick as part of their free students' arts festival. It was nice to play the studio theatre and to remember doing much the same twenty-five years ago when I was a student at Warwick – and we didn't have an arts festival, or a film competition, or coordinated limb movements. Although we were dab hands at 'Maggie, Maggie, Maggie! Out, out, out!' Ah, those were the days: only a handful of politicians on which to focus your loathing, nothing as exhausting as despising an entire parliament.

Back at home, my big author's box of finished copies arrived a few days ago – so that's the next book done. Although I've seen a number of my own books by now, I always experience the same little shock when I unwrap them and they look so . . . well, like a book – a book that anyone might have written – a proper book, by someone else.

One minute they're a buzzing pain behind your eyes, then they're a screen full of gibberish and rewrites, then they're mangled papers in coffee- and red-stained heaps and then suddenly they've scrubbed up nicely and are off to meet the readers. Or the pulpers. Either way, that first moment you meet what is effectively a neatly bound section of your own mind is certainly an excuse for a short pause, maybe a cup of tea and perhaps a bit of hefting, before you slot it into the shelf with all its brothers and sisters. And in August the new short-story collection will be officially launched, at which point plunging into the media with enthusiasm will be pretty much a parental duty – so off we'll go again, more travel, more paranoia. Onwards.

VII

Workshops – I've already mentioned them briefly in my blog, but they are currently much on my mind. Increasingly such things are being called *masterclasses*, which sounds much more impressive and buzzy and vaguely as if they'll involve an opportunity to be in an airless hotel function suite with a minor deity. I've been giving workshops – and now *masterclasses* – in prose fiction for a period of time I will not mention, for fear of feeling wrinkled and reflecting that I had a bloody cheek to try telling anyone anything for at least the first decade. Then again, giving workshops to people who can't write yet, while we can't write yet either, is a traditional way for nascent writers to earn their crusts. And it means we can meet people who aren't characters bent on resisting our will – real, live people – and learn and consider overviews and be near the process in others and see how lovely it is and how a person can light up when all goes well and a penny drops and so forth . . .

I very, very rarely do anything which involves a bunch of strangers and a flipchart, unless I'm the one inhaling the delicious marker-pen fumes and being – nominally – in charge. But, only this evening, I was reflecting with a chum on a *masterclass* I recently attended which has made me reassess how I run my workshops, not to mention questioning the evil which can lie within the human heart.

First, let us think of the horrible temptations inherent in the workshop scenario. There you are, alone with a largely or completely compliant roomful of people who offer themselves up to your help, perhaps harbouring a curiosity about the writing life and perhaps also a touching belief that there is a Golden Key, which will make all well and effect immediate change in their putative vocation. The workshop leader's power can be huge, given that writing is so intimate. Although the scale is tiny, the possibilities for wrongness and corruption can be appallingly extensive: ideas can be mocked, weaklings can be bullied, while tired or apprehensive participants can actively encourage the tutor to blather on about his or her self at revolting length and offer all the most toxic sorts of admiration. The nervous and self-critical (many good writers are both) may not express needs which therefore go unfulfilled, or problems which therefore continue to fester unexamined. Participants may have no idea what to expect and could be fobbed off with any old nonsense. With the best will in the world it's difficult to describe a mental process to someone usefully, without requiring at least a tiny bit that they think like you – when they should ideally think like themselves, only more so. Even without what we might call the intellectual and spiritual pitfalls, there are also the possibilities of technical failures, the restraints of time pressure and the intrusion of acts of God – I once ran a workshop during which a shrew ran up a participant's leg, for example. Things ended badly for the shrew, much to everyone's dismay, including the owner of the leg.

Hopefully, if everything is based on mutual respect and human concern and if the venue isn't inherently evil and obstructive, then the workshop can quickly become a chance for a bunch of interested parties to explore something together in stimulating ways and then go home all the better for it. But near at hand there is always a vile and possibly inviting minefield of behaviour, which frankly puts the **me** into **mental**.

People who've attended my workshops do tend to keep in

touch (in the positive, non-stalking sense) and I think responses are largely good, but there have also been sessions when I've been tired and a bit snippy, or just snippy. I've succumbed to the urgings of folk who wish to avoid a forthcoming task and have chatted on about myself for no reasonable reason. I have made experiments which didn't work. There have definitely been people I just haven't helped, or haven't helped enough. Which makes me unhappy.

But then I think of *That Masterclass* – those suppurating two days spent in the company of a man I, on sight, wanted to stab in the face with a screwdriver. (My Tai Chi teacher was, by way of contrast, the shiniest, most convincing testament to his own abilities that he could be, without actually starting to teach me. At which point he became even better.) In *That Masterclass* I and my fellows huddled in chairs, trying to believe we wanted to make notes, as our Master unzipped and released a tepid stream of narcissistic rage, misogyny, self-aggrandising gibberish and SHOUTING. By lunchtime on the first day we all loathed him. By lunchtime on the second day I was desperately trying to withdraw to my Happy Place, but was being refused entry on the grounds that anyone lovely I could think of, any beautiful location or delightful event would be irretrievably sullied by contact with an apparently endless succession of rants, humiliating exercises and sad little glimpses into a world of horrible disappointments and fear. Ever done something new while strangers observed? Well, try doing it with a real live sociopath bellowing wet comments against your neck. Yes, much easier.

There seemed to be no way to block what was happening. Even my most startlingly distracting pornographic fantasies weren't coming out to play and I really didn't blame them. My entire still-dampened neck had gone into shock and an ever-tightening backward spasm had cranked in, simply to stop my eyes having to look at someone who was, to be kind, a vile waste of skin as he fumbled at his mad display items and unwieldy concepts. Eventually staring at anything other than the ceiling caused me hideous pain. One participant was yelled to the edge of tears as our level of participation dived into entirely negative areas. There were numbed and surly silences. Our leader paced, kicked, sweated and roared. Having been told we were worthless – albeit by someone with very odd personal difficulties – we felt wounded and bewildered. Bored beyond endurance and stunned by rank nonsense, we were strangely unable to leave, or string sentences together. We bonded in corners, hugged, suppressed waves of fury, depression and giggling. I suddenly understood a lot more about the Stanford Prison Experiment.

Even today I can honestly write that I might not be deeply saddened if that particular gentleman was found hog-tied and naked in a car park somewhere, after a number of unpleasant encounters with some thoroughly discourteous bikers. And a moose.

But I did learn a lot from *That Masterclass*. I did see what happens when anything I *could* do wrong *was* done wrong – how penetratingly awful that would become. I recalibrated my understanding of how much a rancid series of thuggish workshop interactions might make me want to wash, and could possibly destroy or seriously damage exactly what I really wanted to do and would deeply enjoy. Whenever I feel myself and a workshop going off the rails, I do now automatically remember: *Ooh no, I can hear that zipper coming down . . . Masterclass on its way.* Onwards.

VIII

The post below referred to research undertaken for The Blue Book *and to all those ultimately thanked on its acknowledgements page.*

For the first time in, I believe, three months, I am not writing this blog on a train. I am not even on a railway station, am not being dragged up a hill by packhorses, am not – beyond the usual inhaling and exhaling and one of my twitches – in motion at all. I am, in fact, safely ensconced in my For-People-With-Bad-Backs Writing Chair. You may, in fact, already know The Chair from a number of newspaper features in which it has taken centre stage. It is galling to be outshone by a jumped-up piece of office-furniture-turned-black-leather-media-whore. Then again, I have to admit that The Chair is considerably more photogenic than I am. It is glowing with smugness beneath me, even as I type. Either that, or it has hitherto unguessed-at properties and I should see if I can find the manual again.

Meanwhile, I am currently going through what we might call a period of acclimatisation. I have spent most of this year doing what more and more writers do more and more – battering around the globe to promote the books, perform in a variety of ways and generally earn the money for which I do not, as it happens, write. But, then again, money can be exchanged for many goods and services I enjoy and so I find it handy. My novel sedentary condition means I can get used to having more than five shirts, having access to all my books and having to dust and make my own bed, rather than expecting Room Service to break in and do that while I'm trying to sneak a lie-in. I have, of course, become immediately and boringly ill – sinuses, neck, ears – simply because my body has resentment issues to work out, but I can make myself chicken soup as a consolation and mainly my circumstances are unusually convenient, if achy. Until the start of August, I will continue to stay at my very own personal address, having baths whenever I want to and being near the park in case I suddenly need to sit in amongst the daisies. Daisy-sitting could be a hobby of mine, who knows – I no longer remember my hobbies, but I do like to keep on the lookout in case one turns up.

Not that I am unbusy. I am now in the run-up to the Edinburgh Festival and so I have rehearsals for the show almost every day. This year I am blessed with a director (rehearsals would be slightly solipsistic without one) and a stage manager/lighting chap, so they're handling many problems I wouldn't understand, but I am still having to deal with the design and arrangement of items such as posters and programmes and flyers. Once again, Room Service has not come to my rescue. In my downtime, when I'm not tweaking at the script, I have a radio play to poke with a stick and much research to digest.

Part of the last fortnight's rush and chaos has been down to research. Naturally, as an author of fiction, I am quite literally paid to make things up, but I still need research. Contexts have to be legitimised, characters have interests and occupations which need to be filled with credible detail, variations of geography or time period will throw up all kinds of questions and I will have to dig about for all kinds of answers. For any given novel, I'll spend around three years – on and off – pondering and picking at worries and researching, before I ever write a word.

Apologies if that sounds like the kind of writer's confession – *I always write my second draft in the sweetest little cabin above Lucerne . . .* – which tends to make me bilious. Fiction takes research and I take my time over it, cos I'm slow to digest things, okay? That's all I mean.

The research I prefer, the type with which I am comfortable, involves me sitting in my study surrounded by a ziggurat of books at which I munch away until they give in. Sadly, if something doesn't appear to be in any book, anywhere – and many things I seem to need for the next novel are ridiculously arcane – then I have to seek out free-standing human beings and pester them, exactly when I am unable to articulate a description of what I don't have and can't understand. Would you let a random scribbler into your premises and then put up with them basically describing a void, the dimensions and angles surrounding a nothing, while waving their arms a bit too much? I know I wouldn't. And I'm only ruining these people's afternoons because they're experts – so this isn't just a theft of time, it's a theft of expert, well-informed time . . . for which I can't pay, because paying is rude and stops a favour being a favour, but you have to bring them something . . . but what do you bring someone who earns – say – ridiculously more than you do . . . ? Do you obsess for weeks trying to figure out what they might like . . . ? You'll then feel slightly grubby if that works . . . or do you take a flyer and get it wrong . . . ? You'll then feel thuggish . . . And if you see them again, should you give them books? You write books . . . but what if they don't like your books, or books at all . . . ? And if you sign the books, that'll mean people feel bad when they dump them in the Oxfam shop – plus, that's a bit up yourself, isn't it, foisting your own signed books on people? But not signing them might seem rude . . . And what if they run over the time they said they'd give you . . . ? Do you interrupt, do you let them go on, do you cry? If they really nail something magnificently, are you allowed to kiss them on the forehead? What if you're bellowing because they're deaf, but they haven't said so, but they are . . . is that rude, or just audible? I have spent a number of fretful hours lately, sitting on patient strangers' sofas and feeling bad, bad, bad about myself.

I can only say that the strangers have, so far, always provided at least sweeties, if not cakes and tea (I clearly look underfed) and have been ridiculously pleasant. I have been hugged, I have been kissed, I have been allowed to play with dogs and I have been given slivers and lumps and handfuls of insight that I sincerely hope I'll be able to boil down into a form I can absorb and use and not spoil too appallingly. And there are few things finer than listening to folk who are at the top of their game enthusing about the things they know and care about. (I vaguely remember that kind of thing being broadcast on telly and the radio in happier times, but I may be mistaken . . . It's good sometimes to have your mind race alongside someone else's, clinging on for dear life, before eventually something goes twang in your limbic area and you fall over happy, while they lope off, hardly out of breath. So thanks to everyone who's helped so far – you know who you are. And you have made me feel good, good, good about my species. Onwards.

I'm still in my flat – extraordinary how boring that can become. Plus, it's amazing how many things have gone wrong since I last really lived here. (I have been mainly away for most of the last three years) . . . So while I sing and hoot through my (no doubt excruciating for the neighbours) voice exercises in preparation for the Fringe, various tradespersons have fiddled with my boiler, my bathroom-sink taps, my gas fires and all and sundry. And it is indeed pleasant not having to brush my teeth in the bath any more.

Meanwhile, the new book, *What Becomes*, is being reviewed, even though it's technically not out yet. It's always good and helpful to be reviewed, rather than ignored, but it is slightly frustrating to think of potential readers coming to the end of a piece and thinking, 'Oh well, I might buy that then . . . wonder if it's in a shop? I haven't seen it in a shop . . . Ooh, look, a shiny thing. And a biscuit.' And they are lost for ever.

In theory, the book emerges, blinking and coughing, on the 6th August, but publication dates do seem to be entirely theoretical these days and I have already given readings where copies were available and am beginning to think publication dates are all designed as some kind of eBay scam – authors sign and date copies before the stated date and then they're worth a florin more than they would have been if we'd left them undefaced. Who can say.

I don't read the reviews until I put them on my website – so that's one, long afternoon of feeling fumbled with, paranoid and queasy and then it all goes away again. And yes, 'I don't read reviews.' Does sound as if I'm happily tucked away in my own colon – but book reviews are odd things. They emerge months, if not years after the book is done with, so they're not that much use to the author. If the book's a car crash, it's already happened and we've walked or crawled away long ago. They are usually written (and should really be written) for readers, but may on occasions wander off and end up being about the reviewer's idea of the author, or a literary theory, or even some kind of personal issue the reviewer is working through. (This seems to be quite common in US reviews.) Yes, I personally want feedback on my work, but I get that from my editor and my agent (who used to be an editor) and from readings of work in progress and (extremely) occasionally from people upon whom I inflict sections of whatever heaving mess I'm wrestling with at the time. I get opinions from people I trust, whose judgement I know and understand.

And just try writing a book of short stories. (I mean that

rhetorically – obviously there are very few commercially or personally viable reasons for your writing a book of short stories. Unless, of course, you harbour a love of the form, you foolish and adorable moppet.) But if you did try it – and my first ever book was a collection of short stories – imagine how utterly bloody confusing the reviews are bound to be. First opinion, 'Story A is rubbish, B is okay, C is middling.' But then you read, 'Story C is transcendent, A's okay and F should be illegal.' And on and on it goes. It's incredibly difficult to review short stories without mentioning individual stories, and opinions will differ and multiple reviews will simply confuse the young and tender brain of the scribbler concerned. So my first crop of reviews was also my last. My publisher tells me how they're going.

And, in many ways, reviews are for publishers – are about trying to get anybody to know the darn thing is out there, whining and weeing on the concrete floor of the big Unowned Books Shelter and staring with big eyes through the chain-link fence in the hope of going home with you. (See what I did there? Trying to get you to buy it. Sorry. Inexcusable. It's been that kind of month. Please ignore me.) And then review quotes are cut out and arranged in ways that will make the paperback jacket read as if the Archangel Gabriel came down to Earth and produced the volume in question with his very own heart's blood, and anyone who doesn't buy it is not only crazy, but possessed of a leprous soul and likely to bite the heads off kittens. Sadly, every other book jacket will read like that, too – reducing the reader to a guilty, cognitively dissonant mess on the floor of Waterstone's café.

It has been particularly easy to not read anything in the last two weeks because I have mainly been battering up and down a rehearsal room, putting the shiny on 'Words' in preparation for next week's previews, and then off we'll go with a show a day until the end of time. Or the end of August, whichever arrives soonest. This means I am fitter than I would usually want to be, louder and currently addicted to bananas. There's nothing like seven or eight bananas to get you through a long day of trying to walk and talk simultaneously.

The whole rehearsal process means that I'm exhausted and yet quite cheery. I do like performing the show – partly because it's an opportunity to talk to people about words and writing and meaning and the silliness of being a writer in an unmediated way. It also means I get to go back to what made me start writing in the first place – hearing and feeling language. Any readers of this blog would, of course, be hugely welcome to turn up and see how it all turns out. Feel free to say hello. Meanwhile, there's hooting to be done. Onwards.

IX

So, here I am in Edinburgh and it's my day off. As far as I'm aware, everyone who returns to the Fringe does so filled with balmy memories of the final few days of it all last time, when the show was run in, the audiences were glossy, contented and oozing with art, and your body knew it would be able to relax soon. Of course, we all turn up for the first week of the new Fringe and suddenly realise we forgot the harried running about of the initial days: the technical glitches, the cuts so that we run to time, the finding of dressing-room space, the snaffling of coat hangers, the stuff that breaks, other people's hissy fits, my hissy fits – not to mention the interesting effect that one hour a day of solid performing has on the human body and brain. I could, for example, now run the show under gunfire or indeed water, but can't recall my own address. And my spine has developed a whole range of aches that are entirely new to me.

Let me repeat that: *I am experiencing back pains I have never had before.* After more than ten years of dodgy backness, during which I had assumed that every possible shoulder, neck and vertebral grief possible had been at least attempted, all kinds of new and interesting kinks and wrinkles are appearing, while all of the places that usually hurt are having a fine old holiday. Who'd've thunk it. Fortunately, the Assembly Rooms provide cut-price massages for performers and – as they are very good massagists and interested in their work – I like to feel I have provided them with some light relief.

Them: 'So, where's the trouble?'

Me: 'Everywhere.'

T: 'Pardon?'

M: 'Go on, just prod your finger there – or there – or I think you'll like this lump. Or this knot . . . or there's a twangy thing here in my neck . . .'

T: 'Oh, my Lord . . . Let me get a chair leg and some embrocation. And the pliers.'

M: 'Knock yourself out. Or me . . . I don't really mind.'

But it's all good fun and lovely to have a pattern to my days: get up at noon, eat a banana, drink as much water as I can fit in, have a bath, eat another banana, wonder if I ate the first one, or forgot – are there fewer bananas? – do Tai Chi, eat a banana, pause to ponder how much I'm beginning to hate bananas – yet their starch, sugar and potassium are so damnably useful – do my hooting, have lunch, get the bus to the Assembly Rooms, drink more water, drink fizzy pop, drink more water, iron my shirt, put on slap, breathe a lot, drink more water, say hi to Mr Draper-Velleut who does my lights, and to George and David who are the techies for the Drawing Room, have a look at the stage, wait for the lovely ladies and gentlemen, perform for the lovely ladies and gentlemen, end show, drink more water, take off slap and shirt, eat something containing no bananas and then go home – actually, it's someone else's home – and off to bed as quickly as possible. Obviously, the day also involves peeing a fair amount what with all that water, but it would be indelicate to mention that. I am also building up to seeing more of other people's shows. Mr Mark Thomas's current offering is, for example, an excellent thing.

So far, I can only commend the quality and intelligence of the ladies and gentlemen – and their often remarkable sweetness. And, let's be fair, some of you are also a little eccentric. But, thus far, only in good ways.

The notable feature of this week – apart from a remarkably romantic older couple in the audience about whom I will tell you next time; no, it's not smut, it would just give away a bit of the show, I'll tell you when we've stopped – was the leaving party for Catherine Lockerbie over at the Edinburgh International Book Festival. Catherine directed the EIBF for nine glorious years and took it from something average and regional to what it is today: far and away the best in the world. And I do travel a lot – I know whereof I speak. She's bowing out now and some of us got to say goodbye and good luck. (The Poet Laureate even brought along a poem – suddenly that job makes a lot more sense.) Catherine is an amazing and amazingly pleasant lady whose statue should be in the middle of Charlotte Square – where they hold the EIBF – rather than the current and, frankly, quite ugly equine statue of a gentleman who I have to presume answered to the name Charlotte at the weekends. He certainly seems to have enjoyed dressing up.

Meanwhile, it's back to the bananas for me tomorrow and another two weeks of meeting the ladies and gentlemen. And gigging a bit with Robin Ince. Huzzah! Onwards.

X

Ah, the tears, the hugs – there's nothing like saying farewell to actors – they're so good at it. Suddenly the room is full of weeping and, quite frankly, it's all uncomfortably inconsolable. So that's the end of the Festival, then: the staid streets of Edinburgh are devoid of unicycles, or flyer-hander-outers, or people eating food they would normally only use to pelt miscreants confined to the stocks.

I do genuinely miss my dressing-room mates deeply at the moment – it's rare to get a bunch of stressed-out artists in, let's admit it, increasingly filthy surroundings who can manage to be so deeply, deeply pleasant all the time. They and the enduring immense pleasantness of my audiences means I am now smiling and chatting to strangers as if everyone is my new chum and human beings are a good idea. (Bear in mind that I usually only see people on telly – made by sociopaths, for sociopaths, about sociopaths – or on the front pages of newspapers abandoned on trains. Which can give you a relatively bleak outlook.) And if anybody out there would like to employ excellent performers, I can recommend – in no particular order – Michelle Gallagher, Billy Mack, Alisa Anderson and Gabriel Quigley. The gentlemen dancers of the New Art Club are extraordinary. And Matt Harvey is the nicest man – and poet – alive. But you probably knew that. He is also proof that a human being can survive on wasabi-coated nuts for a month. But he did look quite peaky for much of that time period. Hope he's back on proper solids now.

And I will miss the assorted kindnesses of audience members – the small notes, the hearty handshakes and kisses and general expressions of affection. *What nice, non-threatening and unstalk-erish folks*, I often thought. (The technical crew tended to circumvent the more mad-eyed, which was sweet of them – I didn't even need to ask. They simply assumed that wanting to speak to me qualifies you as a nutter, which is, in a way, quite sensible.)

As promised, I will mention the older couple who, as I request in the show, wrote I LOVE YOU in the air with their index fingers while thinking of someone they cared about. They then spontaneously turned to each other, smiling, and touched fingers. And then there was the couple who linked fingers . . . I mean, I'm trying to be all cynical about this, but there were some startling expressions of humanity and sweetness going on. Which made Jim Kelman's latest grumbles about the writer's life seem – though justified – slightly more grumbly than they might have.

Still, enough of the luvvy gushing. I dashed back from Edinburgh last night having only scraped the surface of the Stand Comedy Club Party. The SCCP is now an end-of-the-Fringe institution with threatening buckets of punch, comedians of every type, bad dancing and many opportunities for anyone who wishes to make themselves very ill – perhaps in delightful new company – until round about lunchtime the following day. I would have stayed at least half an hour longer – okay, maybe even forty-five minutes longer – if I hadn't been aware that a tide of work was seething and coiling in my flat. So I currently have the washing on as I type and try to prioritise all the scripty bits and letters and emails and bills and post that awaited me. On the one hand, this is a comfort to balance the idea of leaving the Assembly Rooms, my stage being torn down before I even got home, while teams in hazmat suits cleared the more mobile corners of the dressing room. Rather than beginning to think – *Yes, this is the way of the world, all things pass and my presence here will be expunged in moments* . . . a stack of demanding paperwork and enquiries can make you feel – *Yes, my absence was noted. I am necessary. I have a purpose to fulfil in ways that not all that many others could* . . . That pleasant rush of narcissism is, naturally, replaced almost immediately by a sensation of drowning and an interior wail along the lines of – *Bloody hell! I can't do all of this. I'll have a stroke. I can only do all of this if I ram so much caffeine into my head that my heart quite literally leaves and goes to stay with a nice transplant patient – who will, of course, use it as a desk toy, because of it being no earthly use as a pump.*

But to be calm for a moment and assess matters. I have just spent a month standing onstage every day and telling people that I love my job and that words are important. I liked that. And I think it was a good thing to do. Good for the folk who came – students and readers and would-be writers and already-writers and basically people who love words. It was also good for me. I have just spent a month talking to people, telling stories to people, remembering that this is what I do. I usually do it in the absence of readers, I usually do it on paper, but the stories are the beginning and the end and the heart and the challenge and the joy of what I do. It's a simple, lovely, human thing. I tell stories. I like being able to remember that.

I have also liked talking to a whole range of performers and finding out about them, and I am hugely and deeply grateful that I do not have to spend my professional life being prey to the whims of fashion and the megalomaniac fantasies of directors – or, indeed, finding that I go from the intensities of Fringe performance straight into a job giving away free flip-flops on the street to people who agree to try a particular brand of contact lenses. And if you are a writer, I think you have to have a soft spot for actors – the best of them are the best readers you'll meet

– they take words and wear them, eat them, make them into real live, believable people with a bit of glory about them that you had no right to expect. Yes, the bad ones I generally want to hit repeatedly with a spade; but if you're watching a soap opera or one of the few dramas still on British screens and maybe the words aren't that great, or the camera work's a bit dodgy – or you've gone out to see a play and maybe bits of it are creaky – spare a thought for the poor actors who have to be there, anyway. Even if the ship was always going to go down. Or maybe you'll see something wonderful, or a great individual performance, and yet no one else seems to have noticed, and next week or next month it'll be the flip-flops again or temping, minicabbing. Some of them get to be briefly, or longly, famous – and some of them should be, although the problems of famousness shouldn't be lightly wished on anyone – but most of them just keep on keeping on, in an environment where there is less and less theatre, less and less TV drama, hardly any UK film industry. Our loss. And theirs.

Off on holiday now – to Sark. Onwards.

XI

Apologies for this being a slightly-later-that-usual blog – it's not that a good Calvinist like me could ever have got into holiday mood so deeply that I just plain wouldn't file; it's that Force Six gales and changed travel plans have meant that my movements were a little irregular during the earlier part of this week. And if I had a fiver for everyone who told me, 'Well, of course, you could just fly . . .' when another boat failed to appear, or arrived late, or threatened to be bouncier than usual – then I still wouldn't have enough money to go through the extensive course of hypnotic reconditioning and brain surgery it would take to parcel me into an airport after a lovely break away from all vehicles that move faster that trotting pace.

Sark was magnificent, thanks for asking, and is still pretty much unscathed by its recent alterations and trials. (Beyond there now being what looks suspiciously like a helicopter landing pad tucked away on the coast facing Brecqhou . . .)

There is nothing like scrambling up and down vaguely dangerous cliffs for hours and hours a day – with a bit of impromptu abseiling – to turn off the brain. Otherwise I get anxious. Well, I get anxious anyway – about a week into any break I am overwhelmed by a dreadful sense of mental constriction: *surely I should be writing, surely there is a part of me which must be shouting and blathering on at all times, for ever and ever, expressing an internal queue of amorphous people intent on having a local habitation and a name*. . . I take holidays so rarely and work so much of the time and, as it happens, enjoy my work to such an extent that holidays do prove something of a problem. They're a nice problem, but, all the same, the only way to quieten everything down is to be exhausted, over and over again – just knackered – incapable of thought. This means my vacations often involve signing waivers to say I won't mind if I'm killed/crippled/ dented by forthcoming activities and/or bears/whales/eagles/ horses. In Sark it means walking past signs that politely say things like 'Use this path at your own risk.' Or 'Proceed beyond this point at your own risk.' Or 'Sheer Drop' – there's something just gleefully informative and inviting about all of them.

So think of me, Dear Reader, spending days and days at the edges of a tiny island, watching peregrine falcons, or kestrels, cormorants, buzzards, gulls, descending and climbing, climbing and descending, surrounded by shapes of sky and sea lights that would sorely tax anyone's descriptive abilities – things that stretch the mind and teach it humility and let it be content.

I won't bang on about the benefits of feudal living, or the inherent evils of change. I am aware that a fair percentage of the people who enjoy Sark do. They are vociferously and strangely threatened by the UN, 'riff-raff', gels who wear trousers, alter-ations in the Book of Common Prayer and a whole regiment of looming horrors predicted in a number of newspapers and daytime television programmes. I will say that, as far as I can tell, the Sarkese and Sark-lovers care for their environment, are ingenious, resourceful, collaborative and can be gentle and incredibly friendly. And they do like to talk. There are, of course, occasions when conversation is unusually necessary in Sark – it just doesn't feel right to be walking along a night-time path on an island with no street lights and to pass a fellow-traveller without at least a comforting 'Evening'. Sark isn't a museum or an experiment (leastways, they probably are their own long-running experiment), the island has mobile phones, televisions and the Internet, but it also has a remarkably stimulating and pleasant environment and a population that still finds people interesting – that still gossips and asks questions and is moved by the interiors of others' lives. It's wonderful to spend time in a gorgeous setting, but equally delightful to meet people who are not just passive consumers of pre-packaged entertainments, whose environment is largely non-virtual and unaccompanied by backing tracks and the sweaty-eared isolation that gets many of us through our days.

It's good to be reminded of how powerfully we can connect simply by talking to strangers – even quite strange strangers – to know that the blustering man who fears that Christmas cards will no longer show fox-hunting scenes also makes special lunches for his visiting granddaughters, was still quietly surprised by that one time when they didn't visit, by his loneliness. The father who returns, year after year, to beautiful beaches where he played with his children, who loves Sark, but finds the sand less entertaining when he has no excuse to dig holes in it, no companions to scramble with into caves. The widow who used to sit on the headlands with her husband and who comes now twice a year without him. The visitors' stories are often melancholy, the pains of people unable to stop time, addicted to familiarity and seduced by an island which seems to offer the impossible: that first sunny weekend, repeating and repeating like the waves rolling back into Derrible Bay. And I will, of course, go back to Sark myself and have my own set of expectations and my own stories. Writers are very prone to having unreasonable expectations of reality and its inhabitants – used, as we are, to manipulating fictitious characters and environments, we can tend to assume that nothing in the real world should move on without at least consulting us.

Meanwhile, I'm hoping – as I always do after meeting genuinely courteous people – that the habits of courtesy stay with me and that my fear of being stabbed or propositioned in wrong ways will not mean I go back to being brisk and/or savage as soon as I hit London. Then it's back to the typing and, soon, back to promoting *What Becomes* and the autumn festival circuit. Including a plane to Toronto. Doesn't bear thinking about. Onwards.

XII

So. On tour. In my twenties this was all hope and insecurity and gigs that are done and dusted by 9 p.m. and sitting in grey hotel rooms considering the possibilities of self-harm and overpriced in-room porn. In my thirties it was probably about the job, writing as I go and those same bloody hotel rooms. In my forties it seems to be more about meeting people and trying to support the idea of books and reading, the principle of the thing. And, whatever else is happening, touring is about being tired. For the necessary two hours, or three hours, or however many hours with the ladies and gentlemen, not tired – but otherwise – tired. A kind of deep, brain-burrowy, trainy, cary, nicely undefended tired that makes you notice acts of kindness and instances of beauty: Beverley Minster, the Ripon spice bread in Betty's Tea Room, red kites flying over woodland towards dusk.

First stop was Charleston. They get many brownie points for running Small Wonder – a festival entirely dedicated to that endangered thing, the short story. In some quarters they get points deducted for paying writers with vouchers for their own shop. (Not that it isn't a very lovely shop. And not that writers – unlike plumbers and electricians – aren't quite often paid in *things*, rather than *money*.) Additional points for warmth, charm, intelligence and providing a number of highly (almost inappropriately) affectionate animals and a seductive and apparently inexhaustible supply of hand-made food, served around a picturesque and culturally significant kitchen table. For those of you unfamiliar with Charleston's history – it's a rambly country house in an almost numbingly idyllic setting, where a number of the Bloomsbury Group's adherents either lived or loitered and, I get the strong impression, occasionally engaged in artistic activities when they got tired of having sex with men/women/themselves/all of the above. Maynard Keynes – an economist for whom I have much time – removed to Tilton House up the road and, as far as I understand matters, shared his new premises with Lydia the Tattooed Lady. They were both very happy.

I was down at Small Wonder to read from *Freedom* – Amnesty International's anthology celebrating the United Nation's Declaration of Human Rights. Strange to stand in soft and sympathetic surroundings and speak freely about people who can't – to be comfortable and well-fed and discussing torture and how bewildered and distorted human thoughts and actions can become. It made me want to go back and read Zimbardo's *The Lucifer Effect* again, particularly bearing in mind recent revelations of corporate and individual abuses.

I took a diversion after Charleston to see the revival of *Speaking in Tongues* It's always heartening to watch an excellent cast presenting something thoughtful and demanding – and not a musical – in the West End. It's also grand when women onstage actually behave like women, rather than shrill/squeaky things with the interior lives of plants, so thanks to Lucy Cohu and Kerry Fox for that. Lovely work from Ian Hart, particularly in the rather stronger second half. And it always delights me to see John Simm being just vocally and physically *precise*, creatively and generously fastidious. I do also try to remember good voices for later use during the very many occasions when my own interior drone becomes sickening and yet I still have things to type. So I have occasionally borrowed a bit of Mr Simm – that deceptively light, brisk melodiousness with a carborundum centre – to get through the initial stage of loathing each syllable as it oozes out across the computer screen like some particularly vile and luminous personal fluid.

My ability to concentrate on the production was slightly compromised by an essay in the programme from a 'Relationship Psychotherapist' on the howlingly inevitable loneliness of the human condition. I might suggest that something liable to send me rushing for the toilets to hang myself doesn't make ideal reading during the run-up to – and interval inserted within – a lovely evening out. (Of course, the toilets in your average Victorian theatre are only small enough to hang a mouse – which renders the whole procedure impractical. I can never even contemplate anyone being hanged like a mouse.) Beyond that, I didn't at all enjoy being stuck behind an immensely tall man with a head like a volleyball, who sniggered both wetly and at random. Still, the words and humanity smuggled themselves through.

Then on to the launch of the Warwick students' anthology, *Beyond the Bubble*, which I hope will prosper. It was nicely moving to see them giving one of their first readings, beginning the writer's life, hoping the hopes and rubbing at the insecurities. I can only wish them well. And wish that the UK publishing industry wasn't floating belly-up in its own sad, poo-and-algae-filled bowl. All kinds of nasty surprises lie in wait to frighten, dispirit and drain the promise from new writers, but I would like to believe that energy and talent and ingenuity and luck will see the words and humanity smuggled through there, too.

Then on to pretty Beverley, a delightful audience and an equally pleasant readers' group. More of the huge, largely invisible legions of readers who cling on, despite the dwindling variety of books, the disappearing independent bookshops, the expense of all but the hyper-discounted fast-sellers. More words and more humanity in the Minster's war memorial to the nineteenth century's soldiers, dead in Afghanistan – and in the book of requests for prayer, the small records of twenty-first-century gratitude, confusion and grief – and the names of new soldiers, dead in Afghanistan.

And now Ilkley: dusty rain, hospitality, chatting about technical requirements, metallic balloons being delivered for a function in the hotel downstairs – hope they don't have a band – and a show tomorrow. Ely soon, Cheltenham, Toronto, roads and rails and handshakes and people talking about the things that matter to them, writing about the things that matter to them, because how else can we sing out who we are, or were, or could be – all our promises and angers, joys and loves. And now it's time for bed – then onwards.

XIII

Well, you may be as delighted as I was to hear that they *did* have a band – a band capable of penetrating very effectively through two storeys of a large Victorian hotel, all the way to my previously drowsy bedroom. And it played. A lot. Bad covers of good R&B in a function suite charmingly reminiscent of the public areas in the Overlook Hotel, as explored so admirably by Stanley Kubrick during *The Shining*. This is, of course, traditional, both for function suites and for me being on tour.

I do love music, have quite broad – although uninformed – tastes and used to miss my favourite ditties and jingles as I travelled about before the days of MP3 players and iThings. Nevertheless, I am forced to admit that uninvited music, no matter how jolly, burrowing up through my floor between the hours of bedtime and ohmygodwhatanearlystart, is something to which I have never been able to warm. Inn and hotel karaoke nights, marching and/or oompah bands passing endlessly beneath my early-morning window, ceilidhs, shindigs, hooleys, wakes, weddings, birthday singsongs and *Functions* – they have all rendered me psychotically tired during the past two and a bit decades of tarting myself about across the globe on behalf of my books. (The rest of my peripatetic nights have been disturbed by the usual blend of incomprehensible nocturnal pacing overhead, shuddering and scraping lifts and the 360-degree thumping, shouting and larking about of fellow-guests. I occasionally wonder how they manage to gather the additional energy necessary to ruin my few undisturbed hours by also having sex loudly enough to tarnish the night porter's buttons, never mind letting us all hear how *yes* everything is. It's just showing off. And – *yes* – whenever I've had sex in a hotel, I do insist on a full vocal warm-up before we begin. I have years of resentment to work through.)

Then again, the predictable din from my neighbours simply means I travel with industrial-strength earplugs. They're always in my bag, along with the blindfoldy thing for lie-ins when the curtains don't work, camping equipment and powdered food for when the catering doesn't work, the special pillow for when my neck doesn't work and enough pills, instruments, bandages and ointments to deal with a month in the wilderness or a minor surgical procedure – because you never know . . .

Of course, you *do* actually know: touring will be lovely. (And hello to the very excellent ladies and gentlemen of Ilkley – we had much fun. Great festival and sold-out venue, that's what we like.) But the writer's immune system will be exposed to more bugs on tour than you'd find in a poorly maintained plague cart. So when the young chap responsible for cleaning my room in Ilkley staggered past looking like an extra from *Dawn of the Dead* I rightly assumed that his pillow-fluffing and other ministrations would mean that I was basically sleeping in a feathery plague pit and should immediately make my will. Travel back to Glasgow was nasty, sweaty and long, and then what should have been a languid week at home, leading into the next leg of travels, turned into lying in bed having fever dreams too horrible even for conversion into A.L. Kennedy fiction. And the red pills and the white pills and the fawn pills and the inhalations and the endless advice of kind strangers who always assume that I just lie about in my own filth and haven't tried, for example, *a bit of honey and lemon*. Still, at least it wasn't Pig-flu, and after the first few days I stopped feeling as if someone was taking a hand-drill to the top of my head while improvising a lobotomy using dirty biros wedged behind my eyes.

All this feebleness led to cancelled gigs – I always hate cancelling gigs. Not that I think anyone will be particularly distraught if they're deprived of me; it's just rude to say you'll be somewhere and then not turn up. But I got back on track with the very fine Cheltenham Festival, where I have to say that I was anticipating the audience might be the slightest bit reserved and tweedy and maybe even *Daily Maily – not so*. Highly responsive and warm and hugs at the end. Big softies, they were – in a good way. And very fragrant. Which was handy, given that my mum and her pals and my agent and his (business) partner and his partner's girlfriend were all in the audience, too, and I was hoping things would go at least tolerably well.

Ely was lovely – excellent cathedral with two strangely irrelevant shops, pleasant medieval opportunities for tea and a reading at Topping's bookshop – which is the way bookshops ought to be, independent, voluminous, friendly and full of readers. Next on the list is Toronto. Which is a problem. Not Toronto itself – Hog City is a more than acceptable place and the International Festival of Authors is a great festival, highly professional and full of Canadian Friendliness – which is like anyone else's friendliness, but with added layers of eye-contact, sincerity and – well, frankly it's all a bit unnerving. The problem is flying. I have to fly to get there. I have to get on a plane and let it take off with me aboard. And should I survive that, I have to fly back. Or I could become Canadian and just stay – halve my exposure to airborne disaster. Canadian citizenship is a real possibility. (Although I would fail the niceness test.)

I HAVE TO FLY.

I never did like it and then I spent three years researching a book about a tail gunner on a Lancaster bomber who had a 50 per cent chance of surviving any flight he made. I researched sounds, smells, images, tastes, emotions, the works. I spent three years conditioning myself to believe in that 50 per cent probability of death. And now I do. This would be interesting, if it weren't bloody terrifying. And if it didn't make me depressed and unwilling to do any work when I'm anywhere near the prospect of flying. I have spent many an hour reading books on hypnosis and doing exercises and trying to reverse this – the effects thus far have been signally unimpressive. I pray for the intervention of a fork-bearded stranger in a top hat and cloak who's good at snap inductions – and who won't then make me work in Variety during the 1870s. Or a flight attendant with dirty biros to hand . . .

I know I actually have a much lower than 50 per cent chance of being mashed to a pulp or incinerated in a plane, or of flying into a mountain, or coming a cropper on landing, or being frozen to death, or asphyxiated, or otherwise murdered by air transport. Then again, the highly improbable is also very, very unlikely to be survivable. I'm more likely to be in a train accident – but I might survive a train accident . . . I mean, I do think about this stuff. A lot. I am flying on my birthday, partly – and partly insanely – because the chances of my dying on my birthday *and* on a plane are quite low. But not that low. Not low enough.

So, just in case, ladies and gentlemen: do have enjoyable lives, embracing every moment, trying to make a positive difference, and so forth. I hope to blog again, back in the UK and still breathing.

XIV

I am not on a plane.

I am on a train – alive and on a train and on the ground. I am not hurtling miles above my natural height, I am not sweating, twitching and muttering prayers full of shameful bargaining. I am no longer discovering that the proximity of what I feel to be death doesn't make me appreciate the flitter of every bat's wing, or the tender hearts of children – it makes me self-pitying and tetchy. I have flown to Canada and back and have no intention of ever travelling in such a horribly elevated manner again. Feel free to write to me/shout at me/punch me gently if I ever suggest it. Yes, indeedy, I am on a train – a train that has been sitting (at a jaunty angle) between two (now entirely dark) fields since it was broad day. It is now 17.40 and we have little hope of moving any time soon. We have been informed that International Rescue are on their way and are free to wonder whether that means marionettes are gangling bravely to our aid, or if the person making the announcement has a sense of humour that will lead to violence later. Panic-buying at the buffet is well under way and several passengers wearing anti-swine-flue face-masks are clearly under the impression that Patient Zero for a whole new strain of doom is aboard and incubating. Given my current physical condition, they're probably right and should be forcing me into the tea urn for a quick and cleansing boil. And yet still I am grinning like a tired, tired gonk. *I am not on a plane.* (And I won't be the first one we eat when we run out of complimentary mini-pretzels – it'll be the annoying and slow-moving hippy in A23.)

So, as a new religion forms in Coach C and the big-haired pensioner lady in Coach J prepares to become empress of all that stretches between the man watching a Dan Brown DVD and the nasty stain under the bin, I can reflect on the fact that I've done no work in almost a fortnight. I don't see the point, you see, not when I have to fly – writing takes effort, and why put in the effort if you're about to be toast and bits spread down a hillside?

Not that Toronto wasn't, in every other sense, delightful and not that the Canadian audiences weren't even more ridiculously warm and generous than I remembered. I had a lovely time. And – rather disturbingly – many Canadians out there have pictures taken with me to prove it. I was being held together with Red Bull and Sudafed, in an evil combination which held at bay my sinuses and jetlag for long enough to perform, and as I didn't have a heart attack at any point we'll just call that a win.

I also had time to chat with fellow-authors about the whole travel/festival thing and we tended to agree that, although the events themselves are dandy and talking about books to people who care about books is both fine and uplifting, we do all feel as if we've been out of our houses and away from our loved ones (the other writers had lives) for too long. Touring and promoting are more and more important as publishers fire more and more staff, promote less and less effectively and allow sales incomes to be slashed by heavy discounting. This means that when a highly pleasant lady said, as I signed her book, that I must have *a wonderful life*, she was sort of right – I get to do something I love and am often paid for it, I see wonderful places and meet – briefly – people who might be nice. But, then again, there are days when it would be easy to get churlish, if not tearful, and exclaim, 'You want my life? You have it, matey. I'm going to die in a plane crash on Thursday, anyway.' Which would be wrong and sad.

The other topic of writerly chat – I was thinking of you, Dear Readers, and researching as I went – was money. Or its non-arrival. Like other small (very small) businesses, many authors have noticed that those tiny and yet important cheques have started to arrive two or three months late, or not at all. I have even experienced haggling over fees when I turn up for gigs – and, as negotiators go, I'm as resilient as a damp biscuit.

Please don't misunderstand me – I know I'm in a very fortunate position – none of this is as bad as not being published, not being able to find work, being fired in a recession, having my house repossessed, or kids to worry about. If I need more money, I can do more work. And sleep less. I mainly worry for the coming generations of writers. If my next advance is smaller than the last (and it will be), I can try to diversify even more, I can tour more, I can try to ginger up work abroad. I have no idea what a new writer would do now – attempting to burrow into a market that's in free-fall and a literary 'culture' that drastically limits the numbers of books that are published or that will ever be visible in major bookshop chains, in reviews, or in the media generally. Publishers are beyond risk-averse and are currently decision-averse. It is possible that published writers will no longer ever leave whatever other employment they use to subsidise themselves. Meanwhile, the increase in poorly conceived and exploitative Creative Writing courses will continue, and increasingly the writers who teach on them will end up training potential writers to teach other potential writers to teach on other courses, and round and round they all will go – never knowing how good they might be, or what they're missing.

Which isn't what we deserve. There's a place for courses and some of them are excellent – I wouldn't, for example, be an Associate Professor on Warwick University's Creative Writing Programme if I didn't believe in what they do there. But it can't be that our literature relies on false promises and academia to limp along. Established writers surely can't feel morally comfortable about helping new writers to commit themselves to the life while ignoring the fact that the chances of success, or even of publication, are minimal. And we can't pretend that teaching writers to teach writing is meaningful, or anything close to our primary purpose.

At which point I have to say that I don't really have any answers to this any more. I only know that, as I tour and tour about, I keep meeting readers. Not just readers, but intelligent and passionate readers who go out of their way to support books. Over the last few years there has been an explosion in literary festivals, readers' groups and reading series. When the range in your local bookshop collapses, your library dumps its stock and your media barely acknowledge your interests, it seems that you don't, as a reader, just give up and stop reading, or just buy the fast-seller you're peddled by the only part of the UK's publishing machinery that's still functioning – you fight back, you get organised, you dig about for books that you'll genuinely love, you reach out to others of your kind. Which – as a reader and a writer – I find wonderful and promising.

It isn't the readers' or the writers' fault that British publishing (and publishing elsewhere) has fallen on its own sword and allowed bookshop chains and short-term thinking to eat its heart away. It isn't our fault that the Net Book Agreement disappeared. (Although we should have fought harder to keep it.) But we are the ones who'll lose out, who don't get the variety of books, who don't find the unlooked-for pleasures, who don't get to share the new dreams. The dreams and pleasures and the appetite for them are currently still out there. With each generation of poor schooling they'll be diminished – we'll be less and less able to understand what we don't have – but, for now, the part of my job which is consistently inspiring involves seeing and feeling the energy of readers, meeting that immense enthusiasm for wonders – in all kinds of people in all kinds of situations: Ilkley, Ely, Toronto . . . it doesn't seem to matter where. If that energy and intelligence steps up to the next level of organisation, then there could be hope for us. And I need never go on another TV or radio show and find that – however the discussion was described beforehand – what we're really meant to talk about is how poetry is dead, or the novel is rubbish, or the short story is irrelevant. Fuck that, quite frankly. Really. Fuck that with vigour and from a strange direction. It truly leaves me more than annoyed.

Meanwhile, 18.11 – and the train is moving. Slowly, but – against all expectations – we're heading for where we need to be. Just in time for us to get metaphorical. Tiredness, travel, exhausted hyper-sensitivity, rage – they do tend to encourage metaphors. Then again, is this one too obvious, is it a cheap shot? One thing I do know: I'd rather be pondering questions like that than watching us go one better than book-burning. You don't have to burn them if you just ignore them, act as if they never were and hope they go away.

Once again – fuck that!

And especially against the grain.

Onwards.

XV

Now then: the short story. If we're sensible and care about prose, we will agree that it's a fine, exacting and beautiful form. It's perhaps not huge and showy, like making the Eiffel Tower disappear – it's more like someone holding your empty hand until it's satisfactorily and strangely filled with your granny's cameo and the powder-sweet scent of her long-gone lipstick. The short story is small, but can be devastatingly penetrating – quite like, as I almost always say, a bullet.

I'm slightly known for producing short fictions and so, every now and then, folk ask me to give them one. Increasingly these requests arrive with conditions and subjects. 'Could you write a story for next week involving the concept of impermeability?' – 'We need something by Tuesday about fish.' – 'We'd like it this afternoon – do include Plymouth, a small scene in which someone ginger carves a bit of soap, and a left-handed bloke called Simon who confronts his own mortality as embodied by a swarm of moths.'

My answer to the above is often, 'No.' For a variety of reasons. I object on principle to unhelpful restrictions of time and subject being imposed upon me, because I got into writing at least in part so that no one could tell me what to do or think. I neither like nor thrive upon that kind of interference and it doesn't necessarily help me to grow or develop my capacities. I also don't relish restrictions being placed upon a form which should be able to roam free and express itself as it wishes. Sometimes a subject *is* an inspiration, or chimes with an idea you've already got, but often a magazine, or a newspaper, or a bunch of people who say they want to *save the short story* will end up constricting imaginative and technical scope and making sure much of what they receive will resemble slightly over-emotional op-ed articles. This doesn't help the uninitiated to think well of the short story. And would anyone phone up a writer and ask them to write a *themed novel*? The process, however well intended, can seem ever so slightly to imply: 'It's only a short story – you can knock one of them out in a couple of hours – here are some bits to start you off.'

Of course, I am also asked for stories by people who are familiar with my interests. For example, if someone gets in touch – as they recently did – and asks for a story involving sex, then they're probably not going to go away empty-handed. Then again, the wording of the commission could over-concentrate the author's mind on what is not absolutely the money shot. This is because writing about sex usually isn't really about sex – unless you've very wisely decided to produce lucrative porn, rather than cheap and obscure literary fiction. Porn doesn't need (and would in fact be highly disturbing if it included) psychological depth, emotional range, proper characters and a real storyline. Erotica – porn for middle-class people and the timid – tends to follow the same rules.

Literature within which people have sex is, in many ways, curiously like literature within which people grind coffee, lick wet teabags, play the trombone or visit cottages – they simply involve a humdrum physical activity which has to be accurately described with a sense of personality, psychology, voice, tone and plot. Let's say your characters are making a daisy chain: this could be something about which they are passionate and every syllable might be tumescent with heated meaning. Or their subtext could overshadow everything with a sense of impending doom related to the meat-packing facility where one of them will soon be crushed by a poorly stacked load. Their smiles and happily busy fingers could be tinged with tragedy, irritation, somnolence, boredom, *mal de mer*, you name it – up to a point, *it doesn't matter what they're doing.* If your plot compels you to have a protagonist engaged in something as unpromisingly tedious as buffing a German helmet or cleaning up a sticky string of pearls, you retain the power to give that particular activity whatever emotional and psychological colour, subtexts, leitmotifs and atmosphere you and the rest of the story see fit. If you want and need to, those scenes could be – however unlikely this might seem – as roastingly and justifiably hot as forcing one's freshly buttered hand repeatedly in through the letter box of the Society of Authors. Or it could be as dull as the back of your knee.

It's sometimes difficult to explain this to people – and journalists – who read some of my work and then seem to expect I have engaged in all kinds of strenuous research for which I personally would lack, in every way, the flexibility. Fiction about sex is still fiction – standard operating procedures apply. Equally, it is occasionally disconcerting to deal with emerging writers' work when half the notes you have to give read roughly along the lines of 'As far as I'm aware, the average penis doesn't extend to three feet and is unable to go around corners.' Or 'Is this scene followed by reconstructive surgery?' And a percentage of the remaining comments may mention errors caused by embarrassment or a desire to shock. But we, as writers, are already sitting in the nice privacy of the reader's head, enjoying the usual range of necessary intimacies, which we have hopefully earned by being beautiful, interesting, hypnotic, poetic and all the rest. Jumping out from behind a damp bush and ejaculating wildly would almost always be inappropriate and shoddy. And there is, naturally, nothing to be embarrassed or awkward about when a piece of writing involves sex – the reader already thinks of sex a ridiculous number of times per hour without our assistance. We are simply dreaming together – anything goes.

Before the days of scanned-in pages and email texts, I could predict that the number of typesetter-added errors would escalate whenever anything on the page was especially vigorous in its personal areas. This always seemed slightly odd to me because – after the usual repeated, thorough and stretching rewrites – each and every passage has been explored to the point of numbness and has become, on several levels, no more than a test of staying power, a hump to come over, a tricky corner to reach around. This general lack of anything other than a cerebral response to more colourful sections of my texts can mean that I am occasionally surprised by reactions during readings – even though the conventions of a literary event tend to dictate that even the most taboo word, action or subject is admissible, as long as it has been pondered at length and written down before it is mentioned aloud. (Which is actually pretty perverse, if you think about it.) Likewise, responses from readers can be somewhat unexpected. What book-lovers do in the safety and comfort of their own elegantly appointed lobes and parlours is, I feel, their own affair. And I have occasionally been desirous that it should very much remain so.

Meanwhile, I have a story to finish.

Onwards.

XVI

Sorry for the delay in blogging – as the last of the year is rained into submission, I have been travelling. Again. Manchester, London, Brussels, Berlin, Brussels, Glasgow, Edinburgh, Glasgow and a film festival in Cromarty is beckoning, even as I type. Usually I would have taken advantage of the peace and electricity available in this or that train to hammer out something for you, but sadly I was a little preoccupied with sleep, numbed staring, making up twenty minutes of new comedy and fretting about my oncoming novel.

The comedy has been duly delivered to a couple of surprisingly fragrant audiences, my mail, ironing and packing are up to date and I have these small hours of a Thursday morning to ponder.

But before I get to the pondering, I will take a moment to point out that I am aware a number of people who used to be what we might call *friends of mine* now simply read this blog, having entirely abandoned any foolish ideas about phoning me at home for a chat, or actually meeting to do something human. I have been subjected to pathological levels of travel for more than a year now, and whatever relations I had hitherto managed to maintain with non-fictional characters have become almost entirely theoretical. I have even – please forgive me – fallen into the strange pit of gossipy stalkers that is Twitter. At least this allows me to text somebody who might still care – if only because they intend to murder me and then use my skin for cravats. And, as I wandered about in Northern Europe, I was once again struck by how few people on the other side of the Chunnel are welded to their headphones. British high streets are generally packed with what amounts to thousands of competing soundtracks and brave efforts to dodge as much of our prevailing reality as possible. Over There they still do chatting, good coffee and relatively functional public transport. They can also provide civilised, trilingual audiences interested in other cultures and literature in general, at the drop of a jewel-like pastry, and can lavish readers with pleasant venues, varied, well-advertised events and proper media arts coverage. It's boring to have to point this out – repeatedly – but the UK isn't as cool and bright and lovely as we are intended to believe. Our public servants don't just defraud us, they also don't serve us – in detail and day after corrosive, toxic day. And it shows.

But enough about them: actors. Actors are an excellent thing. The Manchester part of last week's itinerary was given over to recording a radio play of mine, and I have to say the proceedings were just a huge joy, parts of which I am still digesting. I knew very little, for example, about the detailed presentation of point of view within sound, and where effects would be live and where they would not and what delicacy and precision goes into the production of radio drama – something I've always enjoyed, since the lovely days when I didn't have a telly.

I very rarely have time to sit in on filming, rehearsals, or even performances of my own scripts. This is very occasionally a blessed relief when I hear later about insane producers, crippling budgets, vicious weather, costumes only fit to be viewed from one side and the risk of death in – for example – improperly choreographed fights, or botched house fires. (No, really . . .) But more usually I find it slightly heart-breaking to never quite know what the last night was like, or to have been somewhere else when a little rewrite might just have helped . . . Manchester allowed me to sit and do virtually nothing for two full days, beyond eating biscuits and listening to excellent performers do what they do, hearing readings develop, interpretations shift and fret and lock, and generally being made very happy. I ended up quite light-headed. This is partly for entirely predictable reasons. If you have Robert Glenister and Bill Nighy flinging themselves into it all day – along with an equally splendid, professional and charming supporting cast – then you will be interested and entertained in the process. Of course. But bear in mind that I fell in love with words because actors said them to me, because they were out loud and happening at me and in me. I hear words in my head when I write them. I sit – in trains, or even my study – building people who don't exist, hearing people who don't exist, until they seem real to me and then perhaps may to somebody else. Imagine what happens when you add actors to that – how very, deeply good it is that the music you couldn't quite hear not only sings in reality, but is far more beautiful than you could have hoped to make it alone. Imagine how permeable proper actors are to language. Imagine people who genuinely possess levels of reckless-ness/talent/training/sensitivity/whoknowswhat and being allowed to hear them let words – your words – penetrate and operate and become what they need to be. It's a strange transaction: on the one hand, the typist (if it's me) experiences sudden rushes of exhilaration along the lines of *I think it, you do it, meat puppets of my brain – oh, life should be like this.* And yet there are also swoops of despair along the lines of *I could do this all again and make it better now I know what you're all like, make it fit better – and thank you for being upset then, and sorry for having to have made you upset, but in that scene it is necessary – and this sounds amazing, but that's you, not me – and that **of** has to go – that **of** doesn't scan at all and should be forgotten and never spoken about again . . . so sorry . . .* And so on. At a certain level, actors are the best readers – it's their job to be. And I hope I can reverse-engineer some response to this whole experience that would improve the reading experience for the rest of my readers. I also need to consider what I can learn from being around people at the top of their game – why are they good? They pay attention, they have a certain type of courage, they are careful of each other, generous, they have interior drives with levels of surprising and usefully applied hunger. What can I apply from this to my own working methods? I don't know yet, but I hope to.

And, otherwise, I am simply full of admiration. As I watched Mr Nighy and Mr Glenister on a monitor, working in what appeared to be a concrete holding cell at Heathrow (the space doesn't need to be pretty, it just needs to sound right) and having to semi-skate on scattered gravel, to produce the necessary effect, while hitting the required mark near the required mike for each cue, while hauling at each other, reading, emoting, taking direction and generally knocking it out of the park with a glorious attention to detail and levels of courtesy and concern for which I will always thank them, I did think very loudly: *bloody hell, what kind of a job is that for human people?* And grinning like a muppet all the while. God bless them, whatever they're up to at the moment.

And onwards.

XVII

I'm just back from meeting and workshopping (let's not mention masterclasses, you know how they make me twitch) with the new year's flock of Creative Writing students at Warwick University. They are, as usual, interesting and thoughtful folk who really don't deserve what the publishing industry will do to them, should it even allow them publication in these apocalyptic times. But, like the inevitability of death, disease and loss, this is a bleak truth we might as well ignore, having little or no ability to amend it. We carry on regardless and find pleasures where we can.

And there are many pleasures to be found in dealing with new writers. I'd like to dwell on two here. The first is the possibility it gives all concerned to examine the craft of rewriting. I wish there were a better term for rewriting, one that was slightly less unappetising and bald – but, in a way, being euphemistic about it would suggest that it is unpleasant and requires sugar-coating. In fact, it is a glorious process. Once you get used to it.

Of course, rewriting does involve writing again – diving back into this or that piece you've laboured at and maybe thought was okay, or at least passable, and you're tired and can't you just leave it? – it's near enough, isn't it? – and yes, there is that section your eye always skips over because it's boring, or unremarkable, or flat-out unbearable, but you're only human, you shouldn't have to suffer for your mistakes – and you're fond of *this* bit – it doesn't fit the story, or the character, not even remotely, but you've had it around in the back of your mind for ages and it needs to go *somewhere*, why not there? Why not let it lurk like an abusive urchin at the blurry end of that sentence? And surely reworking beats all the spontaneity and joy out of your typing mojo, surely this should feel all natural and flowy, surely it shouldn't be so *difficult*?

Oh, but think, Dear Reader, of the dear readers. They've done you no wrong. They have, in fact, sought out your work and allowed it into their mind – deep into their warm, intimate and special personal mind, where they could be thinking exactly what they want to about all the wonders of life. Instead, they chose you. Shouldn't the interaction be – at least in part – about things feeling spontaneous and joyful and all natural and flowy *for them*? They have already been so very kind and inviting, ought they to suffer for your mistakes?

My thoughts would be that they probably shouldn't and that they really ought to be rewarded with all your best and finest, and something better than that. Don't mistake me – I'm not saying that my own attempts at better than best are *the* best, or everyone's cup of tea, or anything other than a failure to live up to my hopes. But it seems only fair to do what we can for the reader. Fair and polite. It's also deeply practical. No one can teach you how to write, or how *you* write or how you could write better. Other people can assist you in various areas, but the way that you learn how you write, the way you really improve, is by diving in and reworking, taking apart, breaking down, questioning, exploring, forgetting and losing and finding and remembering and generally testing your prose until it shows you what it needs to be, until you can see its nature and then help it to express itself as best you can under your current circumstances. This gives you – slowly – an understanding of how you use words on the page to say what you need to. And by making a mental commitment to believe that you are not as good as you could be, you allow yourself to move forward, to mature as a writer. This can seem disheartening and frustrating – why wouldn't it? It involves performing surgery on something which is intimately your own: the way you express your self. But why wouldn't you want to express your voice, your story, your nature more deeply, more beautifully, more effectively? Fretting and worrying at something you made up, an intimate product of your hopes, enthusiasms, passions – it's bound to feel odd, unnatural, but it's also deeply rewarding. In time, you will willingly, if not always happily, put invisible hours and days and weeks of effort into offering someone you don't know, and who will probably never thank you, something which will appear to be 'effortless'.

And don't remind me of the conversation I once had with a prominent academic, who intended the phrase 'But it's so effortless . . .' as an adverse comment on a novel. I simply couldn't rant convincingly enough to ensure that particular book could win a small but useful prize. The narrative's illusion of ease – and just you try creating an illusion of ease, matey – was too convincing. A parallel idiocy might involve refusing to applaud Derek Jacobi or Judi Dench at the end of a performance, because they looked as if they weren't acting.

As our media reduce costs, effort and mutual respect far below a workable minimum, we have become used to programmes, films, broadcasts and reports that appear effortless in the sense that clearly no one could be bothered trying to make them informative, coherent, entertaining or worthwhile. The insultingly slapdash is, at best, presented as being ironic – at worst, it implies that it's somehow what we've asked for, what we deserve. This lack of care is tedious and depressing, but it's also dangerous. The idea that Blair wanted regime change, no matter what, that WMD and the smoking gun were a murderous con, is shocking news again – shocking to the media. Anyone else out there remotely surprised? Millions of UK citizens were more than able to find all those '45

Minutes from Doom' headlines laughable – less funny given that they meant we were about to kill people on a grotesque scale. Simply reading the shamefully weasel-worded dossier, even with no other information available – and other information was massively available – made it clear that the case for war was so shaky that its architects were already shaping phrases specifically to prevent themselves being prosecuted for war crimes. As Dr Kelly said, 'The wordsmithing is actually quite important . . .'

A writer who thinks, who rewrites, isn't just bucking an ugly trend. He or she is also taking control of a power which can delight the heart, encourage, entrance. That same power can deceive, betray and murder and it is a matter of basic self-defence to keep ourselves as literate as possible, as strong as possible in our words.

If you are interested in strong journalism, you might want to follow this link, www.gregpalast.com, to Greg Palast's site. There you can also, should you wish, have the pleasure of donating to a charity dedicated to producing genuinely powerful investigative journalism. Remember Bush stealing the vote – twice? Greg Palast and his team – and *The Guardian* – are why you know that happened.

And the strength of words brings me to my second pleasure in dealing with students: that of simply being near so much *writing*, so much of the energy of individual human beings reaching out to others and defining and uncovering the strengths of their mind and themselves with words and words and words. When you've been locked away with only your own typing, it can be refreshing, if not intoxicating, to feel so much thought, construction, enthusiasm, boiling away on every side.

Meanwhile, spare a kind thought for Sark and the Sarkese – they've just suffered a fairly major landslip that has put Grand Greve Bay out of action. Fortunately, no one was hurt. I like it when no one gets hurt.

Onwards.

XVIII

I do hope the festivities were kind to you. I myself spent the duration lying on the sofa and sincerely hoping that someone would shoot me through the forehead. I find there's nothing quite as effective as Christmas for bringing out all those especially rampant viruses – the ones The Body of the self-employed person saves for rapid deployment as soon as a proper holiday is declared. This is, quite simply, revenge upon The Mind for the rest of the year's truncated nights, double-booked evenings, hair-tearing afternoons and rewrite-and-email-haunted mornings. It is, however, rare for The Body to really rouse itself, dust off its top hat, stop laughing maniacally and playing the organ in the basement (I know, I know) and put together a proper plan for Complete Domination of Everything. This year, however, The Body outdid itself and The Mind's planned break – which was to be filled with nourishing readings from the classics, pottering at the terrifying edges of the new novel and contemplative strolls along the frost-jewelled riverside – actually resolved itself into a tedious amount of throwing up, interspersed by drooling blackouts. Which was restful and cleansing in its own way, I suppose.

And half a mark off to all those of you who briefly thought: *Yes, but surely that's just a traditional Scottish Christmas? The bit after the carafe of Windowlene runs dry and before they start boiling up boot polish with Covonia to release its subtle notes of oak.*

You'll be glad to hear that I was just feeling moderately well and attentive in time for the (albeit strangely/insanely plotted and solipsistic) execution of David Tennant in *Doctor Who*. The Doctor is dead, long live the next Doctor. Meanwhile, as my Inner Child stares, rocks and whimpers in one of my other mental basements (because it's fitting that one fictional construct should mourn another while inside a third – welcome to my brain . . .), the rest of me is back on solids and it's time to look back on 2009's more pleasant aspects. I'd like to at least open 2010 with a touch of zip and to briefly banish any post-Copenhagen conviction that our entire species is doomed and many activities are therefore rather pointless. The more pleasant aspects of my writing life, of course, involve other people. Without other people it would be, in very many ways, impossible to write.

Of course, I now have to break off and agree that writing, particularly novel-writing, does tend to be something one does by oneself. Even those truly, madly, deeply irritating souls who pose with their laptops in fashionable cafés aren't actually collaborating with the baristas. They're – perhaps unsurprisingly – alone. They may even not be utter wankers – they could be saving on their heating bills, or using the dull background hum of cheap dating, caffeinated child howls and Heimlich manoeuvres as a kind of aural wallpaper to block out their internal doubts, or they may simply like being able to look up and find immediate proof that the world contains people they didn't have to make up earlier. The joy and the horror of writing are that it's something you do by yourself – if your name's on it, it's your fault. If your name's on it with somebody else's, it's still your fault. And you'll rarely find multiple authors attached to a literary novel, or a short story – they don't make commercial sense for even one writer. Writers may find like-minded folk they can consult with, or even groups of other writers to support them, but the idea that writers hang out together constantly, taking a deep and involved interest in each other's scribbling as it happens, is less than accurate. Writers can certainly care about *each other* – I'm very fond of my writer chums, for example, and I do love reading what they've come up with. Once it's bloody well finished. Otherwise, I've got my own stuff to write, thanks. Writers who tutor other authors may make suggestions, ask questions, give advice – but eventually the author is alone with the text: every word an opportunity, every word a responsibility, every word another chance. That's at least half the terrifying fun of it all.

So why, if anyone talks to me about my job during 2010 and uses the words *solitary, lonely, isolated* or *the savage wilderness that is your life would make me want to top myself*, do I feel a spot of throat-punching would be in order, if I were not a pacifist? Well . . . for a start, if the writer isn't writing in expectation of the reader, isn't, in some way, offering a letter to an absent love, then why bother? Aiming yourself at a clique of pals, or a market, or up your own private right of way doesn't make for particularly appetising prose. Viciously selfish, compulsive, obsessive and odd though many writers may be, we do everything we do for other people. And then there are the people we make up. Yes, should you watch me writing (for what I can only say would be singularly twisted reasons), I may look as if I'm a bit glum: hunting and pecking away and then staring. And I will have no visible accompaniment. Oh, but inside, Dear Reader – the writer is in minds, under skins, on roads untravelled, and anywhere and everywhere and more. The intensity with which a writer can inhabit a character can make good old reality seem a little bit flat without the use of mental discipline and a will to observe. We have more company than some people will ever know.

Or, we're far too enthusiastic with our imaginary friends. You pick.

And then there are the other people who make sure that our words reach readers and we don't have to shout them in queues, or break in and scrawl them on to sleeping strangers, delightful though that might be. The proofreading may be patchy, incomes may be circling the drain, the assurance and vision may be stunted, but at least we still sort of have a UK publishing industry. *Huzzah!* I've had the same editor for nearly twenty years now. Who can say how my work would have turned out if I'd been slammed stupidly into a niche market, forbidden to write short stories, prevented from making my own mistakes? Who can say how cheering I have found the knowledge of my first reader as that one specific, intelligent and really quite warped personality? Not me, anyway.

Those of you who are familiar with this blog will also be aware that this particular writer couldn't have managed 2009 without, for example, the unsung few who shove refreshment trolleys up and down trains and make a point of actually being pleasant and trying to improve seatless, delayed, boiling, freezing, inexplicable, lost or otherwise disastrous journeys. I would have had much less fun without the festivals in Charleston, Glasgow, Waterford, Edinburgh, Cheltenham, Ullapool, Cromarty, Ilkley, Beverley and Toronto, or without additional audiences in Berlin, Wannsee, Ely, Birnam – and apologies to anywhere I've forgotten. Thanks to the ladies and gentlemen for the notes, emails, letters and gifts of food. Thanks to all the kind strangers who gave me food, in fact. I have often needed it – and clearly looked as if I needed it. And I would have been abandoned like a parcel in all kinds of places without all manner of cabbies, lift-givers and drivers – thanks to them for a magical blend of casual racism, Climate-Change denial, excellent chat, strange anecdotes, health tips and unhinged brooding. Special mention to the madman (in a nice way) who got me from Preston to Glasgow through gales and floods. I can only regret how much CO_2 I must have generated. And thanks to the man who talked about effluent recycling throughout my flight to Toronto – it really was a helpful distraction.

2010 woke up with the start of a new novel for me, so there'll be slightly less travel ahead and a marked increase in penetrating terror at home. Of which more later. Meanwhile, may the next twelve months prove as pleasant as possible for each of you. Onwards.

XIX

So. The New Novel. I'm calling it that in the frail hope that it will hear me and turn into one – at the moment it is, of course, the New Notebook Full of Stuff and a Smattering of Early Paragraphs. A long project is, as you will realise, a massive and potentially ludicrous commitment of time and enthusiasm, which could come apart in your hands at any moment, could promise wonders, cough twice and then turn into ashes and sand at the end of three years' preparation and one year's labour. Its customary horrors have been enhanced this time around by my continuing flu. Many commiserations to those of you who are also still staggering along in the grip of the season's available viruses – you will be well able to imagine how much serious work I've actually managed to get done, whilst feeling that I am trapped on a ship in high seas with someone who is trying to insert a migraine into my face using a dulled Black & Decker router. Round and round the fretting runs: *I should be further ahead. I should get better more quickly. I should have a nice little bundle of pages to ponder and hit with a stick by now. I should . . .*

Well, frankly, I pretty much always *should be* somewhere and someone other than I am at this point. The initial stages of all my novels have always been sabotaged by (in order) my day job, my part-time job, the other writing I was doing while I was writing them, the work I was meant to have finished long before I got to this point and – naturally – the hideous diseases which flesh is heir to, if you persist in making it work and sit on trains and never give it days off and trips to the zoo with balloons. Or even without balloons. And if you have, in general, been unable to continue your programme of inspirational and nourishing treats as you would have wished. I am more worried than usual, but then again I am always more worried than usual – so that must be usual, right?

A greater part of writing than you might suppose relies upon the writer ignoring or temporarily setting aside a whole circus troupe of ugly fears and just typing, in spite of them. Once I've dodged my own novel-related anxieties I can get used to the familiar cycle of enthusiasms and despairs – I wake up in the middle of the night having finally found out the male protagonist's proper name: he promptly stops speaking to me and I lie in the dark wondering what he's up to, if he's found someone else to let him be expressed; I suddenly feel I have exactly the emotional tone and progression for the opening section, it is exciting, clear and inviting: I reach the page and it all veers off somewhere horrible and leaden while I get overly concerned about a tiny and possibly irrelevant description; I think I know the title of the book, I seem to have known it for quite a while and to be happy with it: but is it a *good* title, will it *work*?

Beyond this there is the sense – even if you're entirely well – that putting one word after another is impossibly tiring. Although that's quite likely to be a good sign. Falling asleep in my special typing chair after a couple of pages at the start of a book is, in fact, often an excellent sign. This is because writing prose is exhausting. Not in the way that coal-mining is exhausting, or dragging the body of your frozen companion over an icy Alpine pass is exhausting, but it's demanding, nonetheless. By the end of the novel, things will be easier. Months of concentrating as hard as you are able and then a little bit harder still, of trying to think about sense and musicality and scansion and psychology and tone and metaphor and energy and pace and a number of additional technical doodads will have beaten what's left of your mind into shape and the novel itself will be helping – the characters will be happy to dictate what they will, and will not, stand for and prior events will be contributing their consequences. But I find that, once a book is finished, when I return to it for the first set of overall rewrites after a couple of weeks' break, all of my hard-won stamina has melted away and I am, once again, pathetically feeble. Which is why I'm always happy when a new writer comes to see me and says, in a puzzled and downhearted manner, something along the lines of, 'It's *hard*.' This quite often tends to mean that they have started putting in the amount of effort their work (and the kind lady and gentleman readers) deserves. There are exceptions to this Rule of Tiredness – there are always exceptions in writing. Except when there aren't, which would be the exception to that. I'm never in any way dismayed when something is so anxious to be written that it rips into the page as soon as I give it the chance and won't let me be until it's done – and if I have to load up on Kopi Luwak and Red Bull and hold on tight for a few days to keep up, then so be it. But I've never known that to happen with the start of a novel. In my experience, that tends to be much more like being naked and maliciously observed, while dragging a frozen piano over a muddy Alpine pass, spirit voices gathering on all sides in order to mutter things like, 'You're shit.' And 'This is a bad idea.' And 'You really have no arse to speak of at all, do you?'

Meanwhile, I look forward to being no longer poorly and therefore able to avoid the whole novel-writing issue in a more traditional manner – by dusting, making soup, staring, pacing, repainting the stairwell, dozing, crying, fainting . . . Even so, I'll always eventually end up battering away at the thing until it batters back. It's lovely and it's mind-bending and I wouldn't be without it. Onwards.

XX

Happy New February. I am in my typing chair, surrounded by scribbly bits of paper, bookmarkless books doggedly concealing facts that I need *right now* and data-sticks. You never can have enough backups when you're writing a novel. Thieves may break in and steal your (at home) laptop and your (for travelling) laptop. Hideously unlikely inter-actions of sunlight and magnifying lenses may burn your ecologi-cally shameful, printed-off pages. During an almost inevitable psychotic break you may melt, bend, stamp on or simply eat your auxiliary disk-drive and rats may gnaw to fragments over-night the disks you've hidden under your floorboards. Really you should deposit at least three or four storage devices in the safe-keeping of your doctor, or your bank manager, or someone you can actually trust – and it would be good if you could implant a memory chip about your person, positioned far from any organs valuable enough for forcible extraction by teams of international spare-part thieves, thus keeping your precious chapters free from collateral damage by feral scalpels.

In short, the longer my novel gets, the more anxious I become about its safety and – lunging paranoia aside – the more likely it is that my computer will go into an operatic series of crashes before simply dying in my arms like a concussed gannet. (Readers will remember that I know whereof I speak when it comes to expiring seabirds.) By the end of the year, should all have gone well, my study will be almost impassable and the luggage for any journey beyond the corner shop will include a small fireproof safe.

Not that I believe my novel is any good. I never believe that. And my enduring levels of dissatisfaction can be difficult to explain: telling people, 'I hate everything I produce' seems a tad negative and also suggests that I'm happy to assault the dashing and generous reader with any old nonsense. In fact, I am – believe me – doing all that I possibly can to produce books that are as good as I can make them, and I do believe my work has managed to improve through time. I just never quite climb precisely all the way up my intended mountain – the route gets altered, or the mountain's a bit to the left, or some of the heather's squiff, if not actually broccoli when you look at it closely.

There used to be a delightful pair of older ladies who would attend readings in Edinburgh and loiter until the very end of the signing queue in order to lean forward (to be honest, rather drunkenly) and whisper to unwary authors, 'Yes, but you could do better . . .' Although it was always lovely to meet the pair of them and to see how much innocent joy can be derived from cheap boxed wine, a free evening's heating and applied malevolence, their words were, of course, unnecessary. I already knew I *could do better*. I have *always* known I *could do better*. The one, solitary, mortal thing that I could *not* do any better is knowing that I *could do better*. I'm Scottish. I'm a Calvinist. My cerebrospinal fluid is – I like to imagine – awash with uniquely prickly lymphocytes whose sole purpose is to swim round and round my brain, endlessly carolling: **could do better**.

Okay?

Or rather.

Not okay. *Never* okay.

Which is, perversely, *very much okay*. This certainty of imperfection – in Scots and non-Scots, I'd have to point out – has kept generations of us busily working away, obsessing and convulsing, lest we should fail even more embarrassingly than we fear we might. People like me are always about to be fired, or unmasked, or mocked, humiliated, cashiered, bastinadoed, tarred and feathered and generally knocked about for being dreadful. Believing this too vehemently would – we must surely agree – be catastrophic, but harnessing the little monster in our chests that taunts and derides us can mean that we keep on tinkering and correcting beyond the point at which we might otherwise despair, or surrender, or worry feebly about the bleeding from our ears. We are, in short, a fretting and puzzling fellowship of imperfect perfectionists, flailing gamely through the variously delightful hells of our own making.

Having said all that, I *wouldn't* have said all that if I weren't moderately happy about the tiny amount of typing I've coughed up thus far. If I still loathed it as heartily as I did last week, I wouldn't have been able even to discuss it with you. Had I met you in the street, I would have pulled down my hat and ignored you, weeping inwardly as I loped away to punch myself repeatedly on your behalf. Since then I have erased every repellent syllable of the bilge I managed to secrete over the festive period. (I never do remember not to write when I have flu and am tired, even if I feel I *should* be writing, even if I think I still can . . .) I have started again and am creeping forward between bouts of displacement activity, fourteen-hour jolts of sleep (which do rather eat into the working day) and startling hypnopompic hallucinations. All the above being par for the course. Already, I'm telling my friends about people they've never met, people they can't meet, people who don't exist, people I see in my sleep. As another brace of older ladies I overheard on a train put it so nicely: 'It's better than having your leg cut off.' And how true those words are, even today. Onwards.

XXI

Now then. First off – thanks to those of you who offered expressions of fellow-feeling after my last blog. We are, I like to think, all in this together, and although having written other books with some degree of success may be helpful when you drop off into the abyss of the next one, it can also seem a burden and is certainly, in many very real ways, irrelevant. When we stand at the start of a book, it's not unlikely that we'll all have the distinct impression that we've forgotten to dress and people are looking – and we're up a pole – and covered in angry, greased bats. It may be that we now know how we staggered to the end of the previous books, but that doesn't mean we'll have a clue whether we'll navigate this one to its close or simply expire halfway across its nasty patio, still within sight of its cheap front door.

So here we all are – united and yet hideously isolated by our own bewilderment. And by 'we' I mean those of us who are attempting to type anything – not just those of you who share my species, and with whom I can enjoy a delicious commonality of experiences and dreams. Please feel free to keep reading if you are not a writer, but bear in mind that I will now address you as if you were . . . The point is, it's ridiculous and beautifully unwise of us to even attempt a novel, and anyone who says the process isn't grisly, or won't become so fairly soon, is a big fibber. In my opinion.

Should you be interested, I have clattered out the initial lump of my novel and am now letting it cool – partly so that we can both recover and partly because Other Things have intervened.

Let us discuss Other Matters, beginning with a flashback to some time in the early '90s. Picture me standing, a tyro scribbler, in the London garden of Brian Patten, thinking, 'Ooh. I used to read you when I was at school.' But not saying this, because poets can be sensitive about their age. Mr Patten was a lovely host, but did surprise me by breaking off during our conversation, digging into his pockets and telling me something along the lines of, 'This is what you have to watch for. And *this*. And *this*. *See?*' Out of his pockets he produced . . . almost nothing, mild bits of fluff and nonsense. '*This*.' He waved a palm lightly dusted with what in Scotland we would call *oose* and continued. 'This is what stops you writing. All the *other things*. They get *everywhere. Everywhere.*' And back into his pockets went his fists and on he searched.

I sort of knew what he meant, but as – at that stage – I was still working part-time and believed that a Great Big Full-Time Writer like Mr Patten really had acres of space in which to mentally gambol and invent, I didn't take him too seriously.

He was, of course, right – the main thing that stops you writing when all you technically have to do is write is the apparently gentle stream of minute, but utterly interrupting interruptions. Slowly, all your available pockets do fill with tasks you must perform and which are not proper writing. Some of them are lovely and yet all of them are *in the way*.

Every morning, for example – if I'm actually anywhere near my home town – I must pick up my mail from its maximum-security PO box and then sort it for anything that I might want or understand. Often there are small but necessary contracts and I have to admit that most of them are beyond me, but I do still have to puzzle through them and sign them and parcel them up for posting back. In any week I'm sent four or five books that I haven't asked for and will only have time to read if I do nothing else and, believe me, it breaks my heart that I'm probably not going to give them a quote for their cover, or review them, or mention them in some significant way (the people who send the books think I move in influential circles and cannot be persuaded otherwise) or treat them nicely. I do take some of them home and mean to look at them and then . . . six months later I find them at the bottom of the To Read pile and they stare at me and make me guilty as we run together to the Oxfam shop. This means I'm a bad person, I know that.

And then there are the new writers whose manuscripts need to be supported, and I got support when I was new and so there has to be time made for them, for references and feedback and thinking. And then there are occasionally the students – they need feedback, too. And then there are the emails to and from two different email addresses, very often requesting replies, or attachments, or *treatments* (I have no idea why some people insist on calling a synopsis a treatment, but they do) or some level of coherence.

And then there are the train tickets to be booked – and then the *other* train tickets to replace them, when my plans change and the discount I got for being early turns into a penalty charge for jumping the gun. There are festivals that want information about my technical requirements (I usually have none, but saying I have none takes time, too) and hotels that want me to pay for rooms and make reservations rather than turning up and just crying at them on the night, and then there's the checking and double-checking of both the arrangements I've made and the ones everyone else has, because – believe me – if I don't double-check I'll end up marooned on a rainy Sunday in a disused bus shelter in Ilfracombe. Maybe.

And all this – I do realise – is connected with my being lucky enough to be in work and with my head above water, but it does make me slightly demented before we even add in the things that I do partly because they're interesting and partly because they are 'profile-raising' – all of which seem to involve huge amounts of preparation and *remembering* (when I can no longer recall anything that isn't actually strapped to my body and very clearly labelled) before I straggle about hither and yon and do gigs, or record radio things, or end up being alarmed in a television studio.

I need a PA. I don't have a PA. I can't afford a PA. I've only ever met one PA I really liked and thought was excellent, and he belongs (perhaps literally) to Derren Brown and therefore has much more fun in an average day than I could muster for him in a lifetime. So no PA. As someone once said to a friend of mine at the kind of party I don't attend, 'My people tell me you don't have any people . . .'

But do you know what saves me? Saves what's left of me, anyway? More of the same. (And this isn't just because I'm a Calvinist and the solution to Too Much Work must be More Work.) Either I don't earn a living, or I have to do what I have to do and find ways to make the best of it – at least in part because no human being should ever have to Personally Assist me, even for money: it would be awful for them. So, in the midst of Too Much Mail, More Mail occasionally means that people who've read a book of mine – and who are overly pleasant and supportive – will write me letters and/or send enclosures that are almost always not frightening. And this is cheering and means that for a while I can be less stressed about things which are all manifestations of good fortune and not really stressful in themselves. I can remember that I really have always relied on the kindness of strangers. If they don't read me, all this stops. And since it hasn't stopped yet, I can also fall back on the old, old ruse of using More Writing to make Too Much Writing feel like Calvinist Fun. So, running alongside the novel, I'm encouraging a little radio drama – and when I'm doing one, I can pretend I should be doing the other, and vice versa. It's not ideal, but it's very much better than nothing. Onwards.

XXII

And hello from my hotel room. I can't remember how many hotel rooms I have occupied since I last wrote to you, but they have been numerous and various and have served to confirm me in my belief that I should stick to the same chain if I can, because then I'll always be at home – in somewhere relatively cheap, neutral and suitable for typing. The beginnings and drafts of all my books have, quite frankly, spent more time in hotel rooms than even the most energetic WAG.

For those of you who read the previous blog, my cunning plan to divide my time between the play and the novel (while doing a bit of stand-up and a show in Bath) came somewhat loose on its hinges when the play won, became indecently insistent and ended up monopolising all the parts of last week that I didn't spend either flailing about a stage or hurtling across railway platforms. The play is now with its intended recipient and he has agreed to take care of it – it's probably already peeing on his carpet, chewing his shirt collars and bleating endearingly when he puts it back into its box. For which I, of course, apologise. Naturally, once he's asleep, it will creep out and drink his blood. But only in an affectionate way. Very high-maintenance, plays. And relative peace is descending between meetings – I'm in

London, which is where meetings happen, and muggings, obviously, which are just a kind of vigorous meeting . . . Anyway, I'm overdue for another chat with the novel. A new section is rattling about and needs to be expressed. But, before I start, I thought I'd look at the process of putting one word after another – the process that no one but the author really sees – the process that it's difficult to examine properly, even in one-to-one sessions with students.

So. This won't end up in my novel, but let us say that I have the feeling there's a man about the place and that the place is a room. I wouldn't normally start with something that vague – it would generate an insane amount of rewriting – but this will at least demonstrate that, having written, we can scrabble around and see what the words suggest in the way of playmates they might need and paths they might want to follow. With or without preparation, the picking and grinding and staring that will now ensue are inevitable – prior knowledge would simply make them more informed.

So.

So all over again.

A man and a room.

Right.

A man walks into a room.

We're off then. He's a man, definitely a man, not a lady, or a unicorn, or an urchin – not even urchin-like characteristics – unicorn-like, then? Does he seek out virgins? Not that I'm aware of. Was he at any time a lady? Nope.

A man walks into a room.

Sure it's not *the* man? Bit more definite – *the man*. That being the definite article, and so forth. They're both rather boring, though. What about – *our man*? I quite, for no reason I can put my finger on, like *our man*. It has implications.

Our man walks into a room.

Present tense. Feels appropriate. Doing a lot in the present tense at the moment. Will we argue with the present tense? Not just now. I feel there is something – research, preparation – that tells me things will be revealed about our man, and if he is in the present tense, he will learn of them with us in real time and this seems a good thing. I will keep it for now.

Don't know about the *a*, though . . . The bounce in *our man* seems to render *a room* rather flat and translucent. He isn't a translucent chap. I don't think it's *the room*, either. I think it's *his room*.

Our man walks into his room.

Hmmm. *Walks* is, of course, appalling. Apart from the fact that we may just need the man in his room and may simply assume that he got there in one of the usual ways according to the laws of physics and no entering is necessary – walking is just tedious.

Hopping?

Yes, well, if you're not going to be helpful.

Limps.

Oooh, I quite like *limps* – he may have been to places and done things, our man. He may limp. I may hear the thump of that through a thin carpet and into a wooden floor . . . But I'm mainly having a problem with *into his* – it is slightly difficult to say and therefore to think – it is gluey and unmelodious, somehow. *Into his* . . . I don't like it.

Our man is in his room.

Ah, now then – no mucking about getting there, don't need his life story – well, we may, but not at the present juncture. Yes.

Our man is in his room.

Sort of scans, that does. We need things to scan – presses them so much further and so much more easily into the Dear Readers' brains and they notice them so much less. We need them not to notice, just to open up and let us be. Good. Possibly.

This is a very short sentence – is it a sentence? Are we doing the staccato thing, choppy entrance and then we'll settle down?

He stands.

Apparently we are.

His bottle of rye is in the desk drawer.

Yes, I knew we might wander off down some mean streets in a bit – shut up with your nonsense. He isn't thirsty, he isn't wearing a fedora, although if you want to imagine he's Humphrey Bogart for a while, you're allowed to, because that may help. We like Humphrey Bogart. We have faith in him.

Our man is in his room. He stands.

Is he standing because he was sitting? Or has he been standing all this while? What need we imply?

The leather armchair his Aunt Maude gave him in 1976 squeaks beneath him as he rises in a way that reminds him of his fondness for rubber underwear.

I am going to give you such a slap in a minute. Expo-bloody-sition. Honestly.

He stands by the window.

Okay. Not enough, though.

He stands by the window and waits.

Not entirely unmelodious. Run that all by me again.

Our man is in his room. He stands by the window and waits.

That may do for now.

And it may be that we're a bit choppy, because he's a bit tense, which is fine – he's our man – if he's tense, we all get tense.

The light of the sunrise highlights his broad cheekbones.

Right, I'm filling a sock with room-service apples, taking you into the bathroom and hitting you with it, until you either get a grip or die like the useless weasel you clearly are. *Light* and *highlights*? Because we love helpless and meaningless repetition? And *highlights* anyway? What height is the window – I was getting upper window myself – how is the bloody light striking him? I like that it's sunrise, but I'd prefer *dawn*, off the top of my head, and DON'T LET ME EVER CATCH YOU SLIPPING POINT OF VIEW LIKE THAT — WE'RE IN CLOSE THIRD. HE CAN'T SEE HIS OWN SODDING CHEEKBONES, CAN HE? WHAT IS HE, THINKING ABOUT HIS CHEEKS FOR SOME REASON? LOOKING AT HIS REFLECTION IN THE GLASS, WHICH WOULDN'T EVEN WORK BECAUSE IT'S LIGHT OUTSIDE BECAUSE OF YOUR BLOODY SUNRISE — IT'S THE APPLE SOCK FOR YOU, MATEY, AND NO MISTAKE.

Our man is in his room. He stands by the window and waits and outside the sun is rising and he watches it. There is a slowness about it that he likes.

Maybe. We're less choppy — he seems rather more smooth and substantial here, but I don't like that second *it. Its* can get awfully woolly and, as established, repetition makes me tetchy. *About it that* — bit of a tongue-twister.

There is a slowness to its progress.

Maybe.

There is a slowness in its progress.

Maybe.

There is a slowness in the heat of it that he likes.

And again?

There is a slowness in the heat of it he likes.

We're not shaking the *it*, but it seems more excusable . . . Can't miss that beat, though, I don't think. Once more from the top.

Our man is in his room. He stands by the window and waits and outside the sun is rising and he watches it. There is a slowness in the heat of it that he likes.

And is this a hotel room, or a bedroom, or an office room? Has he been up all night? Does he sleep usually? Is there someone with him? Are they asleep? Why does he like slowness? Does he have a limp? Is it possible to write that without hearing the silent comedy question: *a limp what?*

And on we would go, round and round and round until it's as good as we can manage.

And then some more.

Welcome to the rest of my evening. Onwards.

XXIII

Spring at last, Best Beloveds – and how different those green and airy mornings make my apparently endless battering at the novel.

No. No, they don't: snow, sleet, balmy breezes, my street being inexplicably full of warm and buttered scuba divers – nothing would or could make a difference – with novels, you just have to keep on keeping on. They are a test of endurance. To be more specific, the author does the enduring and quietly harbours tender hopes that the reader will then do some enjoying, or at least get all the way to the end. Although rates of productivity vary, my relatively extensive enquiries suggest that every page in a finished novel will probably represent about a day's worth of scribbling, mooning, prevaricating, really getting into it, shouting at people who interrupt you, interrupting yourself . . . you get the idea. It may not take a day to write 300-ish words, but for every finished, printed, there-you-go-then page, something like a day will have been added to your book's total writing time. So most novels represent a year or more of slog. You may choose to bore your Twitter followers with it – 'novel today' – or to abandon your Twitter followers for it – 'bye for now, I'm writing a novel'. Either way, although it may initially sound a bit impressive as a way to spend your afternoon, it soon starts to seem simply sad, obsessive-compulsive, tedious. Eventually, should anyone insist on asking me what I've been up to, I just pretend I've been mugging pensioners, setting fire to kittens or trying to admire Nick Clegg. (I feel I should be able to; I mean, who else is left?) In this regard, writing a novel is a tiny bit like having a long-term illness: people enquire after it and your relation to it for the first few months and then they don't – they really don't – not unless they're rather peculiar and/or enjoy the discomfort of others.

And then there's the less-visible slog of planning. Well done to those of you who understood what I was up to in the last blog – my attempt to give a small demonstration of the kind of poking and prodding necessary to produce words that are tidy and informative for the Dear Readers. To those of you who thought I generally just wander off into paragraphs without thinking about them first, or that I was – *Sweet God in Heaven and all his furry-toed angels, NO* – showing you something from the novel, then allow me to gently disabuse you on both counts.

First, I plan. I'm a planner. I know I've mentioned this before, but it really is quite important – planning makes life easier and makes something as ridiculously large as a novel possible. We *could* just swim off into one without planning, of course we *could* – we *could* just stick our arms into wood-chippers, or paint ourselves with molten lead – there's no end to the ludicrous and self-harming things we, as human beings, *could* get up to. But, honestly, really truly, novels provide all the ludicrous self-harm anyone could reasonably need. (In addition to all of the good bits.) Set out on a novel without adequate planning and I will bet you considerable sums, perhaps even of money, that you will then fall into a massive chasm, heaving with all the difficulties associated with *not planning*. A novel is a new world, peopled and furnished with the never-were and perhaps the never-could-be. Something as beautifully monumental as that, as founded on thin air and bloody magic, will need preparation. I wasn't kidding about the three years I spend – on and off – fumbling about with settings, finding out about characters, stumbling over lumps of plot and, in every sense of the word, planning. Sorry to bang on about this, but I have, over the last couple of decades, met innumerable people whose novels didn't make it, because they didn't plan. At a certain level, the logic is pretty simple: it's very hard to tell someone a story unless you know what the story is – hence, *planning*.

Methodologies vary, naturally, but being slow of thinking, I would rather potter about for a good long while – as I write other things – and get myself comfortable, enjoy at least two conversations during which my editor suggests that I surely must be ready to get started by now . . . do some more research, have a few panic attacks, do some double-checking and *then* start.

And showing you work-in-progress? Oh, now then . . .

It's not that I don't love and care for you as I would for any reader, but I would be very, very much more likely to have myself filmed while dancing naked across Las Vegas with Michael McIntyre and Jeremy Clarkson and – hey, why not? – Jeremy Kyle than I would be to let you peer at even a paragraph of something I haven't finished. (And, for the more easily confused amongst you, no such film exists – although feel free to look for it, of course.) I have not at any time felt comfortable letting people read my writing when it isn't as close to being finished as I can manage. This is partly because – although my editor is smart as a comfy bag of parrots – someone can only read a book for the first time once. I want whatever happens to him to be as close to the first proper reader's experience as possible, and I'm already having to deal with the facts that he and I have been working together for years, that he tends to get what I mean and that he shares (God help us) many of my interests. He's already much nearer to me than a reader will be, which is potentially fatal when my aim is to be understood by complete strangers – the least I can do is not give him multiple runs through something and a blurry perspective. And other people reading unfinished work? No. Not really. I do run out the opening section of things to editor and agent as a 'Have I gone out of my mind, this time?' test. But, given that neither of them will want to throw me off completely at the start of a book by replying, 'Yes, you've really lost it, give up, it's revolting', I tend to take any enthusiasm with a pan of salt. Anyone else? Any other sections? No. I don't even send the final effort to my editor until it no longer makes me nauseous with fright to get it near a postbox. Or, in these advanced days, near my out-box.

Of course, it hasn't escaped me that I spend a good proportion of my time reading work in progress from new writers of all shapes and sorts – people who are more courageous than me. The first Arvon course I tutored involved me occupying a position of entirely spurious authority, sitting opposite a retired headmaster – a hugely pleasant, sweet and intelligent gentleman of twice my age and experience. His hands were shaking – because I had read his work and was now going to talk to him about it. It's a hugely intimate intrusion, to clomp about in other people's half-formed dreams. Sometimes the dreams are unwise or bewildered, sometimes they need little or no assistance – it's always a privilege to see them, and yet the tutor is always the one who ends up being thanked. And the headmaster? After our hour, he took me outside – being an observant man and a proper educator – and showed me the heaving great rainbow I hadn't noticed roaring overhead. We both enjoyed it equally. 'Help' other people's work and you'll almost inevitably get more help back. Onwards.

XXIV

Dear Christ, just kill me, just please make it stop. Hit me with something solid so that I can lie down, all unthinking, and bleed in a calm and restful manner. Which is to say – *I'm a bit tired at the moment and have stopped greeting people with 'Hello' and am now going with remarks pertaining to and variations on the whole 'Please make it stop' theme.* For goodness' sake, I was in my kitchen at the weekend, genuinely rattling with stress, head ticking away like the Spring Sale window at H. Samuel and *smoking.* I don't *smoke* – it's a vile-tasting form of self-harm which funnels money into the coffers of some grotesquely unpleasant people and is something in which I have never taken any interest. And yet there I was, sucking on a borrowed cigar as if it were my only remaining form of life support and, indeed, a dear and longed-for friend. Obviously, the smoking didn't help – it simply made me feel ill in a mildly distracting manner. I think it is symptomatic of my current condition that this was far more than I could have hoped for.

Don't get me wrong – there is nothing I am burdened with that I don't want to do. I am currently in Cambridge and thoroughly enjoying its Literary Festival. I spent part of my morning reading to kind and attentive strangers with Jim Kelman – who is always an excellent gentleman – and then engaging in a discussion about voice and language that enabled us to mention passion and truth and the nature of humanity and being heard and living lives that are fully expressed and entering into the worlds of others imaginatively in a glorious and healthful manner. There is nothing bad about this. I am simply stuck in a moderately horrifying vortex of novel-typing, other typing, waiting, more waiting, utterly unpredictable rail travel and hotels.

Now, Best Beloveds, I can't bear to think about almost all of the vortex and so I shall now concentrate on its one almost palatable area: hotels. I fear this blog has not, heretofore, paid proper attention to the place of hotel accommodation in the modern writer's life. Trust me – if you have any kind of success with your work, you will be spending more time with carpet toenails, mystery bath hairs, incomprehensible heaters, air conditioners, In-Room Entertainment systems and plugholes than you could have dreamed of in even your most masochistic fantasies. (Yes, plugholes – designers all over the world have clearly spent years perfecting all manner of elegant arrangements which will render you pathetically unable to keep water in your bath or sink and which, given only the tiniest opportunity, will damage you in horrible and permanent ways.) So, let us examine some hotel-related considerations.

First – Food. The acquisition and happy consumption of food in a hotel is always a major issue. Given that you may spend all day getting there and then spend all the next day getting to another hotel – and so on – and may arrive late each evening, outwith the set room-service hours, or there may be no room service, or you may feel that if you have to stay conscious long enough for them to construct a club sandwich and bring it to you there may be a death in your family – yours – then you'll have to take other steps. I tend to prepare myself for touring as I would for camping. I carry a heating element in case there's no kettle, I carry powdered drinks and powdered food with me (either the stuff for building up thin people or the stuff for slimming down fat people: same stuff, different packaging . . .) and I carry cutlery, in case I ever see a shop and can buy real food that I can make into an improvised picnic, or indeed just gnaw in the bathroom while I try to decipher how the taps work. On no account lapse into living on caffeine and biscuits – this will reduce you to a state of weirdly manic malnutrition within days. Hotel restaurants are either full of satellite football games, tattooed men and soiled copies of *The Sun*, or have dress codes and an insistence on staying upright which I usually can't manage when I've been on the road for more than forty-eight hours. There is no comfy and sustaining middle ground. Room service, of course, involves a £300 Tray Charge – which they won't waive even if you give them back the tray immediately or ask that they bring your steak and chips in a carrier bag. Menus vary. A lot. One hotel I know only serves curry in its rooms; I've tried asking for toast, bread and butter, a dish of boiled water – *no, just curry.* I do love curry, but not in a bedroom. Never ask for a cheese and fruit platter – someone will always have left it outside on a window ledge for a couple of weeks before you get it. Never ask for a cooked breakfast, it will have been on the same window ledge since Christmas. Never ask for soup, it will always be unidentifiable and full of *Things*. Hotels within which you basically can't afford to eat at all will provide good and at least warm food, but will justify making you take out a bridging loan to pay for it by adding towers and leaves and twirly, crunchy, confusing adornments and whittled fruit to everything, including your complimentary glass of water. This will bewilder you. The soul-warping mixture of hunger, degradation and/or stupid luxury which results from letting a ghastly range of other people see to your accommodation has led to many scenes I wish I could forget – for example, the tired and withered evening when I simply licked the chocolate lettering off the plate reading 'Welcome, Miss Kennedy', which greeted me when I staggered into somewhere posh in Philadelphia. That and some Cheetos from the railway station provided my calories for the day.

Second – Despair. There will, naturally, be buckets of this. If you have a life, it will seem like a distant and mockingly happy dream. If you – like me – don't have a life, then you will crouch in a corner of your bed, secure in the knowledge that you will now never have time to acquire one. Try to bring things with you which are small, light and also capable of making you happy. Some authors may interpret this to mean booze, drugs and battery-operated aids to relaxation. I might suggest that indulging in these could lead one dangerously astray in an already weakened state. I tend to travel with slippers that remind me of having my feet somewhere I've actually been before and maybe even liked. I carry DVDs and a means of playing them – nothing like Humphrey Bogart or Cary Grant to cheer you. I even bring images of places and people who make me smile, although these can simply reduce me to spasms of helpless longing, so I have to use them sparingly. And I have an alarm clock which doesn't just shout 'Bibbidy-bip!' at me repeatedly. Mine can allegedly provide the sounds of babbling brooks, or rainstorms, birdsong . . . they all suggest a hideous collision in outer space to me, but that's kind of what I was after.

Third – Loneliness. You are mainly going to meet strangers on tour – some of them may be charming, some of them may be revolting; whatever they're like, they'll be gone soon. Some authors find that using a proportion of the available strangers as improvised recreational activities is a way to go – or you may decide, as I have, that this option is inexpressibly depressing and potentially embarrassing, dangerous, infectious, and so forth. Many In-Room Entertainment systems will provide the less-personalised option of 'Films you may wish to enjoy in the privacy of your own room' – which is a very lovely way of saying, 'Fancy a wank? We've got films.' This, again, may well turn out to be the equivalent of digging out your own chest with a melon-baller until your heart is even rattlier and more isolated than it was when you started. The knowledge that others before you may have followed this path with enthusiasm may also make you wary of any objects in your surroundings – especially the remote control. (And for God's sake don't ponder how many people have died and/or shagged and/or thrown up and/or nursed vile diseases in your present position.) You may feel that phoning someone you care for at this point and being offered consolation and diversion would be dandy – it won't. It will simply define your lacks all the more clearly, give you taunting dreams and/or make you wonder what they're actually getting up to without you.

In your spare moments you will be able to listen to the occupants of other rooms dying, shagging, throwing up, nursing vile diseases, arguing, running, laughing and occasionally playing musical instruments. Their televisions will interrupt your fitful slumbers, as will your own room's heating and plumbing and the radio alarm that some malicious bastard set to go off at 4 a.m. and never cancelled.

And when you're not having all this fun? If you're me (sorry to suggest such a thing) you'll either be out with the general public, reading, or talking, or workshopping, or lecturing, or performing and trying to give a halfway convincing impression of being functionally human, or else you'll be clattering away at your laptop, propped on pillows and contemplating the tiny pack of fruit-shortbread biscuits. Biscuits it is. Then earplugs and sleep. And then onwards . . .

XXV

The next blog was written in the immediate run-up to the 2010 general election that brought us the Cameron-Clegg coalition. Which is to say, this was written during the brief period in which Nick Clegg was regarded with some degree of respect/ affection.

Is it that time again? Am I really propped up on yet another hotel bed and nursing my bruised laptop into one of our usual time-delayed chats? *Yes.* Am I at another festival? *Oh, yes.* Am I in Galway, at the very lovely Cúirt Festival, surrounded by still-trembling and weeping participants who had to get here in the non-flying, convoluted, mind-crushing and spine-warping ways that I now take for granted as an inveterate airport avoider? *Indeed. I am.* And may I just mention that I have quite recently decided my accommodation should always feature a small chandelier and a Jacuzzi. I am very fond of my Jacuzzi, it is tender and true, and – in fact – should we grow any closer, I may have to marry it.

I've already mentioned how nourishing it is to attend festivals and meet members of the public who care about books and who greet them with intelligent enthusiasm. It's also great to be away from the *hate-yourself-but-others-more-and-oh-look-an-election-ah-CLEGG* UK media. And, naturally, it's entirely pleasant to have a response to my work which arrives within seconds, rather than years, and to just generally spend time with people I didn't have to invent and then sustain by force of will. (Obviously, I could be wrong about this last point and you may all be projections of my subconscious, but I'm choosing to hope this is not the case . . .)

Festivals also provide an opportunity for writers to meet other writers and this can be a splendid thing. (Although we should always be prevented from breeding – the resultant impoverished gene-pools, interlocking autobiographies and *romans-à-clef* would be more horrible than we can imagine – and we can imagine a lot, as you know.) But there are always pitfalls when it comes to encountering writers, even if you are one yourself.

For example – do you really want to say hello to X or Y author, whose every semi-colon has caused your tiny heart to flutter like a prayer flag in a breeze of pure delight? What if they turn out to be a twat? Then you'll feel betrayed and unable to read them. Actually, it's quite unlikely that someone whose work you really connect with won't be someone with whom you would also get along – their work is of them and from them and will be dibbled all over with things that are, in various ways, highly characteristic of who they truly are. Like the fruit – enjoy the tree. But they may be having an off-day – or a divorce; writers are constantly getting divorced, it's not unlikely. Be careful with yourself in this regard, perhaps observe your idol for a while before approaching and, should he or she cuff an old lady out of their way or step on a dog, then maybe allow them to retain their mystery. And bear in mind that, if you do approach them and interact, you will think that you know them already, even though you don't. Writing and reading are intimate processes and so, in a way, you have been doing an intimate thing together, in your absence. This can be both unnerving and misleading. If you consider that even I – your humble, raddled, permanently weary and deeply unprepossessing author – have encountered a number of gentlemen who decided to be in love with me within moments, purely because my texts had previously interfered with them, then you can imagine what a minefield this becomes for people who are attractive and good at social contact. And, of course, I have fallen distantly and quietly in love with authors myself. It's hard not to – their voice is already in your mind, the walls are breached. Best to run. I always do.

Above all, I avoid talking to other writers about writing. This seems counter-intuitive, but trust me – the last thing you want is to be discussing the thing you love doing most in the world, the thing that is woven up and down your arteries and in the marrow of your bones, and to find *they don't do it the same way*. When you're inexperienced, this dreadful revelation makes you feel you should give up at once because you're an idiot. When you're a little more grounded, it can lead you into terrible, never-speak-to-me-again arguments and, whatever else happens, it will be disturbing. Deeply.

Let me put it this way: I have chums who are actors. They have to do actory things and this occasionally involves their being unclothed and simulating activities which would not normally involve a focus-puller and someone who powders your arse to stop it shining. (I don't mean porn, I mean proper acting. I don't know anyone who does porn. No harm to them, I just don't.) Now, of my chums, some are happy with the whole – if the part requires it – naked and groaning thing and find they can think of it as something sculptural and interesting and they are, of course, meanwhile involved in working and concentrating and remembering what they should do and say, and so it's really no big deal and they are wholly comfortable with the undertaking. (I would have to point out these are people who have relatively high self-esteem and with whom I have difficulty identifying.) Other chums are not happy – they worry that their physical manifestation is unsaveably awful from any and every angle and worry further that when they are pretending to do this, that and

– most particularly – the other, there will be something funda-mentally *wrong* with their presentation. Yes, they're only acting, but somehow the *way* they are acting will let an entire stricken film crew and then generations of nauseated viewers know that, in their own personal lives, they are deeply peculiar and/or pathetic and/or borderline criminal.

I, naturally, identify much more with these chums. And, for me, hearing a fellow-practitioner describe a writing process which is utterly and shakingly alien is always going to be very much like having the director faint and your collaborator throw up in a corner, simply because you've made the noises you always make at home and which seem perfectly normal to you, while going through moves which are the best representation of physical affection you can muster and – again – seem quite reasonable, and why are those guys laughing and why have they called the police?

Humiliating, corrosive, bewildering – that kind of stuff can throw you off for months. I'm more than happy to accept that the multiplicity of writings and writers give rise to innumerable methodologies and there is no harm in this. It is sometimes hugely stimulating to learn from the differences, the conflicts in beliefs and approaches to a craft. But it may not be the best use of your time.

When you meet someone who is in harmony with your aims and hopes, who's up ahead, who's tried things and been brave in places you haven't imagined, who is like you, but bigger and better and finer – that's when I find the real learning begins. Sometimes in a chance meeting over breakfast, sometimes during an event, sometimes as part of a correspondence – you never know when someone will make the whole thing five-dimensional, pressing, new. But you can hope for it, be ready, keep alert – as any writer probably should in general. And there's always the option of reading, of dropping into the minds you admire. I am, for example, currently reading R.L.

Stevenson's essays on fiction and, once again, realising what an altogether excellent thing he was and – in the way of writers – still is.

And the young writer will not so much be helped by genial pictures of what an art may aspire to at its highest, as by a true idea of what it must be on the lowest terms. The best that we can say to him is this: Let him choose a motive, whether of character or passion; carefully construct his plot so that every incident is an illustration of the motive, and every property employed shall bear to it a near relation of congruity or contrast; avoid a sub-plot unless, as sometimes in Shakespeare, the sub-plot be a reversion or complement of the main intrigue; suffer not his style to flag below the level of the argument; pitch the key of the conversation, not with any thought of how men talk in parlours, but with a single eye to the degree of passion he may be called on to express; and allow neither himself in the narrative nor any character in the course of the dialogue, to utter one sentence that is not part and parcel of the business of the story or the discussion of the problem involved.

That's from 'A Humble Remonstrance', Best Beloveds – something to read and inwardly digest. Onwards . . .

XXVI

The post below was written on Guernsey, while en route to Sark.

We can just take the whole hotel room, tiny biscuits, UHT milks, fighting with the dodgy Wi-Fi and eating out of carrier bags thing for granted now, can't we? Although I will point out that I am currently On Holiday, rather than Working. Being On Holiday is something I am very bad at and rarely try. As far as I can tell, it involves not really knowing anyone, paying your own hotel bill and lying on a bed in the evening typing, just as you would at Work. So slightly annoying, really . . . Soon, I will get into the running-up-and-down-cliffs part of the proceedings and my physical exhaustion will cause what's left of my brain to fail and that'll be much more relaxing. (But I'll still be typing. A bit. The novel will shout at me if I don't. Or rather, the people in the novel will shout at me – which is a good, if exhausting, sign.) But now I must, of course, offer deep, head-holding, Brownian apologies to the respondent to the last blog who says I was rude to him at some point. I do, of course, always try not to be rude, but sometimes . . . well, let's consider.

Sometimes members of the public are themselves rude, or want something from me which I cannot provide. (And, Lord knows, that can cover a multitude of what many religions would actually regard as sins.) But this is very, very rare – and I'm sure doesn't include the respondent. The vast majority of people who would bother coming up to an obscure scribbler are already self-selected for niceness. So we can proceed to possibilities A and B, both of which say a good deal about the writer's life and the sad fact that – even if you are fantastically obscure – the usual rules of being recognised will apply: whatever you do or say will be taken as characteristic of your whole life and self, and filed away under your name with a number of cross-references and brought out in casual conversation as a Fact. This is not in any way the full-on horror of being well known and screamed at outside exclusive nightspots, or being asked to sign people's genitals – it is more like wandering your local high street while vaguely under the impression that you should be on your best behaviour. Sort of like being at your scary Auntie's – for ever and ever.

So. Possibility A. I may have been interrupted by a perfectly pleasant member of the public while talking to someone I already know, or on my way to meet someone I already know. This seems innocuous enough and it is – or would be, if I didn't spend most of my life in transit, and if even godchildren and dear friends are people I may see once a year if I'm very lucky, determined and ring-fence a dozen or so possibly compatible dates the preceding Christmas. It may look, to a casual and book-enthused observer, as if I'm just chatting, or strolling with determination in a fixed direction, but I may, in fact, be spending visibly dwindling minutes attempting to remind myself that I am a human being, that I like other human beings and bonding and hugs and mutual affection. (Within reason – obviously; it all gets claustrophobic after two or three hours . . . Ah, but those two or three hours are lovely and restorative.) I was watching *Romeo and Juliet* recently and caught myself thinking: *Star-crossed? Star-crossed is **easy**. They get to dance, joke, flirt, chat, marry, shag, chat and then muck about in a crypt and even die together. Just about. Try Schedule-conflicted: that'd knacker the whole bloody play. 'Well, Jules, I have* *a window in July. Maybe. But if the wind changes and the ash cloud relocates over Gatwick, then the Friar won't get back in time for the ceremony – and the poison merchant's stuck in Tuscany for some reason – can't get him on his mobile . . .'* So, yes – I freely admit there have been times when I have been short with people under those circumstances and afterwards (once it has been too late) I have thought: *Oops, that was a bit brisk.* But by then the damage has been done and, meanwhile, I'm trying to catch up with news about children I last saw in rompers who now have tattoos and degrees in mechanical engineering, or illnesses and mishaps, or instances of serendipity, and impressive successions of husbands, wives, partners and flings, all of whom have come and gone (as it were) without my having met them. I'm still in the wrong, but it's a kind of excuse.

Possibility B. I may have been poorly/tired/poorly and tired. Given that the writer's life is, in many ways, jam and then gravy and then more jam, not a lot is written about the physical demands of something which seems to involve (in a high percentage of cases) not even all the author's fingers, never mind heavy lifting.

Then again, yes, of course, the writer is a pampered and lucky creature and we mustn't forget that, but the occupation does bring with it physical perils beyond the usual self-inflicted overindulgences. Writers tend to be cerebral and not entirely excellent at expressing their emotions in a healthy manner. This may partly explain all that typing, but it may also give rise to tension – especially spinal tension. Add in poor posture, badly positioned screens and keyboards and unergonomic everything elses and you'll find you have a profession full of people with more or less wrecked backs – a profession which expects its practitioners to travel, to sit on planes and trains and in ferries and cars and do, now that you mention it, a fair amount of heavy lifting. Unexcitingly strange beds, long hours, insane schedules (and – *Christ!* – German schedules . . .), jetlag, frequent-flyer's lung, sketchy nutrition, sleep-deprivation and visibly frayed immune systems can swoop in to hammer a writer at any time. These sound like High-Class Problems – and they are. You have to be published and sort of at least making it as a writer a little to be seriously afflicted. But it's less than joyful to find that serious illness halves your income, stops you travelling and punches a hole in your plans for sustainable self-employment, simply because you were in work and doing all the nonsenses that involved.

The days of averagely successful writers being able to earn a living simply by writing have probably gone, if not for good, then for the foreseeable future. The tiny percentage at the top of the iceberg will be okay, everyone else will be cold, or cold and underwater, or cold and underwater and pale and bloated. This will mean more hours for huge numbers of writers, more work to subsidise the work you want to do and more risk of falling apart while you push yourself too hard to get that extra inch forward. Stress, unwise use of a laptop, over-long working hours and general lack of forethought left me with ten years of chronic back pain and the unpleasant impression that one decade would follow another until I just coiled into a knot like a worm left on hot crazy paving. Fortunately, I'm almost always pain-free now, but, all you fellow-writers out there: don't let your love of the words drag you off into unsafe practices, strain and long-term damage. Spend a bit more for a decent keyboard, or a good chair, take breaks. Defend yourself. Make your boss look after you – you're the only workforce he, or she, has got.

Which is a long way of saying: *I may have been rude because I was in pain and wanted to lie down in a darkened room with a TENS machine and some feeble over-the-counter pills, because ten years of effective pills would have been a problem in itself.* And, if that's the case, I may not even have noticed the incident and I probably didn't regret it. I probably wanted to kill whoever else was involved for breathing too loudly, or looking healthy. Not nice, but true. Being unwell is shit – and I hope I never forget it, partly so that I'll look after myself and partly so that I'll be vaguely tolerant with other people who aren't well – even if their not-wellness is the long-winded and vaguely invisible sort.

Hence the holiday. So I can be grateful that I can scale cliffs, so that I can actually stop for a bit, so that I can stroll back of an evening and enjoy the company of the imaginary people – or leave them to get impatient for a while. It may do them good. Onwards.

XXVII

Okay, those of you out there who are kind and lovely – and that's many of you – please either stop me from ever taking another holiday, or stop me from taking a holiday during an election which will unpredictably generate long hours of suddenly requested scribbling, or stop me from taking a holiday which involves cliff-scrambling all day and then typing all night in a warm Sarkese Hobbit hole and then feeling all wibbly and translucent through the complicated ferry and train wanderings to which we flight-phobics must submit in order to get home from anywhere. Because that kind of holiday makes me so tired that I eventually end up living entirely on Red Bull – which stops me sleeping – to get through the complicated, nervy days of doing vaguely media-related things – which means I *need* sleep – and the continuing novel-tinkering – which means I *really need* sleep . . . The media things may help my publisher remember who I am at the end of the year and treat my novel gently when I hand it in. Or at least it will mean the marketing people may know who I am, even though I can't play football, have a tediously windswept sex life, couldn't dance underwater for a place in a West End musical if you paid me and am highly unphotogenic. (All disadvantages for the modern novelist – Graham Greene never had these problems, you can bet . . .)

I trimmed my nails today – fingers *and* toes – and reflected on how long it's been since I last gave time and attention to those tiny details which prevent one from looking like a mad-bag-cat woman. I think my most recent haircut was in February – the guy knows now to just hack at me savagely whenever we do meet and then we can try to last out the next four months. Not how to look your best when, well . . . basically you're never going to.

But – despite the surrounding chaos – it was lovely to sit on Sark with the ravens and the bluebells and the Sarkese and to have six uninterrupted evenings with nothing but the novel, improvised dining on buttered digestive biscuits, peace and more novel. It made being under a deadline almost cosy. And the lady who was renting me the Hobbit hole eventually worked out that the dusty, peering and mumbling thing occasionally clumping past her door was relatively safe, if eccentric and biscuity. I have now reached the traditional Aboutathirdofthewaythrough Stage when I run everything off on paper again and hit it with a stick before going back into the next Stage, which I like to call The Horrifying Slog.

Meanwhile, I took an evening off when I finally made it home – via Weymouth, London, Chichester and London – and trotted out to see Derren Brown doing the range of excellent things that he does onstage. Now this is slightly because I have an interest in magic (Grandpop gave me a book about Houdini when I was tiny and it all went downhill from there), but it's much more because I have an interest, of course, in story – in pure story and how powerful it can be. Why was I actually, in fact, reading *The Hobbit* in my burrow on Sark? Because the best of the children's stories are so very, very vigorously themselves – they aim to transport, to suspend reality, and they do. They penetrate and delight and return us to ourselves, slightly altered, slightly more than we thought we could be. I read and believed *The Hobbitt* when I was young – it was company and exercise and joy – and reading it again reminds me of the uncomplicated faith I had in books, a faith that is useful to a writer. It also reminds me of the pleasure in the pages. I always hope (despite the filth and misery of which my narratives consist) to write in the spirit of that first enthusiasm and certainty and to try and pass on something of that fun to the reader – even though I write for adults and even though I'll never succeed as I'd wish to.

And Mr Brown? Well – more of the same really, except played out in real time, in a very hot, very full theatre. Professionally speaking, Mr Brown is himself a story – like any very fine magician, he doesn't throw out a succession of tricks, which, however wonderful, would still be just a number of ways of being clever using more or less layered and skulduggerous means. He tells us a story of himself and a story of where and who we are and of what is occurring, and he tells it so well that we believe it – even though we are all grown-ups and we know we should never, ever believe a magician. And, within the right story, magical effects can sit up and shine and become emotionally charged and personally significant and much more deeply and pleasantly misleading. The hand isn't quicker than the eye – our eyes are really very quick – it's just that the story makes us misinterpret the hand, forget the hand, assist the hand, whatever is necessary. The story is both an unlooked-for beauty and a lovely misdirection and – along with many other secretive and sneaky elements – it means that, for a while, we can believe in miracles and nonsense and people who've never existed and a range of exhilarating and puzzling and moving possibilities. As an audience member, this always makes me jump up and applaud like a happy sea lion. As a writer, this always reminds me that the magical fraternity have rather deftly (and typically) pocketed the term *thaumaturgy* – the working of wonders – for themselves, when really all the arts should have access to it, including the writers and – for goodness' sake – shouldn't I be trying to learn from those stories, from those illusions, when I'm in the business of making my own? I would say so.

Naturally, Mr Brown is – in his professional capacity – a great big fibber and delighted to say so. His dark arts aren't really dark at all. But the dark is, of course, out there. I also like to explore the work of people I find entirely unentertaining, thuggish and morally repugnant – to examine the dark. (And I hope you know by now that I have no illusions about how high my moral high ground is, but even so . . .) The world is full of hucksters who want to sell you their way of cranking out hypnotic prose that'll get clients to pay over the odds, or buy rubbish, or believe your self-help system/diet/philosophy/return from the dead/redemption, and so forth. They lie to you about your lying to other people and hope your greed will satisfy theirs. They offer you the letter format they suggest will guarantee replies, the way of presenting yourself that will guarantee you get the job, or win the poker game, or dominate your colleagues, or sell you a way of talking that's meant to guarantee you can shag your chosen victim before they discover how dreadful you are . . . stories about stories about stories . . . And need I dwell on our latest election and all those words and words and words? *Trust me, don't trust him, blame them, be scared, be proud, be angry, be quiet . . .* the interwoven narratives within narratives that we either buy, or don't buy. It's grubby and appalling and I don't visit often, but I do nip in now and then, just to check what they're peddling and how. In a time when art has to justify itself and when craft in prose is overlooked, or seen as foolishness, I like to stare at the undeniable power behind it all, the huge amoral force of story. We are the ones who chose to be dark or light, chose the stories we tell ourselves and others: in work, in play, in love . . . in all of our lives.

Then I go back to whatever temporary address I'm borrowing, get the head down and try working back to the wonder. Onwards.

XXVIII

Glad I had the holiday then, cos the seemingly eternal trains, deadline-haunted scribbling and trying not to cough while speaking for Her Majesty's Wireless kicked in immediately thereafter and hasn't left me alone since. I did manage to batter the existing bit of the novel into a slightly less horrifying shape – mainly going to and from Inverness – but the thing is now chewing doggedly at the back of my head and whining for attention while I have to ignore it and get through a week of more short-term writing and seeing the students at Warwick. It's my last visit of the year to the university, which is always slightly nerve-racking, as another crop of new writers prepares to plummet off what we might choose to call the savage cliffs of optimism, hoping to land in what we might choose to call the urine-filled thimble of British publishing. They are nice people, they work hard – I can only wish them well and try not to get tearful. And they may make it. Eventually. Send them all a kind thought, if you have time.

But after that – more novel. Ish. Kind of. In someone else's house. But definitely novel. As far as I can tell.

At which point I usually compare my life to those of so many other novelists who are (perhaps inaccurately) quoted as saying they 'always complete the final draft in my suite at the Carlyle' or 'my writing room faces the smaller of our lakes and has a delightfully inspiring view across the Chilterns/Dartmoor/the Swiss Alps/Dollis Hill . . .' or 'I always get up at 4 a.m., sip my organic mint tea – dew-kissed leaves fresh from the sunken garden – and then five or six thousand words can tumble forth before Freddie and Timmy and the dogs wake up and I have to oversee Marta while she makes them breakfast – she's from the Philippines and simply doesn't understand toast . . .' and so forth.

Eventually, if you type anything at all, you will – of course – be asked about your Typical Writing Day and you will have to say *something*, or be sneered at and mocked during writerly social occasions. (Which may be why I avoid writerly social occasions.) It is never accepted as being factual or sincere, if your answer to the 'What is your Typical Writing Day?' question runs: '*Dear God, I would beg for the ability to even contemplate a typical writing day, I would offer up my eye teeth – and my eye teeth are big, you could make scrimshaw snuff-boxes, if not children's clogs, out of my eye teeth . . . I would offer up my entire supply of Kopi Luwak for the chance to have my typical writing day – help me, help me, bits keep dropping off . . .*'

But I do have an Ideal Writing Day, a Hoped-for Writing Day, and sometimes – when I really do need to get cracking – I arrange one, if not more. After roughly twenty-five years, this is the best I can come up with.

Morning – I avoid it. I'm rubbish in the mornings, I can't think, can barely speak and shouldn't be allowed to type. I don't want to eat breakfast, I want to be asleep and dreaming of my happy place – and, let me tell you, my happy place is really bloody happy, so don't arrange unreasonably early meetings, don't phone me, don't buzz the doorbell, leave me be behind my blackout blind and go away.

Lunchtime – have shower. Wake up gently, but not so gently that I get confused in the shower and inhale soapy water. Dress in something comfortable; it should preserve me at an appropriate temperature and not chafe, annoy or depress. Then have first meal of the day. Ideally, this should be small and taste of nothing that's distracting – porridge, oatcakes, play dough, styrofoam, maybe toast. Then eat toast (or less-stimulating substitute) and drink something containing a gentle amount of caffeine, while looking at my emails and discovering that none of them need to be answered and at least one of them is funny.

After lunch – put on shoes, nip down to get vegetables and sundries and to pick up non-email from the nice people who guard my PO Box and look askance at lumpy and/or oozing envelopes. Bring home spoils, go through mail and find – to my delight – that all of it can be thrown immediately into the recycling bag. Take off shoes. After that, do Tai Chi, because it does seem to help with concentration and gives me an important sense of smugness, balanced by the humiliation of wobbling and falling over if I get mentally or emotionally waylaid. Then do voice exercises because they are good for me, because without them performances have less welly – and I need all the Wellington I can get – and because cramming your brain with oxygen while feeling your own voice rattling your skull and being a tangible and forceful thing does no harm. If you're about to head off for the study and yet another attempt to slap your voice down in print, then it probably does no harm at all.

After that – have slightly more caffeine, put on some suitably encouraging music and then waste time playing an incredibly simple game on my computer; this is almost like work, but not quite. Having promised myself one more game, suddenly open the current file for the novel (or short story, let's not forget the short story . . .), tip my good-for-a-bad-back chair into the fully recumbent writing position and slide into the text gently via whatever is already there, inching forwards towards what is not there, but really should be by the time I have to cook dinner. Stop just before I run out of things to say. Turn off the music.

Pre-dinner – cook something which is fiddly and tedious, like stew or curry, while allowing the subconscious to fumble about at those things left unsaid in a manner which will encourage them to grow large and invite their chums round.

Dinner – eat while watching an uplifting and pleasant DVD with proper actors and a real script. Try to relax. Try not to think about the book. Finish meal with slightly more caffeine and possibly some fruit – which is good for me – and then lie on the sofa until the DVD has finished. Be as happy as possible. Hope that no one phones me and interrupts.

After dinner – go back to the study, turn on the music and write like a bastard, because I'm awake now, it's getting/has got dark, I'm slightly wired with all that coffee and the idea I was studiously ignoring while I watched a movie is so keen for attention that it has actually agreed to cooperate.

After that. *Shit!* – look, it's 2 a.m. How did that happen? Quite tired. Must remember to save work, to make multiple backups, to place the backups in locations that will be subject to different and, hopefully, non-simultaneous accidents, turn off computer, turn off music and then have a bath – total submersion if possible.

After that – sit on sofa, dripping gently and watching another nice DVD to chill out a bit, or I won't sleep. Then tiptoe off to bed. Hope for dreams of a) Happy Place b) relevance to novel or the characters therein.

Repeat as necessary.

It doesn't happen often, but when it does it's such a help.

Hope your days are at least approaching your ideal. Onwards.

XXIX

Now then, as a variety of sporting events continue to annoy me and my novel turns its petulant head from me as if I were an unsatisfactory and clumsy-thumbed lover, I must find something writing-related with which to (hopefully) beguile you and (rather pathetically) distract myself from the savagely pointing and giggling paragraphs with which I am now faced on a daily basis.

Yes, it's The Middle Bit of the novel – a completely soul-grinding and exhausting tramp across rewrites and rewrites and rewrites while I recalibrate my instruments to take into account the changing value of the Yen and the position of Venus, neither of which should exert a massive effect – but then again, over time, any slight discrepancy means I'll end up taking an unwary walk into a chasm, rather than enjoying an amble amongst honeysuckle and endearing woodland creatures.

But enough of that . . . Mustn't focus on the idea that my whole plot is only inches away from dropping off a cliff. I do. But I mustn't.

So let's distract me with a different brand of savage pointing and giggling and the question of appearance. My appearance.

Time was, writers didn't have to *appear* – they didn't need to support and maintain *an appearance*. Leastways, they may have – reciting around the cooking fire or across the banqueting table

– being storytellers and storymakers, perhaps even simultaneously (or, in the case of Homer, perhaps being many storytellers, or a collective of some kind, or – who knows. – a cave full of Mediterranean orphans forced to invent plotlines . . .), but that wasn't really *appearing*, not in an aesthetically onerous sense – everyone was equally covered in mammoth blood and filth, or olive oil and filth, or leprosy and filth, and all was well. Authors existed, but were anonymous – their stories were fiddled with and added to and improved as necessary, which the authors partially prevented by making them rhyme and scan – but still, the emphasis was on the stories themselves, the characters, the heroes and heroines and excitingly unlikely animals and the monsters, deities and events.

Then the ages rolled by and parchment and reading and writing and professional scribes and so forth became possible and so books existed, in various forms, and this meant that they could influence, delight and speak *without their authors.* They could even – accidents and fires in Alexandria aside – outlive their creators, which may have led many authors to conclude: *I shall leave all that public-appearance malarkey to troubadours and players and fools and recline here in my hermitage, making up stuff and being as ugly and ill-kempt as I see fit.*

Later still, authors became more prominent. Chaucer was a bit of a star in his day, for example, but still didn't undertake any broadcast interviews of which I am aware. He wrote *The Canterbury Tales* and they were funny and wise and moving and rude and people spoke in them the way that people actually spoke, so the people who read them, or heard them being read, or simply heard of them were rendered happy – end of story, no air-brushing, or HD-friendly preparation and fluffing required.

Moving on again, authors and publications and printing presses proliferated, but there still wasn't a lot of *appearing*. Even though Shakespeare, for instance, was an actor and did perform onstage and give elegant little speeches at court, we have no idea what he really looked like – possibly fat-necked and brain-dead, as in his memorial bust at Stratford – possibly dapper and a bit louche, as in the latest re/discovered maybe-portrait. That portrait is interesting because – if it is of Shakespeare – it was made during his lifetime and may show early signs of what I term Author Appearance Anxiety: he's wearing somebody's very best doublet, if not actually his own, has a beard so well combed it's alarming, and his hairline has been adjusted in a series of repaintings so that its desperate retreat from his eyebrows has been not only arrested, but radically reversed.

And then we arrive at the age of lectures, recitations and readings. Dickens – an actor manqué with complicated reasons for wishing to be mobile and earning – trod the boards extensively. He may even have toured himself to death. He may also have caused publishers to notice how well his backlist sold after he'd been in town, giving his all to Little Nell for the admiring multitude. This may have helped to herald in the modern age of author-with-audience-related shindigs – and their accompanying on-the-road fatalities.

Now, those of you who read this blog regularly will know that I have no objection to reading or performing – both can be lovely, life-affirming and useful things. The hideous travel between gigs and the horrors of infectious, debilitating and frankly threatening accommodation have been dealt with elsewhere (and you can bet they will arise again), but the *appearing* . . . that's a different matter.

As more and more events are billed – both dreadfully and wrongly – as *A Chance to Meet the Author of* . . ., cosmetically challenged writers such as myself have more and more opportunities to find themselves disappointing. You have no idea how guilty I feel when I consider the photographic reproduction of my head at the top of my *Guardian* blog or other newspaper manifestations, and the likelihood that you will have to look at it. I can and do – of course – avoid mirrors and dodge snapshots whenever I can, in many ways living like the owner of an ugly house in a lovely landscape: I get the delightful view and everyone else has to suffer my vile pinkwash, ill-considered storm porch and horrible proportions. But the business of being a writer requires photographs, is pathetically delighted by television outings and contractually insists on the public exposure of folk who otherwise sit alone with imaginary pals and fidget their hands about.

So I make an effort. It's only polite. Over the past twenty-five years I have genuinely tried to find a way of scrubbing up that would actually look as if I am scrubbed, or at least up, rather than simply highlighting my available deficiencies. My own Author Appearance Anxiety has created a number of imaginatively disastrous 'looks', including the *my fatter, taller sister is a social worker and lends me her clothes*, the *reserve policewoman*, the *apparently lesbian solicitor*, the *yes, everything is leather because it's warm and doesn't crease – it doesn't mean I want to tie you up or hit you for your, or indeed my own, entertainment – please go away now* and my current: *this is quite a nice shirt and at least I've been able to get a haircut now my neck's better – and I have a nice coat: it's willing to tolerate me until a better author comes along.* Add in the variously benign, malevolent or over-enthusiastic attentions of TV make-up personages in a number of locations, the effects of exhaustion, jetlag and a poor/odd/worrying diet and the ability of all photographers everywhere to catch exactly the angle and expression to immortalise me for ever as a demonic gonk/idiot non-savant/ botched facial-transplant case – when, from the best of angles, I am usually close to all three – and you can understand why I would prefer to – very literally – draw a veil over many proceedings. As age and gravity assert themselves, my incipient goatee becomes luxuriant and my teeth remain as equine as ever, I can be sure that matters will only deteriorate. Although this should have very little to do with me, or my job, it does. And I am sorry for it. I will, in fact, take this opportunity to assure you, Dear Readers, that I am as sorry for it as I can be and will remain so. There is no more that I can do. Onwards.

XXX

And as the summer asserts itself, albeit damply, I am reminded yet again that there is an optimum temperature range for typing. If – as I have been lately – I am trapped in bad-tempered, green-aired and broiling old London, the chances of my being able to batter out more than a paragraph without lapsing into a shallow coma are almost nil. Suddenly, the ghastly similarities between typing and what I imagine to be the irritatingly intermittent joys of auto-erotic asphyxiation come galloping to the fore. *Oh, this is all right. Think I'm getting somewhere. Yes, quite nice, probably – especially if we fiddle about round that corner bit for a while and then – Hello . . . now why am I on the carpet?* Even when I'm conscious, I spend an unhealthy amount of time battling urges towards languid strolling and trying to find a snake I can look at while I'm in pyjamas.

(That was a literary reference, not a euphemism.)

This means that I am working mostly at night – which does not sit well with the numberless work-related things I am supposed to do amongst people who operate – perversely, in my opinion – during the hours of daylight.

Naturally, my earliest years as a typist (in Dundee) were characterised by the opposite problem: an inability to keep even slightly warm. Dundee is cold and basic rented accommodation is colder. Sitting/crouching/lying still and thinking and occasionally writing illegibly (because you have no computer – they were rare in those days – and you are embarrassed to even look at what you're producing) is particularly cold. And at that point in my life all forms of heating beyond huddling under blankets were unaffordable. I spent a great deal of time looking as if I had been prised loose from an outside toilet on the Trans-Siberian Railway. I write lying down partly because my spinal column was designed by a drunk monkey, but mostly because I have spent so many long, sniffling, miserable hours lurking in my own bed or those of cheap B&Bs, or bleak borrowed houses, trying to stay alive long enough to reach the end of the next paragraph. I have become accustomed to writing in bed and in several layers of clothing. Not that there is any shame in wearing hats, coats and/or scarves indoors – this can be bracing and dapper. It's *having* to do so that can be depressing. I still feel the cold more than the average person and, during the winter months at home, I may still leave my living room briskly, putting on my jacket and shapka as I go, whistling merrily and feeling that the journey along the corridor to my study is all I ever really want to know about walking to work. It would only be colder outside.

I only mention this in case any of you have been experiencing unusual difficulties in putting one word after another and have, perhaps, not considered that you may simply be paying inadequate attention to your operational parameters. Perhaps a cold shower would be advisable. Or else a hot one. You decide.

Meanwhile, some of you may have noticed that I have been spending rather more time than usual on the radio. This is always a pleasure – radio people take care of words, are generally very courteous and offer room for more reflection and flexibility than you might find in other media. In fact, the only drawback is one I bring with me – the immense need to swear.

I do not swear much (unless provoked) and wouldn't normally swear at an audience at all – unless I was giving a reading and there were Bad Words on the page in front of me. Or possibly in the context of a comedy club, where swearing becomes a kind of comforting descant on everything from 'Hello' to 'Why is your hand in my pocket? And your leg in my trousers?' (And goodness knows why it's less offensive to have someone say *fuck* at you when they've carefully written it down first, pondered it lovingly, considered other alternatives and then settled on *fuck* very firmly all over again – surely that should actually be *more* disturbing that just hearing them exclaim *fuck* spontaneously when they, for example, stub their toe on the lectern – but I digress . . .) Should I, however, be doing something live for a radio programme – or, as also occasionally happens, for the telly – there will always be the moment when someone charming with a clipboard appears to gently murmur, 'Of course . . . not that we think you would, but . . . you would want to avoid swearing . . .' Which naturally fills me with an unbearable desire to do nothing but yell obscenities and blasphemies for the duration. This would be why, for example, I spent a portion of one evening last week hopping up and down a corridor in Broadcasting House, quietly reciting every allegedly appalling word I could think of – just to get them out of my system. It's the only way.

Apart from anything else, the murmured requests for verbal restraint are more than averagely heartfelt at the moment, if you're involved with a BBC broadcast. Even the slightest additional misstep from the Corporation – perhaps caused by an obscure Scottish novelist getting all Anglo-Saxon and causing a retired and much-loved ophthalmologist in East Cheam to choke on his suppertime rarebit in the absence of anyone qualified in the Heimlich manoeuvre and provoking *Overpaid, Elitist BBC Bastards Kill Popular Friend and Uncle* headlines – could mean the entire licence fee is redirected to fund bankers' bonuses and the hunting of immigrants through woodland for sport. And, although it has many failings – we all do – I like the idea of the

BBC, and we could still rebuild it and make it better and happier with itself and therefore kinder to its viewers and listeners – all could go well and is not past saving. I'd hate its demise to be in any tiny way my fault.

I have – as a person interested in words – been informed of the BBC's graded list of Words That Will Get Us All Fired. You'll be relieved to know that *orgasm* isn't listed, and perhaps surprised to learn that what I will voluntarily choose to call *the C-word* is only in second place. The very worst thing to say is currently a term implying that a person and his mother are involved in relations frowned upon by conventional society and which force any subsequent offspring to search card shops for the *Happy Father's Day to My Loving Brother* options. Obviously, the Beeb interviews a lot more 1970s pimps than I had hitherto realised.

Not for the first time, this has led me to reflect on my own ambivalence towards swearing. On the one hand, many of the words involved are melodiously and perfectly formed for the purpose and, frankly, there are few things more dandy – and indeed stimulating – than hearing someone who is genuinely good at swearing, someone who works with imagination, eloquence and poise. On the other hand, the words English uses as terms of abuse are almost universally terms for lovely (or at least interesting) activities and areas of the body which it is either wonderful to have or delightful to be offered for one's temporary recreation and/or mutual fun. So I have decided, as an exercise, to try and adopt words that would be more logical for me to use when stressed or outraged – and not just flirting in a shouty manner, which would lead me back to the usual repertoire. I have, during readings where the young and tender were present, already used *Blair*, *Blairing*, and so forth, but I truly don't want that in my mouth regularly, so I don't think it'll do. *Death* is short, to the point and something I don't enjoy in others and will probably find oppressive for myself . . . *Poverty* is definitely offensive and has a good feel to it as a word . . . as some of you may remember, I have a soft spot for *'sblood*, but that would sound massively eccentric when I need no further help in that direction . . . And, given the burden laid across my every waking minute, there is always *novel* to consider . . .

Perhaps you, Dear Readers, can assist. (Without swamping the poor old site with offensiveness, which will simply be disappeared.) Or you could try to construct your own lists at home for improved entertainment and expression. Onwards.

XXXI

Ah, there are days when you leave me moist-eyed and jolly, there really are. (There are other days when – a very few of – you make me want to change my address and wear a knee-length hat, but we'll let that pass.) You made me proud, you did, with your ready responses to the last blog: your *twunt* and your *frigbiscuits* did my heart good. Thank you for reinvigorating my already enthusiastic faith in your imaginative and pleasing use of language and for making me reflect, yet again, that politicians, advertisers and fibbers of all varieties really don't know how massively they underestimate you and your linguistic sophistication. And a special hello to Ian Lawther. Both my sainted mother and I are now using *fox cakes* in our everyday exchanges and it is working well for us.

I feel we must all have another targeted exchange of views soon – perhaps with a real prize for especially excellent involvement. Although, of course, Mr Lawther does in a very genuine way now possess the reward of having made my mother grin. Very few people – apart from noisy children who have fallen over and hurt themselves – can do that. And, naturally, the cash I have available for prizes and postage is limited, so not winning might be less of a disappointment than opening a recycled envelope full of personally signed elm leaves – which is about what this month's surplus would run to. Meanwhile, I have just (I hope) put the finishing touches to an essay on writing workshops and have therefore knocked away the last major obstacle between me and the novel and our being welded ever closer, as I desperately try to get everything done and as it should be by the end of December. I do indeed catch myself telling those kind enough to enquire about the beast, 'It'll all be over by Christmas' and then shuddering appropriately. Not that typing more than anyone healthy ever ought to is in any way comparable to being under fire at the Somme – I am simply squirming under a slightly tighter deadline than I am used to.

In fact, now that we mention it, I've never really had a deadline for a novel. But this time around, the health and sanity of the British publishing scene mean that I am already discussing covers and cover blurbs for something which is roughly half-completed and for which I have only just signed a contract. One minute I am ambling along with my hands in my pockets, flirting ardently but gently and with no legal obligations, and the next I'm roughly handcuffed to what may – I'll admit – develop into a lovely, warm and clean-limbed partner, but which I, as usual, fear may turn out to be, at best, a corpse and, at worst, some kind of brain-eating undead gentleman who will embarrass me at parties. If I miss the deadline, I miss the mystically calculated ideal time for novel release in 2011 and my editor has to disembowel a whole field full of goats and consult their entrails before he can select another in 2012. (The goats aren't, strictly speaking, essential to the process – he just gets tetchy when publications don't go to plan . . .)

I am trying to remain calm and to kid (sorry!) myself into thinking: *Well, if it has a cover and cover copy, then it must exist . . . All must be right with the novel.* I have played a similar trick on myself with my notebooks for years – each book I intend to write has a notebook containing . . . well, yes, notes – but nothing that finished or, as things progress, that massively helpful. The notebook seems to be a way of getting to the point where I can start – and I know everyone is different in this area, I'm just saying how it is for me. Despite it being full of scared nonsense, illegible essentials and unhinged suggestions, I like to stare at the (tightly closed) notebook and pretend that it is, in fact, full of the novel, neatly written down by hand, and all I have to do is type it up again and maybe do a spellcheck. There are mornings when this is convincing. Not many mornings, to be sure, but I cling to their spasms of dewy hope.

Turning back to that essay, I am glad I put an end to my major distractions by writing about workshops. This isn't so much because I like them – in fact, much of the essay was taken up with detailing what can go wrong with workshops and how unuseful the standard *let's sit round in a circle and read ourselves and each other with inadequate attention in a strained setting before allowing the blind to lead the deaf* type of workshop can be. But it also allowed me to remember the sheer wonder of a successful workshop. Apart from anything else, a good workshop can allow us to see – as closely as we ever will – writers writing, writing happening, the thing itself. There are few things better than sitting in a room which is suddenly united in action, which suddenly has that tingly, ozoney feeling of something on its way – of whatever inspiration is taking shape, of words struggling, or plummeting, or bubbling through. When we work ourselves, we're too engrossed in the process to really be aware of it – to be frank, once we're aware, it tends to have gone away. When we see it in others – perhaps as part of group authorship, perhaps in a series of solo contributions – then there are moments when we can actually grasp the ungraspable, when we can see a very specific type of joy: the way a face clears and becomes beautiful when it is absolutely focused; completely itself and yet open to something other than itself, touched.

Part of what annoys me about the deadline and contract side

of publishing is that it really has nothing whatever to do with writing, nothing to do with that beauty – the same beauty you see when someone is really reading, completely engrossed. I always say that writers and readers are misunderstood, because if you glance casually at people who are reading and writing, you may simply see people who appear serious, frozen. But if we happen to glance at people just before they kiss (not in an intrusive or unpleasant way, I would hope), then their expression is the same – oddly solemn, intent. And yet nobody ever suggests that kissing is dull, or pathetic, or a bit of a waste of time. I happen to believe that giving and receiving a kiss operates very much along the same lines as giving and receiving a word – it's simply that the giving and receiving are done in different rooms at different times – they are still an attempt to touch, be touched, be recognised, to exist in passion, to be human.

I was reminded of this when reading *Last Words of the Executed*, a very fine book edited by Robert K. Elder. One fragment records the mass hanging of thirty-eight Dakota Sioux men. The *St Paul Pioneer* stated, 'We were informed . . . that their singing and dancing was only to sustain each other – that there was nothing defiant in their last moments . . . Each one shouted his own name, and called on the name of his friend, saying in substance, "I'm here! I'm here!"' It occurred to me that when we write fully and honestly, when we speak from who we are, mortal human being to mortal human being, it comes down to this – that we sustain each other with musics and dreams of motion, that we say who we are, that we reach out to the friend who is beyond us, out of sight – and this is perhaps defiant in the deepest possible way and is perhaps a type of love and is certainly very much alive and – I think it bears repeating – beautiful.

Onwards.

XXXII

The stomach trouble referred to in the post below was, in fact, an undiagnosed ulcer.

Ah, it was bound to go pear-shaped, Best Beloveds – all major obstacles to our sweaty unification had been tumbled away, all chaperones had been dodged, misdirected or anaesthetised – finally, it was just me and the novel in the smallest, brownest London hotel room I have ever suffered. (And those of you who know London will realise that England's capital is heaving with minute, dun-coloured cells and establishments generous and imaginative only in their provision of misery with an added option of mild disease.) It was going to be a lovely weekend – possible cover designs had been emailed, an actual real live contract had been signed (for some reason I had been finding it light and relieving not to sign a contract and simply to write) and a genuine coin-of-the-realm advance had been received and banked – we were all set . . . You're guessing there were tears long before bedtime? Well, of course. It's always awkward: that first time when there's nothing in the way, you've been hoping, expecting, daydreaming, but now – here it is. Here *you* are – one half of a couple. Ish. You've dumped your bags and coat and suddenly an inviting tryst feels very like waiting alone with a stranger for something possibly awful to happen in a cramped space which includes an embarrassing bed. Perhaps you fumble about round a paragraph here and there and find that you're not in the mood – many of the words are in the wrong place and a bit, somehow, chilly.

You try turning on the telly, reclining gingerly against the too many pillows. (Why does everywhere have too many pillows? Even places with no sink and holes in the shower stall have too many pillows, when surely they could be investing their pillow budget in mousetraps and bleach?) You mumble that maybe there'll be something on pay-per-view with some *hot and heavy plotting* or perhaps an *achingly wide range of inspirational characterisation and credible psychology* – it's not an ideal option, but perhaps it'll slap some ginger and mojo into your mood.

It doesn't – possibly because pay-per-view tends only to offer vampires, men who blow things up, young people with impossible skins intent upon falling in love and/or being murdered and nurses/air hostesses/dancers with surprisingly repetitive personal lives. You abandon artificial stimulations and potter off to the tiny bathroom – perhaps a shower will relax you – if you can ignore the fact that there seems to be eyebrow hair everywhere. (Finding other people's pubic hair in bathroom areas is, naturally, unpleasant, but somehow much less disturbing than finding what amounts to handfuls of what is clearly eyebrow hair.) Meanwhile, your novel rests sullenly on the bed, peering at you as if you are the worst mistake it has ever made and it may throw up if you touch it.

Yes, the Dark Night of the Soul had arrived. Well, Dark Night Number One – there are usually several. This one involved page 153 – all the other pages weren't helping, but 153 was especially off-putting – plus unwise accommodation, a hideously nervous stomach which was preventing me from eating and sleeping (two things I enjoy), a number of oncoming onerous tasks for 2011, a marked inability to focus when trying to read illuminated signs and the complete failure of EVERYONE to email or call as and when expected. No sleep, no food, novel-wrestling and radio silence from all manner of previously lovely, useful and important folk left me surveying the ruins of my career within minutes, envisaging a sad and unremarked death up an alleyway in Streatham, my withered corpse later consumed by feral badgers. Before the day was out I was chewing my own ankles for relief.

I came home. I got an eye test. (I now need glasses – just a bit – for illuminated signs and, if it's small, the telly.) I went to the doctor and scored a prescription for stomach-pacifying medication. *EVERYONE* got back in touch. I sat in my comfy chair and stared at page 153 until it giggled and scampered up to stroke my brow in the manner that (unlikely though it may seem) I find irresistible.

This does not, of course, mean that all is well – or that page 153 is in any way readable – but at least my pages and I are trundling along once again, holding hands and looking at pictures of beach resorts where we could stay, if we didn't mind the fact that we would kill each other before the initial sunset's end.

And we are actually heading for foreign parts, Dear Readers. Should everything go to plan – and I needn't say that I anticipate it won't – then we will soon be aiming for the US and Canada. As my novel and I are both phobic about air transport, this will involve a boat, a number of trains and then another boat – all spread out over a significant period. The cost of travelling this way means that my entire tour will only break even, but does also mean that my entire stomach won't combust, I won't become hysterically blind and I won't find myself unable to write even a postcard for the duration of my residence abroad, deafened as I would be by the internal monologue which – trust me, I've heard it before – runs as follows: *What's the point of typing anything if the plane's wings are going to fall off as you try to get the novel home, or the tail fin is compromised, or the rudders get jammed, or there's clear-air turbulence, or a head-on collision, or all of those other things you've studied on* Air Crash Investigation? *Why would you bother when it's hard to write books and you could be concentrating on drawing up your will and being nice to toddlers and puppies in ways that mean your afterlife – should you get one – will be moderately comfy and not conducted in a small, brown hotel room, filled with eyebrow hair not your own and a vile-tempered novel.*

Which is where I came in. Except that – forgive us – me and the pages are currently not unhappy and, in fact, are heading off at this point for a little time together where you can't follow. We have some issues to work out. Onwards.

XXXIII

The post below was written soon after I celebrated middle age by discovering that I needed glasses. Much of the stress mentioned was, in fact, caused by the previously mentioned ulcer and its associated difficulties.

Dear Readers, I am outside at the back of a cabin in New York State with – I kid you not – a crimson dragonfly perched attractively on the top right-hand corner of my laptop. I am wearing my glasses, which means the surrounding trees are now so in focus that they're mildly trippy (the dragonfly, at this point, is getting it on with another dragonfly . . . ah, nature . . .), and much is well with my world. Over the last few months I was aware – especially when I caught sight of myself in shop windows and other cruelly reflective surfaces – that I was slightly stressed. Slightly blurry and slightly stressed. I am now unblurry and unstressed to the extent that I realise my spine was actually making arrangements to slip away in the night if I cranked it up any nearer to playing high C every time I acquired a new unease. It is, apparently (and who could have guessed) not quite possible to pinball around the UK and Europe while writing slivers of journalism and essays and doing spots of teaching and stand-up and a touring show and bits of radio and fragments of telly and to write a large and complicated novel and to *worry* without becoming poorly as a result. I apologise to my workforce – I am a bad self-employer.

And I am trying to make amends: crossing to America by boat has begun to ease the condition my condition is in. I'm aware that some people were incredulous about this travel option, and I'm aware that yet others thought I was simply making an effort towards a niftily upmarket lifestyle choice. If it *is* a lifestyle choice, then my lifestyle is based on fear – not a desire to join large Germans and orange Brummies on deck three for a duty-free perfume sale. I fear flying and yet I must travel . . . I have solved my problem as best I can and am not pretending to be classy. Plus – for some reason, being rocked to sleep by a potentially fatal ocean while strangers take tutorials in napkin-folding does me no end of good, and there are few things better than sitting on deck – in a *deck chair* – and chiselling at your novel while blokes in uniforms bring you bouillon. You did not know you wanted bouillon, you are not an habitual bouillon-drinker and yet, 'Yes, thank you – oh, and crackers. Why not? Thank you again. Can you arrange for the rest of my life to be like this, but not cost me the price of a healthy kidney per week? Or just throw me overboard now. My spine would bless you for it.' So the novel and I spent a dandy six nights traversing the Atlantic, battering away at the pages and looking out for porpoises. There were rumours of a gannet, but as some of you will know, I have a history with gannets and tried to avoid it.

I am now – in the nicest possible sense – being patronised. A very pleasant individual has offered me (not for the first time) accommodation and food and time in a wooden house with wooden furnishings in a wood. It's a bit of a wood-themed experience. Writers may not get the freebies and refreshingly frank sexual encounters offered to sportspersons, actors, musicians and politicians, but we do get accommodation. For some reason charities, acquaintances, institutions and collectors of curiosities are often just falling over themselves to give us rooms that aren't our own. So here I am. I sit and write uninterruptedly during the weeks, and at the weekends I appear at the big house, get proper dinners, say hello and meet people who might want to meet a novelist.

There are many things that are good about my current circumstances: a) I am in a radically different time zone and location from many people who might otherwise want me to write novel-interrupting things, or perform novel-interrupting things for them. b) If you don't have to cook, clean, shop or attend to your usual life, you will find you have enormous amounts of time to both potter and type. (Suddenly the huge volumes, complicated love lives and ornate hobbies of the servant-wielding authors of bygone ages become explicable, if not much less impressive.) c) I am surrounded by scampering animals, alien birds, wiffling greenery, pleasant walks and many of the things that delight my gnarled and weary heart.

Of course, what with me being me, there are also a few drawbacks: a) My extremely palatable surroundings, flexible hours and general lack of any restraints mean that I pass my eccentricity event horizon about three hours after I arrive here. And then I spend hours and hours with people who don't exist, trying to scribble round them . . . My dress sense (what there was of it) evaporates, my sleeping, eating, strolling, bathing and typing happen at increasingly random points. (Which, when they appear to check on me, can be highly alarming for those people we will have to refer to as 'the staff' – although obviously they are not *my* staff.) I talk to the animals. I talk to the people who don't exist. I talk to the staff. 'Hello. Yes. Does this work, I don't seem to be able to . . . Oh. And when I do that . . . Oh, I shouldn't do that, then. And what day is it? Oh, meatballs. *Great.* Sorry for eating with my hands, I've lost the fork again. Why are you crying? Well, I'd be wearing more if I hadn't been in the bath. Sorrysorrysorry . . .' I celebrated page 250 with a small al-fresco dance involving Mr Hendrix on the extremely effective stereo. I am basically now in a feral condition. b) Even when I'm not in an animal state I don't really take well to meeting people, and if I am being presented exactly and precisely as a novelist in unknown company, then I tend to come apart like a chocolate hammock. I have, during previous stays, demolished a number of dinner services and sets of glasses with my generally nervous flailings and have not – I feel – given anyone an even passably good impression of writers as a species. c) This is a cabin in the woods. It is, indeed, surrounded by nature. And as soon as the sun goes down, nature spends every moment of darkness scrabbling, thumping, tramping, breathing, creaking and generally impersonating every possible type of assassin. I have never packed a flimsy negligee, high heels and a broken torch for my stays here and so have been unable to 'just go outside and check on that funny noise' and therefore I have not been murdered even slightly. I have a functional torch, I have boots, I have my grandpa's patented self-defence moves, I am surrounded (appropriately) by a large fence. Nevertheless, it has taken me a number of stays here to acclimatise to the bloody racket caused by peaceful countryside.

But mainly I am writing. I sleep soundly because I am deaf with exhaustion, and then I get up and write again and then I write some more and this is lovely. This is what I do, what I always wanted to do. I'm lucky to be here. Patronage isn't in any way a replacement for proper arts funding – I'm a UK citizen, very temporarily in the US: a land of private funding, of savage poverty and savage wealth – enjoying the effect of an individual's generous whims on my professional life. In the UK the government we pay for doesn't want to prevent us from dying or help us to lead even tolerable lives, so you know that arts funding's a goner. I repeat, I am lucky. Currently lucky and generally lucky. I am able to do something I love and sometimes the circumstances in which I do it are more than pleasant. I would love it anyway, should always remember to love it, and at the moment I have the energy to do so. I wish you all your own versions of the same opportunity – the space to express what you need to express. Onwards.

XXXIV

Welcome, to the 8.35 a.m. train out of Richmond, Virginia – heading for New York and Pennsylvania Station, one of the very few rail termini to have been demolished in the real world and then reconstructed within Satan's colon. Lately, I have been spending a good deal of time in Penn Station and have wondered – not for the first time – whether 65 per cent of the people waiting for trains there appear to be seriously mentally distressed because they arrived that way, or because they have stepped into an alternative universe of heat, bewilderment, pain and ambient evil. You may be aware that many US rail stations are grand expressions of generous respect to their users, full of stately perpendiculars, handy benches and lots of gold leaf – high-ceilinged temples to mass transit and the communal hopes of a bygone age. Penn Station is there for balance: to remind you that this Depression will not produce a New Deal and that many members of the general public are surplus to requirements, and to hint that your train will travel at the speed of lazy treacle on a cold day, will shudder along rails that even Railtrack would call poorly maintained and that will give priority to freight, cars, pedestrians and any animal above the size of a healthy adult woodchuck.

Yet I continue to love American (and Canadian) trains. I am trying to rebrand my debilitating and expensive fear of flying as Steampunk Travel and – at a certain level – I find I am convincing at least myself that rail transportation is a good and lovely, as well as an ecological, option. US trains are roomy, their passengers have no expectations and therefore often eschew UK train travellers' lapses into frenzied disappointment and rage when they are delayed, misled or ignored. Plus, US trains are still rich in the iconic elements that I – lover of black-and-white movies that I am – find intoxicating. They are monumental, they still roll majestically into stations with their bells ringing like harbingers of strange mortality, they still hoot across the countryside in the manner of wistful mechanical whales, the conductors still wear little round blue conductors' hats and the Redcaps still wear red caps – although sometimes they're baseball caps . . . From my initial exposure to a real live US train around twenty years ago in California I have been in love with them. I can still remember that first high, silver locomotive as it glided and wailed along the sunset into a wood-canopied rural station full of cicada songs and moist heat, and my heart was lost.

Of course, this only slightly mitigates the fact that I am back to business as usual – typing on trains and rattling from city to city, performing readings or the one-person show while trying to keep the novel on track in spite of tiredness and an increasingly cranky spine. This isn't ideal, but life rarely is, and I'm up over the 300-page line which is a comfort – the pages may not be great, but they are there and I can always rewrite a page that's there. I would have to make up a page that isn't there from scratch . . . Currently, of course, the 350-lb gentleman in front of me who is thrashing in his seat, sighing and occasionally exclaiming 'Phnnah-urr' isn't helping matters, but I have come to expect this on trains. Trains are where people speak to themselves with loud enthusiasm, trains are where those listening to MP3 players airdrum without shame, where those not listening to anything do much the same, and trains are where people eat hot dogs made of reconstituted protein substances illegal in many countries.

I can particularly recommend travel from New York to Montreal – the journey takes around eleven hours for no really good reason, beyond a type of shyness that will leave your train hiding, loitering and then simply fainting to a halt at regular intervals. When you are travelling north it will wait like a faithful lover to meet and be passed by the southbound train, and when you are travelling south it will also wait. You will do a great deal of waiting. But you will also be beguiled by the autumn foliage (should it be autumn), the picturesque wetlands and gentle vistas – all slightly distracting if you're trying to write a sex scene and are already freaked out by your somewhat intrusive surroundings and the fiddly technical matters you have to consider. But you will be able to spot great blue herons and egrets and red-tailed hawks aplenty, as you wonder who should do what to whom first and from which angle.

As usual, it's much easier to leave the US than to enter it again. On my return, US Border Control began with the usual questions, 'Are you travelling for business? How long were you in Canada? How long will you be in the US?' But then escalated to the kind of enquiries I never handle well: 'What kind of writing? Would I have read you? What kind of novels?' I find it oddly difficult to give an adequate definition of literary fiction to men with guns, and yet it's surprising how often they seem to need one. And I am always alarmed when the first option they reach for as a genre suggestion is, 'So . . . you write romance?' This leads me to believe they are poor judges of character and therefore unsuited for their jobs. On this occasion the interrogation moved forward into areas including, 'What about *Braveheart* – was that historically accurate?' Something which could be a normal conversational gambit, but which seems to develop dangerous significance when delivered in a tone one would imagine should be reserved for poorly trained drug-mules and parrot-smugglers. I had no idea if I was being given an opportunity to prove my Scottish credentials or simply chatting with someone unable to not be *violently earnest*. It was then decided that the carriage 'smelled weird' – of course it smelled weird, it's a railway carriage. After a small discussion about whether the aroma was, in fact, 'weird' or 'just bad', reinforcements were brought in with inadequate tools and a sniffer dog, travellers were evacuated and the next two hours or so were spent hanging about and listening to the noises of a train car being disassembled.

Meanwhile, my chum with an interest in contemporary fiction and Mel Gibson then loped down the aisle shouting, 'Scottish novelist?' in a way that led me to be both nervous and hurt that he hadn't remembered my face. I then had to present my passport to be rechecked by a more senior and rather languid official, installed in the buffet car. Arrival by boat is rare and therefore leaves unusual traces on one's passport. I was forced, once again, to reflect on my student days when I had the idea that putting 'Writer' in my passport would somehow challenge and unsettle officials of all kinds, prove my interior fortitude, and generally involve me in sticking it to The Man and degrees of personal risk. In fact, I tend to become craven when anywhere near The Man, and The Man, in return, seems to regard my vocation as a mildly amusing indulgence. Writing can, of course, unseat governments, free the soul and prepare the mind and spirit for all possible rigours and joys – but I did not find myself or my vocation especially uplifting as I plodded back from the buffet car to a seriously interfered-with carriage that now smelled both 'bad' and 'of warm Alsatian'.

And now, Dear Readers, as we wait in Washington Union Station, I must leave you. I have a few more days of woodland scribbling to try and get my characters into physical synch and all shiny for the end of their book, and then I will begin the long journeys to Oregon and New Mexico. More landscape, more scary food and more sitting and writing . . . Onwards.

XXXV

Dear Readers, I have just got lost for a dizzied ninety minutes within something like 200 square yards of Santa Fe. Last night I spent another goodly portion of time (I don't know how long, I had forgotten to wear my watch. I had, in fact, temporarily mislaid my watch . . .) trying to enter my loaned apartment. As it turned out, I couldn't open the door because it wasn't the door to my apartment. I live somewhere else – somewhere with a lock that my key can open. I would have become tearful, but I was tired and dehydrated and coated with (hoping to ease my withering skin) what turned out to be hair conditioner and not body lotion. Oddly, it seemed to work quite well and was fragrant. After a while, all the little travel bottles look the same . . . In short, I'm at 7,000 feet where the air is thin and water boils too quickly to make you a nice restorative cuppa that isn't lukewarm, and am writing to you from a fragment of my former self. Happy, but a fragment.

I'll get to the happy later – the drive to defer gratification: it never wears off, even when I'm crumbly and my oxygen levels are below par. First let me take you through a wibbly, retro flashback, à la Alfred Hitchcock, to somewhere around 5,000 miles in my past – or someone else's past, at the moment I'm not sure.

Two weeks ago, my novel and I plunged once again into the

muggy near-death experience which is Penn Station, all set to trundle off, Steampunking it for Chicago and Portland, Oregon, then LA and Santa Fe – not a plane in sight and all was almost well. I wasn't expecting *North by Northwest* – the *20th Century Limited* stopped running long ago, in every sense, but even so . . . it was something of a shock when I met my roomette. Did I in any way suggest that US train cars were roomy last time we spoke? Did I? The Amtrak roomette – ugly, ugly, ugly word – is quite small in the way that leptons and quarks are quite small. It has no room for most of the normal activities a human being might expect to enjoy: standing, breathing, thrashing in and out of a foetal position while begging for an aneurism to intervene . . . Up and down the passageway as you sink into a compression-induced fugue state you will hear the tiny cries of other passengers as they contemplate their own accommodations, or simply wonder numbly: *Where the fuck did they put the rest of it?* And roomettes are designed for two – even the ones which incorporate a prison-style sink and toilet combo that also acts as a handy set of steps. I feel I cannot be alone in believing this would remove every shred of helpful mystery from even the most resilient relationship. I cannot think of anyone I love enough – and I do have large capacities for affection – to spend hour after dank hour with them while learning too much about all their previously adored places in what amounts to a cross between a tea caddy and a commode.

There were, of course, compensations. There would have to have been.

First Compensation. Train travel has allowed vast tracts of America to limp past at a wonderfully detailed pace. I have watched a misty pink sunrise across gentle Indiana, seen the farms and autumnal dells of Wisconsin, the wheeling perspectives of corn fields, pumpkin fields, harrowed earth and prairie roads. I have sat and stared out at the Columbia Valley cliffs, seen the sun set on the rolling Pacific Coast and the surfers' bonfires lighting up thereafter, watched the tawny plains of Montana and North Dakota, the blue distances and wind-worn mountains of Arizona and New Mexico . . . I mean, I could go on, but you'd get bored. I should also have witnessed a setting sun in the picturesque Glacier National Park, but massive delays – this is Amtrak – meant it was dark long before then and the sun had, in fact, burnished and gilded the delightful brown oil-processing facilities of Shelby, Montana. Shelby granted us a 'fresh-air stop'. These have generally brought me both relief and anxiety. I come from a small town myself, and I know they're hard to escape. Many's the time I have alighted from the high, safe, silvery railcar and felt that tingle of panic: *what if the train just moved on without me: this is somewhere you'd never be able to leave: this is a kind of nowhere: this is fading amateur murals declaring the dangers of drugs: this is stray yellow dogs and hand-painted signs reading 'Cold Beer. Good Food. Band every Saturday Night.' This is a savage place in a savage time.* Local newspapers along my routes wrote of electoral candidates who hadn't bothered attending community debates, of foreclosures and soup kitchens, unprecedented demands for assistance, homelessness. Outside the windows, a nation has fallen in two.

Second Compensation. Amtrak staff behave with extraordinary and democratic levels of courtesy, charm and attentiveness – this being all that prevents their benighted cargo from re-enacting *Night of the Living Dead* within moments of boarding. Their kindness quite literally keeps everything going. En route announcements blend humour, menace and levels of enjoyable psychosis, and I certainly never will ever dream of spitting at fellow-travellers, nor will I alarm children, wander about with my shoes off, or smoke. I am fully aware that smoking on a train will involve my being disappeared to Diego Garcia and not heard of again. So hello to Paul, Victor, Louis, Tiffany, Joyce, Moses and everyone else. Yes,

I remember their names; the last fourteen days have been, among other things, a crash course in hardcore friendliness.

Third Compensation. Friendliness. I usually see this as a threat, but Amtrak is determined that I should adjust and embrace it. Apart from being thrown on the mercy of uniformed strangers simply to survive (and I'm aware that I wasn't trying to sleep in coach accommodation – I have seen the coach sleepers, they will haunt my dreams . . .), Amtrak is determined that everyone should sit together, be together and eat together. If they ran the UN, then ceasefires would be gruelling and yet weirdly binding. Antisocial curmudgeon that I am, if I wanted to receive actual hot food on a plate I had to batter along to the dining car and be forcefully seated at a table with three other people, all of them terrifyingly convivial. Before I could even sit down I was barraged with other people's personal details, affection and warmth, and I suspect it has altered my make-up, perhaps for ever. I now find I am unable to eat without first reciting, 'Hi, I'm Alison. I live in Glasgow, Scotland. Not Glasgow, Montana. I am both travelling and working. I don't fly. I am writing a novel. It is book number thirteen. I am right-handed, forty-four, single, I have no children and I don't drink. What about you?' And so hello to the lady who worked in one of the many posh Minnesota rehab clinics. Addiction, like any illness, is an income-source in the US – it will bring you bills, not help. If you're wealthy, you may recover. If you're not, you'll die. And hello to the mother of a serving soldier who has survived Iraq and Afghanistan, and hello to the WWII veteran who listened to her pride politely, although his war was not like her son's war – destruction all they have in common. And hello to the man amazed by his country's capacity only to destroy, and then apologetic that he'd talked about it for so long. Hello to all the decent and friendly and promising human beings currently being shafted by their government, much as we are being shafted by ours. People like Wayne, who asked me for money in LA Union

Station, which is a poem of a building, extravagant in the beauty it offers everyone who enters it, First Class the only class available – the product of a lost philosophy.

Fourth Compensation. The first draft of my novel was finished aboard the *Empire Builder*: my pages and I trundling together somewhere in the dark, I think across the little bit of Idaho that protrudes north between Washington and Oregon. We were not riding the 20*th Century Limited*, I was not Eva Marie Saint and neither was my novel Cary Grant, but we did sit quietly for a bit, side by side, and enjoy the end of our initial adventures. And in the morning, car 2730 celebrated with me and we had hugs – all human beings together. Onwards.

XXXVI

As I write, two comedy TV programmes, *The Daily Show* and *The Colbert Report*, are hosting a non-shouting political rally in Washington, and outside my New York hotel, Central Park is filling with nippers dressed as a variety of demons, ghosts, witches, insects, pirates and cartoon characters. It's the Halloween weekend, US political discourse has appropriately crumpled into a terrifying shouting match within which anyone can say anything – the loonier, the better – and there is, of course, at least one witch (retired) on the campaign trail. Having just trundled round the country, reading local newspapers and meeting regional reporters as I progressed, I am aware that conventional politicians are, at best, simply mud-slinging and, at worst, dodging arrest and/or releasing whatever witless and scary mouth-noise their reptile brain can conjure, secure in the knowledge that they will never have to defend any assertion, no matter how manifestly unhinged. Journalistic oversight is scant – and seems to come largely from the two light-entertainment shows above – and many candidates are being held in seclusion lest they tell waiting reporters that the Liberal Media Elite are controlled by al-Qaeda elk (those aren't antlers, they're communications antennae), that Obama's healthcare reforms cause cancer, that Jesus hates left-handed people – all of whom could choose to be right-handed if they really wanted – and that gravity is only a myth put about by atheist 'scientists' in order to restrict the righteous and their natural ability to fly.

This isn't my country, but I am aware that UK politicians borrow all their plays (even – if not especially – the cruel and dysfunctional ones) from the US. Never have I been more tempted to opt out and join the merry throngs in the park, possibly dressed as (why not?) Scooby-Doo.

'Do you think UK politics has plunged into a new nadir of secrecy, sleaze and sadistically damaging cuts?' *WrIdunno*. 'Do you feel that while recreational fiction – a vital source of imaginative exercise, energy and companionship – is being devalued on all sides, political fiction is setting us adrift in a hideous bubble of dangerous crap?' *You have scoobysnax? Me want scoobysnax.* 'You do realise you're not really a cartoon character, right? You're a forty-five-year-old adult. You have responsibilities.' *Scoobyscoobydoo . . .*

I should, of course, never be trusted when I'm hopping about on the moral high ground. I am not a moral person – I am much more comfortable saying that my objections to political bullshit are professional. I have spent more than a quarter of a century trying to use words in ways that are communicative and precise. I have led I can't begin to count how many workshops and one-to-ones with the hope and intention of increasing accuracy and fluency amongst others, and have seen how liberating and powerful language can be when operated with honesty and generosity. (I know I'm in the fiction business, but honesty of approach and an understanding of reality are vital in the writer's relationship with the reader: the reader does agree he or she will be lied to, but nobody wants their intelligence insulted . . .) I also know that human beings are malleable and porous – subject us to malign and distorted fictions and we do not prosper, we become cruel. We can go very, very deeply wrong.

I have also spent more than a quarter of a century defending my corner of the arts against ridicule, censorship and cutbacks. As of Monday, I'll be returning – slowly – to a country where the arts have gone the way of education, adequate healthcare, transport and the rest. The means of communication that the electorate can use and enjoy are becoming more and more inaccessible, while the fantasies of those who seek to influence us become more and more powerful. As a reader and a writer and a voter and a person, I would rather this were not the case.

Sorry for being glum there, but I do get tired of the people I vote for acting like occupying forces as soon as they gain power, and if I don't tell you about it – remember, I've been in a lot of railway stations and trains in the past weeks – I will end up simply ranting and twitching at strangers in public places, which will render them uneasy. And it's not too late – that's the thing about imagination: wake it up and feed it and it'll change the world. Always.

Meanwhile, my own circumstances are not too gloomy. I am newly forty-five. (Like the pistol – as they delightfully say in Santa Fe . . .) Which is fine by me, and I am scribbling all over the initial manuscript of my novel and swaying, as usual, between tentative thoughts that the thing might actually just work and the impulse to seek out someone who will beat me severely for even attempting to impose upon the brains of others with more of my rancid nonsense. Yes, my last blog was all gussied up (not by me) with an air of finality – but you and I know that the end of the first draft is barely the beginning of the tinkering, fiddling and fretting, the rewrites large and small and frantic and middle-of-the-night and despairing and problem-solving and problem-generating – the ones that maintain continuity, the ones that adjust backwards for something you didn't quite find out until page 230, the ones that seem just a much better way of getting from A to F, the ones suggested by reading work-in-progress to audiences of (I must say) remarkably tolerant strangers and the ones that simply save me from myself.

And why is it that I can enjoy these happy torments? Because I got an adequate education, because I grew up in a house with access to books, was a child who could visit my local, well-stocked library and know it was full of wonders, unguessed-at beauties, the dry, exciting, papery scent of other worlds, because I got into publishing in 1990 when it was (barely) possible to bring out a collection of short stories as a first book, because there were magazine and anthology opportunities there for me which now no longer exist, because I could make ends meet for the first decade during which my writing did not in any way support me, because I was immensely lucky and a workaholic.

I would like today's new writers to have the chances I did – better chances than I did. I would like today's readers to have more choice, a wider variety of voices and subjects and characters. I can't say that I currently think they will. I also can't say we are powerless to alter our circumstances – imagining change is the first step towards creating it: the first act to reclaim our strength is only to think, to practise the habit of thinking, of exercising our interior liberty. Onwards.

XXXVII

Well, it had to happen eventually – I am surrounded by washed and ironed clothing and accompanying wreaths of condensation. I am listening to the silvery banjo stylings of Mr Steve Martin, as relayed to me by my personal (heavy on the bass) CD player, and reclining on my purchased-along-with-the-flat-because-it-is-huge-and-therefore-irremoveable sofa in what I am reliably informed is still my very own address, with none of my furniture subject to governmental compulsory purchase in order to fund another bank bailout or repairs to the Conservative Party offices. In short, I am home.

My novel and I did, in fact, run from room to room calling, 'Honey, I'm home!' until we realised that at least one of us was an inanimate – and, as yet, unpolished – object and then got all bashful and had to have a cup of tea.

Being back home is, naturally, lovely. I had left brand-new socks waiting here to delight me and I can lie in for ever without anyone at any time yelling, 'Room service!' and forcing me to be me at too nasty a speed. It is also, of course, depressing: if I'm stuck here for more than four days I'm going to get bored, or have to redecorate, and why is no one barging through in the morning yelling, 'Room service!' and cleaning up after me? Although, oddly, the flat isn't that dusty, given that I have been away for three months. For reasons I cannot explain there have only been massive accumulations of dust inside my fridge. This is a mystery I'm sure only Penn & Teller could explain with any kind of clarity.

Since we last spoke I have bobbed back over a strangely kind Atlantic and – finally – stood on the port side and watched completely healthy and alive gannets flinging themselves about in search of fish. (Long-term readers will remember that I was scarred, perhaps for ever, by a dreadful succession of gannet-carrying, gannet-death and gannet-burial-at-sea mishaps, which mightily amused the lovely town of Ullapool, but which will mean I am never again able to look a gannet in its mad-blue eyes without flinching and, at the very least, offering up a herring as a belated apology.)

Meanwhile, the first requests for Book of the Year nominations are coming in from assorted newspapers, I am wearing a coat indoors and it must therefore be nearly Christmas. I am not a great fan of the festive period – I hate the colour scheme, I hate the waste, I hate the mass-media implication that anyone not gathered round a glistening and bonhominous board with seventy of their dearest and loveliest is somehow an irredeemable failure, I don't want to send cards to people with whom I would otherwise never communicate, I don't think recycling the cards afterwards is really the point – why not simply *not send them in the first place?* – I hate the Celebrity Special Xmas Editions of 'Are You Smarter Than a Pebble?' and even if I were a hyper-devout Christian (or perhaps especially if I were) I would be aware that the 25th of December was a fairly random date selected for a variety of politico-religious reasons and means we are all cele-brating something deeply pagan, as well as our ability to shove the calorific equivalent of a fried rhino into our heads at every meal. One mince pie and a good sing-song and I'm more than done with the whole thing.

Not that I am in any way against outbreaks of peace on Earth and goodwill to all men. I am very much in favour of both the above actually getting together over the Christmas period, so that we can all play the equivalent of football in No Man's Land, rather than be locked into a permanent recreation of its court-martial-threatening aftermath.

Meanwhile, Christmas 2010 is the Big Deadline for my novel and me. We could – if we absolutely must – cleave to each other until the first week of January. (It's a question of whether my holiday is ruined by one last rewrite, or my editor's holiday is ruined by having to read me . . .) But basically when the Christmas Special mistletoe is swinging over the TARDIS, things really have to be in good order with the magnum opus. I completed the second draft in my cabin as I came across to Southampton and may always associate this book with missed opportunities to attend scarf-tying workshops (bring your own scarf) or sit at a dinner table in evening dress while wanting to hang myself with my napkin. (The napkin-folding session may have included a special *how to tie a genuine Pierrepoint hangman's knot* section. I don't know. I missed that, too. I was busy typing.)

Picture me, Dear Readers, locked in my little cabin and scratching at the printout of Draft One with a violent red pen. You are all aware that pages which may look passable, or even charming, onscreen turn into vile, vile, nauseating, heavingly awful sewers of rancid excrement as soon as they are printed off and their traumatised author can see them properly. (Which does lead me to wonder what nonsense we scribblers could get away with, if books all simply make journeys from the author's screen to the readers' and never hit the paper pulp.) Many's the hour I have wept and snarled through trying to get the soggy to become snappy, the maundering to become sprightly, the utterly incomprehensible to become something communicative and suave, or simply not illegally bad. And then, of course, there are the rude bits – which have to be sexy, rather than silly, or crude, or impossible, or incorrectly funny, or incorrectly disturbing – or, ohgawdhelpus . . . The jury is still out, but I am moving on to Draft Three in the coming week. Once again, the pages will be printed off and – given that we are now much closer – if you go outside and listen very carefully at sunset with your children (or borrowed children, if you have none of your own) you will be able to turn to them and say, with due solemnity, 'There now, little ones, that moaning and whimpering is the sort of noise you would make if you decided to be a novelist.' Onwards.

XXXVIII

The only thing less fun than sitting with another round of pages to be red-penned and rearranged is doing so while ice complicates the inside of your windows and your immobile extremities slowly sting, then throb, then turn numb, then become perhaps irretrievably blue and fragile. Writing is not a mobile activity and – rampant hypochondria and/or genuine illness apart – historically, it seems to involve being in bed more than might be considered entirely reasonable. The onset of winter always reminds me of my early days as a scribbler, reading about all those Russian and Irish and Parisian writers' lives in suitably louche and tormented novels, or short stories, or memoirs. One element they shared – beyond narcissism, absinthe abuse and athletic sexual angst – was the presence of one (or more than one) writer in a bed and occasionally putting pen to paper.

This week, I have a choice of bed-writing in a Holiday Inn or sitting next to a tiny portable heater in a university office so cold that no one else ever seems willing to occupy it. The office part of the equation means it's time to meet Creative Writing students at Warwick University again, and time to be reminded again of how horrible it is to begin seriously considering writing as a profession. I spent years either being mocked by a gnawing desire to write, well . . . *something*. Or having ideas which were bloody terrifying, or unwieldy, or just plain beyond my technical capacities. Panic was never far away. I started to write before I knew what I was writing about and then fell into a pit of aimless and bewildered prose – or I scared myself silly because it seemed entirely unavoidable that my protagonist would be a man, or an older woman, or a child, or just someone other than me, when I didn't feel up to creating someone other than me that morning – or else I'd need to write in the first person, or cope with a major timescale, or lollop off into an experiment in magic realism.

Christ, it was appalling. And, of course, numerous psychological logjams and nervous perils never entirely leave, but just at the point when I was as inexperienced as I could get, I was doing all the most punishing and self-defeating and unpleasant things that a writer can to themselves. I was worrying that my eventual readers would hunt me down and cause me harm. I was refusing to interrogate what had come to me to be expressed and therefore – unsurprisingly – finding myself unable to express it. I was doubting every word before it emerged. I was neither considering the overall structure and meaning of pieces nor really focusing on the practical details of making them communicative, in case they just melted away under scrutiny. I was, in short, being scared.

Being scared is perfectly normal when starting to write – it would be foolish not to have qualms about entering another person's mind and perhaps not being as entertaining and moving and eloquent as one should when given such a splendid, generous and intimate opportunity. And handing over what is, in effect, a dream – that's stressful. *Here is something of me and from me and I have committed to it utterly and it is now nakedly in your possession and if it doesn't please you, then I will have failed on many, many levels.* That's a hard thing to even consider, never mind putting it into practice. And yet, without asking our ideas to tell us more – and risking that they won't – without throwing ourselves into the matter completely – and risking that our very best just isn't good enough – then we never fully know what we can say and how we might say it best. We never find how good we can be and how we can grow beyond that. We don't do ourselves, or our work, or our readers justice. Which would be a shame. And – scary though it feels to work passionately for absent strangers – it's not coal-mining, it's not being a nurse, it's not marching in London to defend the possibility of being a student, even though there might be bother, or batons, or horses.

That's the other memory Warwick University campus consistently awakes – one of being a largely pathetic, but occasionally active student. This is the place where I took part in my first demonstrations, first found out how large and unpleasant police horses can be, first realised that a policeman can shove you repeatedly in the back because he wants to, because he can, because it will annoy you, because he would like to start a fight, because he would always win the fight, because he's a policeman and you're not . . . It was an education. I wasn't at Warwick studying Creative Writing – such courses barely existed then and I wouldn't have dared go near one if they had – but I was studying. I was able to do so because I received a grant. No grant, no university: it would have been that simple. No three years to start learning how my mind actually operated, to become slightly familiar with how I think, to strengthen my ability to analyse and criticise and imagine, to present my thoughts with any kind of confidence. Who knows how long it would have taken me to begin writing without the university experience, or if I would have been able to subsidise myself before my writing earned its keep without the, albeit slightly evanescent, backing of a degree? And I am otherwise unemployable. And I do love writing more than almost anything else. And I am not in any way domestic, or fond of permanent children. So perhaps a life wasted, a life unfulfilled.

And yes, my life is – at a certain level – a big arty nonsense that can be sneered at from many angles. Being a student will

163

always involve self-indulgence and silliness and blagging and there are other paths to enlightenment and confidence, but a university education isn't something I would lightly deny a fellow-citizen. And the lack of an adequate primary and secondary education is already stifling, crippling and – I don't mean this metaphorically – killing a generation of people I personally have no wish to injure.

Without analysis and criticism, we can't get to grips with what may or may not be wrong around us – without a muscular capacity to imagine, we can't construct better alternatives – without support, we can find it difficult to believe what we have to say should even be heard, that who we are should be expressed: whether that might involve a sonnet that proves you're as human as everyone else and therefore entitled to consideration, or a love letter, or a job application that changes your life, or the novel that sustains someone recently bereaved, or the joke, or the song that made someone smile after a shitty day, or the slogan that will tell a nearby policeman: *Your jobs are next.*

I'm all right. I got my education, my library books, access to my voice and those of others – so many wonderful others. Which is partly why I feel others should have that joy, too. Something to boost the National Happiness Index, minimal investment required. Onwards.

XXXIX

*T*he post below was written near the beginning of sustained protest actions against government cuts and capitalism's dysfunctions. This was around the time that Alfie Meadows suffered a head injury as part of a demonstration and Jody McIntyre was shown being pulled from his wheelchair by Metropolitan Police.

I am tired. I'm almost too tired to talk about the things that are tiring me. Then again – as with bad dentistry, unpleasant personal experiences and unpleasant gentleman callers – there's something minutely empowering about writing down the source of your woes and peering at them in effigy. It can become a small rehearsal for future change.

So. Let's start with a small woe. I am tired of my printer. It's a tiny gripe in these days of mayhem and threatened water-cannons, but for more years than I'd like to mention my printer has been the Nick Clegg of office equipment. It promised it would fax – it has never managed to send or receive anything like a fax. It talked to me through my computer in a cloying and yet convincingly masculine voice (until I turned that bit off) about switching it on when it was switched on and connecting it when it was connected and supplying it with paper when its paper supply was entirely adequate and, above all, it told me big, fat, narwhal herds of lies about ink. When it could still talk it would warn me, within hours of receiving new cartridges, that my coloured ink was low and that my black ink was exhausted and that swingeing cuts in page output or desperate foraging for cartridges must immediately ensue. I used to believe it. Then I got curious, let things run and discovered that, on average, my ink supplies actually last three months longer than my printer is willing to admit. Now it can no longer nag me audibly, it constantly pesters my computer with alarmist messages while displaying its own scrolling alerts across its irritating little display screen. Since I've decided to switch brands, it also repeats dire threats relating to my use of non-proprietorial inks which have voided its warranty, threaten its health and may cause me to become sterile shortly before the building implodes. I hate it. It's only still in my office because – beyond being a money-grabbing, conniving company shill – it is, unlike Clegg, basically functional and I need it to hiccup and whine its way through what I hope will be the last paper draft of the novel.

I am also – let's be careful here – not tired *of* the novel, but certainly tired *because of* the novel. I can't quite remember which draft I'm on, but all of them have seemed to involve struggling and fumbling on the living-room sofa (the living room can often reach habitable temperatures) and slathering recalcitrant pages with red scribbles, or else thrashing and grim silences in bed (also occasionally warmish) or simply giving up, pacing, consuming medically unwise quantities of caffeine and then starting in again with thicker socks, a different soundtrack on the stereo and a hot-water bottle. I spent – for example – Saturday evening, Saturday night and the early hours of Sunday tickling, wheedling, gnawing and praying through my last 200 pages – again – before crumpling like a wet manifesto and texting a chum in another time zone for moral support. (It's important for writers to cultivate chums in enough locations to cover their usual writing/panicking/despairing hours. I know from bitter experience that you don't want to be stuck for a week in Hungary with a manuscript that reads like a migraine and no one you can call.) Even as I type this in my suitable-for-middle-age glasses and cardigan with washable elbow patches (Christ, how did this happen?) I can feel myself folding deeper into scraggled monomania. When I go outside I simply fall over – either because of the sheet ice and uncollected bin bags underfoot, or simply because my brain can no longer sustain coordinated movement while obsessing with adequate enthusiasm over the twiddly bit on page 308.

I have reached the point at which I can't tell if the book is all right, or vile, or moderately interesting in parts. I can't even tell how many fingers I'm holding up. (That's a trick question – I'm not holding up any, I just haven't noticed yet.) In short, I'm almost ready to hand the thing in. I have corrected and smoothed it and almost tested it enough to be slightly confident that it will be consistent under variable conditions. I've worked it over in hotel rooms and on trains and in my house. I've leapt at it with energetic vigour and while begging inwardly for a minor but debilitating injury that would hospitalise me just enough for a wee rest. I've peered at it while in a sunny mood and while trying not boot my television through the window on learning that my government really has decided to screw everyone with whom it is not on first-name terms.

I hate to repeat myself, but none of the fun I'm describing above – and it is fun, it is beautiful fun, it is the time of my life, it is years of sheer bloody joy and a mercy and an income and a way of being useful – would be happening if I hadn't had a chance at tertiary education. And I'm tired of turning on my television, my radio, going and talking to my friends, the people I work with and counting off those who wouldn't have got to university, who wouldn't have been able to go back to study in later life, who wouldn't have been able to train for what they do best under Cameron and Clegg's new fee regime.

And this makes me more tired than I can say. As tired as hearing the word 'free' – as in 'Free Education', when we never have had 'free' education, just as we don't have 'free' healthcare – we all pay for both, in advance, and have done for generations, because it was thought that both ensured the social cohesion, the stability, the economic security, the intellectual development and the moral centre of our country. Soon England and Wales will rely on charities to educate its young people. I hope Scotland will continue to pursue a wiser course – I hope it can begin to demonstrate how much wiser, but I truly would rather it didn't have to.

And it makes me tired to hear kettling described as a method of crowd control; if it controlled crowds, it would be routinely used on football supporters – they turn up in crowds every week, but react rather more badly than most when penned in a crush for hours without explanation. Kettling is designed to punish insurgents – sorry, demonstrators. (Including potentially dangerous wheelchair users and schoolchildren.) It humiliates, panics, frustrates and its results are entirely predictable – anyone who wants a fight will get one, and God help those who didn't. Like Alfie Meadows. Tired, tired, tired. But I'm writing this with an income and a good life and a fresh book nearly finished and plans for next year – which is more than I could have dreamed of when I was twenty. I'd like more twenty-year-olds to end up with more than they dreamed of – not head injuries, not stupidly wasted energies, not a lack of hope. And we can arrange that. To quote William Beveridge, 'The door of learning should not shut for anyone at eighteen, or at any time. Ignorance to its present extent is not only unnecessary, but dangerous. Democracies cannot be well-governed except on the basis of understanding.' Britain was in ruins when he wrote that, in debt and shattered after years of war, but its government respected its people, its government remembered it wouldn't exist without its people and it acted with justice and it acted with grace. And it could do so again. As Beveridge also said, '. . . that which is made by man can by man be prevented'. Onwards.

XL

Happy New Year. I sincerely hope that all goes well with you and that you're not nursing a Public Service ninety-day redundancy notice, or wondering if your children have a future, or wondering if you have a future, or wondering if you can pay your fuel bills, or sitting in a heap of recalcitrant snow. Or perhaps you just have flu. I have the distinct impression that being, if not happy, then grimly amused will be one of the lower-cost items we need to get us through the next twelve months of support-slashing, book-burning, rioting, outrage and attempts to divert our attention with shiny things. Are there any more royals who could get married? Is there a long-running soap opera that hasn't suffered mass casualties and apocalyptic emotional trauma? Could the few, loveable survivors get married? Could said survivors front populist campaigns to generate massive phone-in votes for new bills that favour the reintroduction of trial by ordeal, serfdom and the twenty-four hour projection of Sky News onto the surface of the moon? I suspect that if we don't laugh – and come up with some imaginative ways of saving ourselves – then our only other options will tend towards tears and self-loathing. And, as a Scot, I can confidently state that both become extremely tedious extremely quickly.

I have been as jolly as I get during the festive period. Those among you who are self-employed will be aware of how annoying public holidays can be: you want to get on, maybe you have to get on, and yet everyone you deal with who has a Proper Job has suddenly disappeared . . . or been fired . . . it all seems very peculiar . . . To pass the time you may even try *resting* . . . something bound to induce the kind of felling medical difficulties that always appear when you *stop working* . . . I duly ran a comb and mallet over the last paper rewrite of the novel, loaded the resulting stack of hope, fear, loathing and scribbles back into the computer and then consigned it to the ether (I'm with TalkTalk, I won't use the term 'sent by email' with any kind of confidence) just before Christmas. As the last files disappeared – perhaps for ever – I felt my body weaken, crumple and search about for some really trail-blazing infection. Oddly, all it could come up with was a mimsy little bout of sinusitis – perhaps I was tired. So I settled back with a box set of Basil Rathbone *Sherlock Holmes* movies and some mulled Ribena, suffering no more than stabbing pains in my forehead, which prevented me from regularly exclaiming, 'God bless us, every one!' and wondering when our first new workhouses will be constructed.

I was, of course, also noticeably oppressed by the fact that I was *waiting to hear*. The research, the writing, the rewriting, the fretting and tinkering: they all end in this – *waiting to hear*. I have never met anyone who even remotely enjoys this part of the book-producing process. I've been writing professionally since 1989, but this will only be my thirteenth book. (And let's ignore the implications of thirteen.) This is only the thirteenth time that I have footled about, gone for walks, tried to start other things, sketched hollow-sounding plans for the coming months, stared blackly at the ceiling and generally failed to avoid the constant, low-level nausea generated by *waiting to hear*. I woke up in the morning and waited, I prodded at lunch and waited, I watched Holmes subject himself to a number of unfortunate triple-comb-over options, and still I waited. For those of you unfamiliar with the heady emotional tumble drier that is the post-handover-pre-verdict hiatus, try to imagine one of those insultingly lengthy TV elimination-round pauses which somehow elongates over days or weeks, blends with your driving-test outcome, the announcements of every important exam result upon which you have ever relied, every time you've asked someone lovely to have a coffee, or hold your hand, or subject you to intimate forms of relaxation and every naked-on-the-roof-of-Sydney-Opera-House-while-your-parents-and-in-laws-and-primary -school-teachers-render-you-in-watercolours anxiety dream you've ever had. Only it's less pleasant than that.

Don't get me wrong, this isn't the same as waiting to hear if someone you love is okay, or if your scan came back clear. But waiting to find out if my book successfully scrapes past my editor does mean that three years of research, one year of full-on typing and a whole range of ideas, technical developments and experiments and personal commitments are being assessed simultaneously. The fact that things have gone well before doesn't mean they will again. And if they fail, then there will either be a mountain of additional and disheartening work to do – when 2011 is already looking very full – or the beast is past saving and I lose a significant portion of my income. And I'm a big, rubbishy, shameful failure in an area of which I am fond. On a more personal note, the *waiting to hear* phase of things seems always to remove my ability to celebrate the completion of a book. The moment when I have, in many ways, done all I think I can bleeds effortlessly into the moment when I start to wait and when, if the outcome is good, the book begins to leave me and belong to a succession of other people. This time around I have a friend who has seen fit to cheerlead through all the stages of construction. In effect, he has done my celebrating for me and I have, in turn, been happy that he is happy. That's as good as it has ever got. Which is, perhaps, perfectly fine. The end of a book marks the point when my mind consents to become obsessively interested in whatever's next – and it's healthy and necessary to move on.

At which point, Dear Reader, I can confess to feeling slightly grubby for having kept you yourselves waiting. The many failings of the Christmas telly schedules (and the shocking preponderance of sofa ads, to say nothing of his devotion to the editorial arts) meant that my editor set to and read my offering with alacrity and an email recently arrived stating that the thing has been deemed acceptable. This doesn't mean that anyone else will like the book, that I won't tinker with it more, that the novel genuinely is any use, or that it will prosper, but I am not unrelieved to know that it will get a chance to go out and make its way in the world without me and I can see how it fares.

And – setting my friend aside for a moment – I would like to thank all of you who were supportive during 2010. It was very kind of you to take the trouble. And we are all in this together – as I've heard said elsewhere – trying to make things properly for people we'll probably never meet, being in favour of creation rather than destruction. I hope, if you're writing, that all goes well. If you're thinking of writing, then a new year is as good a place to start as any. And if you're reading, I hope that you have all you need and unlooked-for pleasures besides. There's nothing like writing a novel to get in the way of sustained reading, but now I can get back to the stacked volumes beside my bed and start enjoying the particular miracle of eloquent marks on paper pulp again. Onwards.

XLI

Now then – book signings . . . I spent a goodly portion of yesterday afternoon sitting in my study and signing book-plates to be pasted at a later date into (I have to assume) books that I have written. On the one hand, this spares the readers involved having to be in the same room with me – which many would say is a mercy – and, on the other hand, it does tend to magnify the high levels of absurdity that book signings have always impressed upon me. There I was, in my own home, producing well-wishings, congratulations and comments for people about whom I know nothing at all and trying to pretend that the addition of my cramped and childish scrawl will in some way make a book more lovely. If I am told, for example, to recommend myself warmly to Maureen with, 'I know you'll enjoy this', I am aware that I'm really speaking on behalf of the kind (if misguided) friend who thinks Maureen's life will be improved by a spot of ALK typing. If I have to say, 'With love and kisses to Sidney', then love and kisses will be copied out and presumably reach Sidney, but the whole procedure will leave me feeling a little as if I'm suddenly thinking more of myself than is wise or accurate, and indeed handing out favours of a more intimate nature than I would associate with a business transaction.

There are, of course, worse signing scenarios. Much worse. I am not a genre writer or a major seller, so I have rarely been left behind a table in a bookshop simply in hopes that would-be readers will spot me – like an unlooked-for phalarope, or a bargain set of kitchen containers – and be immediately moved to make an impulse purchase and have it defaced by the author forthwith. But this doesn't mean that I have absolutely avoided the hour after humiliating hour of waiting, trying not to make eye-contact with browsers who are plainly wondering who the hell I am, and being presented with perhaps one, maybe even two copies of my work, either by people who were clearly feeling sorry for me or mad-eyed stalkers who try to touch me inappropriately before stealing the mug of cold tea I have been nursing in order to give myself anything, anything, anything at all to do, because there's nothing I *can* do. (Make notes? For what: another book no one will buy? Read someone else's book? Which is clearly doing better than yours. Read your own book? No one else will. Hide behind a newspaper? They can still see you. Cry? And so you bloody well should . . .) Nothing else at all that won't simply make my position even more excruciating.

More hopeful are the signings that take place after readings – unless you're reading with someone ridiculously successful, as a kind of warm-up act for them . . . How clearly I recall that evening when I was on the bill with Martin Amis and Richard Ford. Dear God . . . Average Ford and Amis queue-dweller, 'We've been waiting for three months outside the building – so glad we got in. This is little Martina – she was conceived in the queue. And Richard – he's two now . . . We love you. Can we touch your hair? Sorry we've talked so long – we know you still have 3,000 other people to deal with . . .' First person in ALK queue, 'Hi. We met when we were both on holiday in Jordan. Um . . . I thought I'd turn up. So . . . You write books, then?' Second person in ALK queue, 'I work here. You might as well sign this . . . keep you busy.' And that was my queue. And Mr Ford got me to sign a book for him, because he is a kind man. Not that Mr Amis isn't – he was just being borne shoulder-high across the foyer by admirers and didn't have his hands free.

Size matters. And you can't just walk away when you're done. Nobody leaves until the last book is Sharpied . . . if that means you have to engage your tiny clutch of people in deep conversation, sing songs from shows or open your wrists to pass the time, then so be it. This is literature, baby – nobody said it would be easy . . .

Signings after events where you've been flying solo may be slightly less soul-destroying. It could be that book-buyers, or owners, will attend a reading by you to deepen their experience of . . . well, you don't really want to consider, but perhaps something that might mean they need a book to be signed. On long tours – especially in Germany, for some reason – this may combine tiredness and repetition in a manner that means I actually forget how to produce my own signature, and experience all manner of existential chaos while dutifully scrawling, 'Viel Glück, Heinrich!' and then something that would mean a cheque (in as far as such things still exist) would be instantly invalidated.

And then there are the imaginative readers and venues with extravagantly leather-bound visitors' books who will wait until your ebb is low and chuck in a casual, 'Oh and just draw anything you want . . .' And suddenly there you are for all time on big posh pages between Václav Havel and Maya Angelou or suchlike, simply proving that you have no artistic ability at all, shouldn't be there and are a fraud, an upstart impostor and someone whose volumes should be burned at every opportunity.

Add in my long-running inability to know what on earth to say to people who have been kind enough to stand in a queue in order to speak to me and whose names I will inevitably misspell (oh, the number of wrongly dedicated books I have had to hide away and pay for later, after providing replacements . . .) and you have a whole bundle of nightmares and possibilities for failure and offence.

But better to have the opportunity to be publicly shamed and to go wrong horribly than not. Of course. Better to be published than not. Of course. And – even more of course – the printed dedication page, the one I get to have neatly printed in every copy beforehand, provides me with an opportunity to do something useful in a book, something I can be happy about. Over the years and the books, I have been able to thank my mother for being my mother, to let my grandfather be happy about a small memorial to his wife and to remember him when he was also gone – to express the affection I never adequately articulate in person. It's the best I can do. Onwards.

XLII

The post below appeared at a time when the sale of public forests was being seriously considered.

Defending the arts – it can seem a peculiar and foolish thing to do. I've been working in the arts since what retrospectively seem the kind and smiling days of Thatcherite funding cuts. Now I'm watching what amounts to the UK's Closing Down Sale. Soon, the public forests and rights of way will go, as will the post offices, the educational opportunities for the weak and the regional and the poor. And people with disabilities who live in residential care will lose their transport benefits, because why would anyone in residential care ever want to leave the building and, goodness me, wouldn't 'normal' people be mightily disturbed if strange and possibly non-voting social outcasts did get out and about? (Obviously the homeless non-voting outcasts will continue to be outside all kinds of buildings in increasing numbers.) And on it will go, like the original type of juggernaut. So why, when everything seems to be threatened – health, education, heritage, sport – even mention the arts?

If you've been reading this blog for any length of time, you'll be aware that I do feel very strongly that it's legitimate to defend the arts, even in the harshest of times. You'll also be aware of the usual arguments fielded against anyone positioned on the side of the arts – views which have been endlessly recycled in the media over the last decades and which now mean the principal activity within many arts is apology. This is, I would point out, a land-scape which many observers abroad with an awareness of European history find both alarming and bewilderingly self-destructive.

You're just defending your own job. You're an artist and therefore a middle-class tosser with no idea of the lives ordinary people lead and should shut up, because everything about you is suspect in ways I can't quite describe.

You know what? Yes, I am defending my own job. It's a great job – and I would like other people to be able to have ones like it: long, but flexible hours, adaptable practices, poorly unionised – it's the kind of job Neocon Capitalism wants me to have. Sadly, it also involves reasonable experience-related pay and very few industrial injuries, or diseases. It's work that does not depress or demoralise the worker. It involves dignity and high degrees of job satisfaction, both of which tend to give an artist the energy and ability to have and express opinions – sometimes political opinions – should they wish to. While a high-profile piece of bad art, self-indulgent art, patronising and watered-down art, uncommunicative art tends to produce blanket condemnations of all arts everywhere, the pieces of art that people love: the songs on their iPod, the design of their iPod, the Angel of the North, the mural at the end of their street, the play they saw on a school trip that made them into a slightly different person, the stained glass in their church, the picture on the card from someone significant, the movies they've collected on DVD . . . that art tends to be so personally and deeply enjoyable and loved that it becomes a part of individual personalities. Good art stops being art – it becomes a way of being happy, of receiving something beautiful and human from strangers, of exploring one's identity, of being not alone. This is the average end-product of a good-quality and satisfying job in the arts sector of British industry. Why would I be a tosser for defending this?

Yeah, but you're an artist – I repeat, you don't know about ordinary people.

Wherever an artist comes from, the default classification for an arts worker tends to be Middle-Class. This means that people can come into the arts from all kinds of backgrounds and places and be granted (or be cursed with) Middle-Classness. This kind of social mobility can be hugely confusing for observers who want everyone to stay where they're put. (And, while we're about it, the arts are relatively gender-blind. Women can do very well in the arts without being punished for it too heavily.) Having gained an income and a trade through the arts, artists who suggest that others should have the same opportunities are dismissed as Middle-Class wankers for saying that access to the arts shouldn't be restricted to the Middle (and perhaps Upper) Classes.

My personal experience – which is actually nobody's business but my own – would be that I was brought up by working-class parents who had educated themselves into Middle-Class jobs. I got through the last years of my schooling and all of my university education with the aid of the state – being, by then, the child of a divorced working mother with limited resources. I then spent around ten years working with people in prisons, hospitals, daycare centres, elderly care homes. I even worked in the homes of people with special needs. Together, we used the arts to improve our lives. And lives really were improved. Finding a means of expression when people usually shout at you or ignore you is something significant. Creating a piece of art which means others view you as human, rather a problem or a freak, is a remarkable thing. (Although it can scare the crap out of politicos who want to shut down your facility, or who are trying to pretend that just because you have cerebral palsy, or use a wheelchair, or are very old and will die soon, you won't mind losing what few pleasures you have, or jumping through increasingly arcane and humiliating hoops to gain the minimal aid that would help you contribute to your society and gain a minimum level of comfort and contentment.) The arts aren't about self-indulgence, they're about being fully and visibly alive.

No, the arts are elitist and self-obsessed. What about the baby who needs an incubator? Would you take the money away from a baby?

As I've just pointed out – and as I have pointed out for more than two decades – it takes a great deal of effort and what amounts to wholesale economic censorship to make the arts elitist and, even then, because they are nourished by personal enthusiasm, they can still break out in unexpected ways and among unconventional people. The arts communicate the humanity of others to us and our own humanity to them. Dictators, police states and every colour and composition of oppressive regime seek to control the arts, because they know that will give them enormous levels of control over their population. The book-burnings, the intimidation, the arrests and executions of artists, the specific targeting of much-loved artworks – they serve a purpose. They reduce those private and sustaining joys that a population can cling to, unite around, and they reduce the information we need to remind us that other human beings are human, that they shouldn't be robbed of dignity, shouldn't be harmed or destroyed.

In the UK, increasingly unresponsive and self-regarding governments have imposed ever greater financial and moral burdens upon the electorate, while coincidentally suppressing the arts – muzzling one of the few ways we have of communicating with each other at emotional depth. The arts also represent one of the few ways we have of communicating with our leaders – of representing ourselves in a public forum to people dangerously isolated from the consequences of their own actions.

A straight – and completely mythical – choice between the baby's incubator and a poem? The incubator wins every time. The poet would write the poem anyway. Poets will write less if they never get paid, thrive less, or give up. So we get fewer poems and, long-term, the poems are part of why we try to make sure there's an incubator there for the people we don't know, will never meet, don't understand, don't like. The arts are part of what gets us through the day, especially in the harshest of times. Onwards.

XLIII

*T*he post below refers to the occupation of the much-loved Hetherington Club for postgraduates at Glasgow University. The renamed 'Free Hetherington' occupation continued until August 2011 and was marked by a varied programme of events and lectures, shared responsibilities and imaginative cooperation. The occupation focused particularly on cuts to educational provision at Glasgow University and the imposition of higher student fees.

For the first time in many weeks, I am typing on a train. As I wandered the aisles, trying to find a functioning power point for my laptop, it all felt very much like home. In fact, it felt very much more like home than my home currently does. As you may recall, I have for some time been threatening to redecorate my flat in a meaningful way and with professional assistance, rather than just running up and down a ladder myself armed with Polyfilla, misplaced hope and magnolia emulsion. Long-term exposure to my own residence, something to which I am not at all used, eventually made chaos and dustsheets inevitable.

Meanwhile, I was sitting in on the recording of a radio sitcom, finishing the rewrite for a radio play, tidying a magazine essay and coordinating with the students who nominated me as their candidate for Rector of Glasgow University. So a quiet little spell for me, then. As the roofer (suddenly, I needed the roofer) and painter chatted, I lapsed in and out of consciousness, typed and prayed that order would restore itself before I got enough rest to rally and become distressed.

Actually, distress was a relatively distant possibility, given that my study and the books were safe. If you're a writer and have ever undergone domestic disruption – been burgled, evicted, forced to renew your heating system, subjected to savage replumbing, joined by demanding and messy visitors – then you'll know that scribblers, as a species, have curious priorities. The only thing I was able to find amusing about being burgled (on two occasions) was my instinctive rush to check that manuscripts and backups were okay. My priorities make sense to me, but might seem unusual to others. We all have something precious we'd rather not lose, which sustains us, allows us to be ourselves.

As it happens, the roofer also has what might be considered unusual priorities, by someone who perhaps knows little of roofers. Fred (that's not his real name, but roofers need their privacy) is a chum of mine and, apart from being a proper artisan and craftsman of roofs, he is also an artist. He paints – in the sense of producing paintings, rather than refurbishing window frames and coving – sells his work and has recently been to Stockholm, taking in the qualities of light. Fred isn't the kind of guy who's supposed to take an interest in nineteenth-century European masters. If he was portrayed on telly, he'd drink too much, or be in some way criminal, because working-class people – like students, like the disabled, like anyone outside the tiny, perceived mainstream – only seem to merit public portrayals as blurry threats, or dysfunctional souls, lost among the deservedly helpless. At best, a low-budget British movie might remodel Fred as the golden-hearted, but comfortingly stupid father of an attractive and upwardly-mobile youngster. According to our current culture, Fred shouldn't be widely and well read, shouldn't be capable of analysing newspapers with amused cynicism and disgust, and shouldn't be able to have coherent and interesting opinions on art, culture, politics, philosophy and spirituality, to name but a few. Fred would be great on *The Culture Show*, or *The Review Show* – he would be interesting, coherent and dignified. But he's an autodidact with a working-class accent. And he's a roofer. They wouldn't want him. (And, I'd have to say, he has more sense than to want them.)

If I think about it, I'd estimate that 80 per cent of the real human beings I know are appallingly misrepresented in the media. For more than a generation, reality TV has focused on increasingly freakish freaks, intelligent drama has withered and the definition of current affairs has become depressingly literal, limiting itself to the coverage of car-crash celebrities' couplings and media-induced meltdowns. It's unsurprising that public policy has meanwhile become less and less beneficial to the public and our leaders have been drawn from a smaller and smaller elite.

Fred comes from a tradition of self-education and personal dignity that's still lively in the west of Scotland, but which is, of course, under threat. I've lost count of the number of people I know who didn't receive a great education, but who then simply went to their local library and started reading at A. This was possible, because they had a library nearby with an extensive stock of free books, free heating and reasonable opening hours. This was also possible because the culture surrounding them helped them believe that the getting of wisdom was worthwhile for its own sake and that it would help them to live better, not simply increase their earning potential – although it might do that, too. In the UK today, it's harder for those who want to become more fully themselves to even start their journeys into what could be a lifelong process of education.

And, of course, universities and their students are under attack as never before. Students go into debt to pay for courses with decreasing levels of support from professional staff, while greater and greater teaching burdens are placed on postgraduates.

Emphasis on revenue-generation alters priorities in such a way that the reputations of institutions and qualifications declines and a generation mortgages its future to emerge less fitted for adult life, less self-aware and less able to survive in a savage marketplace. This isn't about ivory-tower notions and creating an intellectual elite – although the genuinely powerful elite always seem to manage to get a very thorough intellectual grooming – this is about making the most of our collective abilities and ensuring our commercial survival, as well as allowing fellow-human beings to achieve their fullest potential. The phoney internal markets and fake business practices which have broken the NHS, public transport, the BBC and primary and secondary education are poised to destroy tertiary education, too. They are the same business practices that have dragged the UK into recession, but still we are expected to trust them with our nation's future.

Which is why a portion of my last few weeks have been spent trying to air some of these issues as part of the Rectorial debate in Glasgow University. The media found the idea of a Kennedy (Charles) versus Kennedy (A.L.) clash attractive, as the ingenious and admirable students who nominated me knew they would, and both Kennedys have been able to speak about the need for free education and radically altered priorities. Our team haven't been playing to win – we won't – we've been playing to try and alter the agenda. The students would have made better speakers on their own behalf than me, but it has been an honour to collaborate with them. They will go on occupying the Hetherington Club in a spirit of cooperation and real education and they will go on opposing the Glasgow University cuts. They have no choice. They're fighting for something precious they'd rather not lose, that sustains them, that allows them to be themselves. In many ways, they're fighting for their lives. Onwards.

XLIV

I'm lying down. This is as close as I get to a hobby. Over the weekend I attempted to establish sleeping as a further leisure activity, but I'm afraid that the vast list of things I have to do before most days break – or, indeed, I myself break – made that impossible. So lying down and working: it's almost as good as a rest.

Not that I am complaining about being in work. Being in work is a good thing. Being in work when you are self-employed and me – and your employer is therefore almost as mentally sturdy as Charlie Sheen – is a less good thing. Not that I'm in any way chemically enhanced, or unhanced. I can forget why I've ended up in the kitchen again and am holding a single shoe without any assistance from prescribed or clandestinely imported substances. When I shake my head my brain thumps against its sides like a neatly parcelled corpse in the boot of a slewing car.

Meanwhile, I have been asked to write a little about the typist's progress from hoping-to-be-published-anywhere-at-all-ever to dear-God-shoot-me-just-in-the-shin-then-I'll-get-a-day-off. This is, of course, both a happy progression and something that should be much better organised in my case. Here, I'll try and look at what we might call the very early days. The awful and wonderful early days.

So, to begin at the beginning. My own experience of starting out was haphazard and almost certain to fail. I didn't really intend to write, I was simply living in a tiny, cold bedsit with no other ways of being constructive. (And if your only way to prove yourself useful is by producing a steady trickle of maimed and ugly short stories, you should probably take a good look at yourself.) I joined a writer's group and then remembered that I don't like groups. I sent off stories without really researching my target magazines, which duly returned my efforts, often accompanied only by a scribble on a square of paper slightly smaller than a commemorative stamp. I had occasional successes and an encouraging letter of rejection, or – dear God – an acceptance, or – good heavens – not just a free copy of *Quentin's Quarterly Gallimaufry*, but a cheque for twenty quid could light up my month. I was more often disappointed than not, but I was also learning that I cared about this. I cared so much that I would start again after every sad envelope flopped in, write something else, forget that it hurt to be knocked back.

I was writing by hand with later multicoloured corrections as nervousness and tinkering racked up rewrites. Rewriting in the days before personal computers was something of a grind . . . A bit of planning before I'd started and then stepping back for an overview would have helped me much more than altering things blindly and investing affection, rather than criticism. As it was, I ended up with page after page of Jackson Pollocked nonsense. I didn't know any better. I wanted advice, but I was afraid that someone well informed would simply tell me I shouldn't bother because I was incurably dreadful. I felt lonely and pointless and hungry.

If you're at that stage now, then you have my sympathy – it's horrible. And it's worse now – opportunities to get involved with tutoring, or reviewing, or workshops are evaporating, the publishing landscape is ever-shrinking, as are advances, there are fewer magazines out there and fewer anthologies, there are fewer places for new books in bookshop chains and, yes, it may be that you don't ever get published and reach anyone's shelves. You may be a risk that someone would have taken ten years ago, while today you seem unaffordable. You may be a good writer, but unlucky. There may be a day when you fold that set of ambitions away and turn your mind to something else. We have to consider this.

But if you haven't given up yet, I can say – and I think I am being honest about this – that even this initial grimness needn't turn out to be 100 per cent horrible. Really. It needn't. When everything about writing is a slog and you seem to be getting nowhere, your lack of pressing demands from numerous admirers does mean you have the time to sit back and consider why you're putting all this effort into what appears to be an unrewarding relationship. You're flinging out the best love letters you can, you're breaking your heart and no one's answering, but on you go regardless . . . why? If your answer is that you love what you're doing and couldn't abandon it without being someone other than yourself, then you probably have to keep on. You would be less than yourself if you did otherwise. The certainty that you have to write can be a pain in the neck, but it's also a great, firm truth to build around – the shysters and manipulators and compromise-peddlers won't be able to shake you later, if you fasten yourself to that.

And if you are eventually successful and your work as an author does take off in one direction or another, it's not unlikely that there will be other times when, for other reasons, you come to doubt if the effort is worth it, or if you're suited to it. Your experience in those first, hard times will be there for you then. If you've not had enough money and not had enough support – or any support – if people have thought you were crazy and yet you've pressed on regardless and tried to learn your craft, then it could be that you just are a writer. If you've taken notes and practised observation and made horrible mistakes and pondered giving up and listened and puzzled and fretted and wasted your time and woken at three in the morning being shaken by the best idea you've ever met and fought sentences for days until they've actually rolled over and let you win, then you may already, deeply know that you're a writer. You certainly know that you kept writing, even when you had no reason to. You know that writing calls in you, that it's a good thing, a life-changing thing, and that you'd be foolish to ignore it.

Way back when I was at my beginning I summoned up the courage to find my local Writer in Residence – we had one, funded by the Scottish Arts Council – and he read my material while I felt nauseous. Then he showed me how to make cocoa. Thinking back on it, making cocoa is probably all he could think of to do with someone who was clearly a ball of pure tension and liable to cry, if not faint at any moment. I've been in his position since and it's hard to be correctly tender and correctly firm with someone who's just handed you an armful of their dreams – cocoa might not be a bad distraction. Someone who has fully committed to their work, pressed everything they can into word after word – because half-measures won't cut it – will have more than a little interest in what you think of the results.

I sat and pondered my gradually cooling mug while he talked me through the two or three stories I'd handed over, and was factual about their flaws and kicked the crap out of one of the endings – I still remember – and generally bludgeoned me. I was sore by the time we'd finished, but I felt wonderful, too. Here was a writer who was talking to me as if I were a writer. I wasn't a good writer – what I'd done was full of flaws and holes and silliness – but somebody qualified had read my work and thought it had enough merit to deserve close examination.

I left knowing how to make cocoa (I still use his method) and feeling bruised. But I also knew it was all right. Somehow, it was going to be all right. I would start again, and again and again. I would rewrite.

Which is why I wish you the very best attentions of a reader you can trust. Quite possibly this won't be all thirty-eight variously deluded members of your workshop, or your partner, or a secretly embittered relative, or a stranger on a bus, or anyone you have to pay. You'll need somebody who cares about writing, who wants to help, who probably wants to pass along the help they received when they were starting out. I wish you a Good Reader. Onwards.

XLV

T *he post below was written during the first bout of labyrinthitis and while my immune system declined without my
particularly paying attention.*

Those of you who indulge in Twitter as well as this blog will
be aware that I've spent the time between my last piece and this
being mainly in bed and feeling like someone who really does
need to take things more easily. Several people have, in fact,
shouted at me to that effect and I am taking their advice. April
may be the cruellest month, but I am planning to render it
civilised and to take my antibiotics in a regular manner.

Meanwhile, let us progress – if that's the right word – from
last time's little sketch of the writer's Very Early Days to the
Less Early Days. One might expect that these bring with them
inrushes of professional assurance, public acclaim and cash.
Well, no. Not unless your first book is not only accepted for
publication, but also instantly taken up as a soul-clattering work
of genius that should be sold to every sane and able citizen.
Which is unlikely.

Your Less Early Days will bring you – if all goes well – into
contact with your first agent, your first editor and your first
advance. These are all fine things which you will need, but they
will also be at least a little terrifying. Back in the Precambrian
Era when I was a neophyte scribbler, publishing houses weren't

quite the fortresses they are today and you could almost get by – or rather in – without an agent. (And editors eager to save cash could almost persuade you to do so.) Nevertheless, even I had worked out that signing a contract without assistance was something I should never do. My first 'agent' was entirely self-appointed and had a habit of accumulating injuries while 'not drunk', or providing the inadvertent floor show at social/literary occasions by – for example – igniting a whole box of matches while fumbling to light her cigarette. As I am inept enough at social/literary occasions without additional chaos, I sought to divest myself of her attentions – especially as I hadn't asked for them. And, believe me, there are few things more embarrassing than writing to an editor who has just rejected your first attempt at your first novel, in order to explain that the manuscript was sadly returned to someone only claiming to be your agent . . . My second agent was more successful, up to a point, but managed to let my foreign rights rest with my publisher. Allow me to begin a new, important paragraph about that.

Never, ever, ever sign away your foreign rights. Foreign rights allow you to be published abroad and in translation. They give you to the world and the world to you. And they mean you earn more money without doing more work. Unless you are the Archangel Gabriel with new instructions for mankind, if your publisher retains your foreign rights they won't particularly have the time or focus to promote your work elsewhere. Your agent needs to do that for you. Really.

Of course, choosing an agent is tricky – and horribly important, as they represent pretty much your only path to an editor and a published life. On the one hand, you need to select someone who will suit you, who will be about the same age as you (this is a long-term business) and who will support you in the ways you need. And yet, at the start of your career you probably have no idea how best you should be supported, what kind of person you would get on with in this capacity and – above all – you will be pathetically grateful if anyone even replies to your begging letter, opening chapter and synopsis. Happily, someone who likes your work will probably be a good fit for you: the person who produced it. Likewise, the editor who is excited by your writing will probably share many of your interests. Still, I think it's a good idea to avoid compromising too deeply, too soon. If your agent can't remember your name and doesn't listen to you, or seems anxious to rework you into someone else, then perhaps go elsewhere. With your editor, you'll have no choice – unless they're flirting with you, but not committing to a contract – so an amount of grinning and bearing it may have to take place.

Through a combination of accident and design, I have ended up with a male agent and a male editor – I work better with men. They're both roughly my age – the way things are going, I'll probably die before both of them, which will save any inconvenient rearrangements. My agent is willing to suffer and assuage my voluminous range of fears, will catch some of the hassle and madness that can accrue when working with others and can handle the full range of writing I produce. My editor is someone whose judgement I trust absolutely and I work on texts with him. That suits me. But it took about fifteen years for me to feel comfortable with either party as a collaborator, rather than someone who was putting up with me as a charity project. This would be why it's very important that my agent also negotiates my fees.

Talking of which – back to that first advance. Miracles aside, if you weren't a sexy-looking unknown during the late 1980s or early '90s, the chances of your first advance being anything other than frighteningly tiny are slim. Try to be happy that you're about to be published, that you'll have free copies with which to amaze your family and hit your friends. Don't stand there holding the cheque and thinking, 'I'll never earn a living, will I? This is a joke. I will never up give my day job and write, write, write.'

Yes, there you'll be, still working to subsidise what you want to do and perhaps feeling tired and unappreciated. But, then again, your day job will keep you connected to the real world, and no one – not even me – can write, write, write all the time. That would kill you – trust me on this, it really would. And maybe you'll want to get reviewed, which is a necessary thing. But then again, being reviewed badly or oddly, or even well, is quite disconcerting and weirdly irrelevant – it all refers to work you did so long ago . . . You may begin to realise that exposure isn't called exposure for nothing. For a while – if all goes to plan – you may feel both pestered with fame and utterly and permanently invisible. You may despair of your work ever finding a little niche where it can grow and flourish. You may wonder if you're any good, if it's worth the bother, if you'll be able to manage it all over again with the next one. Of course.

And yet – you're a writer, you have written. There's a book out there with your name on it. Imagine that. You did imagine that. Every word of that. And in the moments when you're undistracted, you can feel that the other books are waiting, the ideas that will come to you to be expressed. This is a vocation – it called to you and you answered and now it calls in you. If you are quiet enough to hear, it always will. You have that and you are lucky, beyond lucky. Which is – I often have to remind myself – nothing to complain about. Onwards.

XLVI

Well, the antibiotics weren't exactly what I needed, should you remember them from the last blog. I had/have viral labyrinthitis and the only response to that is lying down a lot and taking pills to counteract the worst of the symptoms. The worst of the symptoms being panic attacks, nausea and generally feeling as if you are strapped to the prow of a ship in a Force Nine gale whenever you stand up or do something reckless like turning your head. And then there are the muscle cramps and the immense tiredness . . . this health bulletin seeming horribly appropriate as we reach what will be the last sketch of Stages in the Writer's Career, which we might entitle: When You Have Been Doing It for Ages and Are Knackered.

And may I hope sincerely that all of you writing readers don't take my precise path to being knackered. It is in every way not worth it and contravenes all the healthy and good advice I give to other people. Of course. Imagine the scene: I am being tended in Warwickshire by my mother. (You know you are ill when you are a grown-up and your mum is looking after you.) I shuffle about, sometimes check my email and take short strolls. I feel old. (To be fair, I am old.) I have forgotten many of my hobbies and the possible strain of arranging any of them leaves me worrying that I will worry and feel worse. (Labyrinthitis both causes and can be caused or worsened by stress. This will be funny. Eventually.) I am self-employed, but have done no work since my last blog two weeks ago. This doesn't exactly mean that I haven't earned anything for a fortnight, but it does mean that I'm further behind schedule than during the weeks building up to Complete Illness, when I was only moving at the speed of chilled glue. I assumed I was simply a bit poorly and tense – which is to say, my standard self.

I forgot one of my most fundamental rules, Dear Readers, which is that I have to look after myself in order for myself to be able to do anything. Even writing. I forgot that I am a horrible self-employer and should be dealt with by the kind of harsh arbitration that only ever really happened during the 1970s. Whole swathes of what used to be the TUC should be picketing me, even as I type. I also forgot that I need to arrange nice little outings and trips and inspirations, or just a few hours off for myself, to preserve maximum efficiency. I have mentioned this practice of inspiration at other times, when I was sane and functional. I can ignore it – I have ignored it – but I only ever do so at my peril.

It's not the first time this has happened. One of the issues that must be addressed when you're writing is the enduring conflict between other people's agendas and one's own. The urge to keep working while the work is there can quite simply steal your life. But it's hard to resist. It may be that I want to watch a box set of *Babylon* 5, but perhaps someone else is offering me a bit of a trial in a new medium and now isn't ideal, but the creative possibilities do seem interesting . . . Perhaps I have been working on some odds and ends for radio, and more than the average number of pitches have been accepted and I don't want to now refuse tasks I have essentially been humbly requesting the honour of undertaking (the BBC requires precisely that attitude) for months, so the schedule thickens . . . Suddenly a novel-free year looks as if it may kill me before the novel that nearly killed me last year has a chance to come out. (This would, naturally, increase sales into the high dozens.)

And then there are the rewrites. Rewriting is as much a part of writing as being mugged is a part of walking about in an urban environment at night looking happy. Sorry, I'm feeling a little bitter about the wrong kind of rewriting. The right and improving kind is a gruelling delight, as I feel we have established. Anything of mine will have been rewritten until it squeaks before anyone else has to put up with it. On collaborative projects, there will then be necessary changes that deal with technical issues, changes of location, or cast, lack of funds – the possibilities are horribly variable and numerous and yet oddly fun. There are also the good ideas and happy nudges from people who are providing a healthy outside eye on a piece of work. I can be joyful about all of these.

But then there are the other kind of rewrites – the wrong kind. Many of you out there may also be familiar with these and will be wincing and twitching already. These are never to do with the script and always to do with whoever is demanding them – and, trust me, they will always be *demanded*. They come from people incapable of suggestion. They will be required to address the demanding party's personal difficulties with their lives, their need to feel involved and powerful, their need to crap on other people's days, their need to add hours and weeks and even months to projects which might at one point have been pleasant and alive. Sadly, no literary process can ever cure any of these ills and so the demands can and will continue until the writer does the only thing the writer can do – he or she withdraws, accepts that vast effort has been wasted, that the struggle has been in vain and that the script, text, article, limerick is now a dog's breakfast that cannot be saved and is nothing anyone would wish to bear their name. At which point everything will always become the writer's fault and they will be, for ever after, branded as 'difficult' – even if they are already folded into a pretzel with the strain of accommodating increasingly self-contradictory and mentally peculiar instructions. One scriptwriter friend of mine counts it as a victory if he gets through the terminal conversation without crying – and he's a veteran of the Korean War . . . If nothing else, the stress and personal offence this kind of nonsense builds up can remind the author that he or she really does still care about what ends up on the page. And it can act as an emotional reminder for future occasions when work is questioned and probed by others. There's all the difference in the world – and it's more than palpable – between the sting of someone noting a weakness you missed and the stabbing pain of someone deciding to wedge something witless into your personal sentences because they had, for example, a funny relationship with their dad.

As my years of writing pass, I find that the only thing I really resent, regret and generally deplore is the number of months – perhaps even years – that I have wasted on projects that could have been okay if everyone involved actually wanted them to happen and to be as good as it can be. Choose your collaborators wisely, would be my advice. And – then again – take no advice from anyone who can't take their own. Onwards.

XLVII

Well, I am still not what you'd call healthy, but I'm not as ill as I was when I last blogged. Every morning I take a handful of pills and every evening likewise, and I no longer feel as if I am going to fall off the world if it goes any faster. I am operating through the tail end of labyrinthitis, while I nurse a brand-new sinus infection and submit to a regimen of major antibiotics to knock out the *H. pylori* that my doctor had forgotten to tell me was busily swimming about in my interior and preparing to give me stomach ulcers. I can breathe and see and the tinnitus has stopped, so I can hardly complain, although naturally I am complaining at every possible opportunity – it fills in the time I would usually spend overworking. Yesterday – while I was feeling suitably sorry for myself – I received a letter from HMP Long Lartin, a prison which houses, among others, a number of inmates who are being detained without trial. They haven't had their day in court, their guilt or innocence has not been established, because they have fallen into the legal and moral vacuum that holds people who are thought to have been associated with terrorist activity. You'll probably be aware of how strangely easy it can be to end up somewhere more or less unpleasant, more or less indefinitely, and branded as a terrorist threat. Recent revelations about those held in Guantanamo tell familiar stories of information obtained under torture, of captives taken for money, of minors and pensioners being detained, of a number of innocent Uighurs held prisoner for years and of how simply choosing to wear a particular brand of watch can be seen as definitively incriminating. It's somehow unsurprising that for some time the Navy spokesman for Gitmo was one Lt Mike Kafka.

My letter was from Syed Talha Ahsan, a man with Asperger's syndrome, who campaigned for, among other things, the release of former Guantanamo detainee Moazzam Begg. Ahsan has been imprisoned since July 2006 following an extradition request from the US Government, using the 2003 Extradition Act. The act means that requests do not have to be supported by any prima-facie evidence. He has not been found guilty of any crime in the UK.

Perhaps you find all of this as disturbing as I do, but Talha's letter wasn't about his situation. It was a letter like many others I receive from a writer who wants advice. Talha Ahsan is a writer: a poet who wants to transfer his skills to short fiction. He doesn't know when he'll be extradited and so wonders if a correspondence course would be a good idea. He tells me another prisoner has now been held in detention for thirteen years – plenty of time for study – but perhaps he doesn't have that long, he has no way of knowing.

When I write back to Ahsan this evening, I will tell him what I would tell any other writer – that courses aren't necessary, that the idea of teaching creative writing is relatively new and, in some cases, simply a way that institutions can make money from the hopes of would-be authors while delivering very little of use. As beauty and happiness and sex have all been commodified, so, to an extent, has imagination. A whole plethora of courses, magazines, DVDs and computer programs have sprung up to extract funds from people who would formerly have simply found themselves unable not to write and would have proceeded accordingly.

Those same people rarely have funds to spare and should, above all, be defended from shabby tricks, spurious 'methods' and intellectual manipulation. I'd be the last one to suggest that artists should be indulged, or that their whims should be taken more seriously than anyone else's. Still, I have to say that writers – especially new writers – are horrifyingly vulnerable. They are caught up in a passion they can't yet control, they are generally unable not to read whatever they can find, unable not to seek any kind of guidance that might reassure, unable not to chase the sense of an unexpressed voice in their lives, unable not to embrace the joys and pains of a way of life devoted to making musics and wonders and worlds for others. This means they can be very easily abused and, of course, makes the abuse repellent.

Fortunately, just that voracious reading and experimenting and searching and fretting will eventually turn them into writers. It will fit them for a life of changes and of perpetual education. In twenty-five years of writing I have come across countless hopeful authors who doubted their abilities because they hadn't gone to university, hadn't a library of How To books, hadn't sat at the feet of a master and imbibed wisdom in a suitably furnished study. In fact, they were no more or less able than the others who had done many, if not all, of those things. There are courses that are worthwhile and books that are helpful, depending on the writer's personality. There is still a little free assistance out there, despite the unending cuts, and more-established writers are often quite generous with their time if they are asked for it moderately nicely. I would also recommend Raymond Carver's *Fires*, a book which prepared me for writing before I even really knew that I wanted to be a writer. Chekhov's letters, if you can find them, are full of insights, humour and proper humility. R.L. Stevenson's essays on fiction are wonderful, passionate, sensible and humane. Reading a book about writing written by someone of whom you have never heard, who wants you to visualise gardens, or polish your aura, or indulge in make-work exercises, or shut your eyes and try scribbling with whichever hand would be least natural might not be a good bet.

I will tell Ahsan these things. I have never met the man and only know him through his poems, tender and fierce pieces that deal in part with pleasures he can't have: a choice of food, the touch of a lover's skin, the ability to be wherever he would like. I know that writing has always been a consolation to me, a refuge and a source of strength. I know that writing can express the humanity of those who are written out of life elsewhere. I know that the simple act of sending a letter to a prisoner can change him or her and how they are treated. Amnesty's and PEN's work is centred around the effectiveness of the written word. But how do I talk about these things to someone enduring something I can't imagine and know that I couldn't withstand? How do I talk about the humanity of writing, that it is a triumph of beauty, when humanity's treatment of Ahsan has been so ugly? Onwards.

XLVIII

S o I'm walking along a railway platform in Lancaster and it's all good. The rain falling is not heavy rain. My train should have gone clear through to Glasgow and has nevertheless decided to end things here, but there'll be another option along any time. I have been assured. The bag I am carrying is light and comfy and I am not ill. I am not even a bit ill. Last night I did my one-person show in Liverpool – first gig in a couple of months, since the labyrinthitis took hold. I didn't fall over, or blank out, the audience seemed pleased, and my hotel for the night was very cool in the nice way, not the way that means I had to break out the emergency foil blanket which, yes, I do carry with me in case of nocturnal freezing. And my iPod is – *Dum-dah-dum, da dah-dum dah-dum* – playing me 'I Want You', because this is a morning for being cheery, yet mellow. I tend to play Elvis Costello on the way to events, for a touch of drive. Mr Zimmerman is more suited for occasions when the work is done and I need to walk slightly slowly and even with a minor drag-step, because this is one of those days when I can appreciate my job.

Yesterday I spent an hour and a half talking to an audience about what I love, which is working with words. I am, in fact, paid to keep words around, tend them and give them to other people. My performance was happening as part of the Writing on the Wall Festival, so I was pretty much singing to the choir, but still it's always great to be in a big room full of human beings who are exploring alternatives to what can often appear to be the Standard-Issue Way of Thinking: *What happens if we don't agree that TV was invented to let us hear strangers yelling about having sex with relatives or how we are constantly threatened by dangerous scum? What if we don't believe our newspapers, or do maintain an affection and respect for our own species not currently shared by many with power in public life? What happens if we have free imagination?*

Before my Liverpool trip, I was up in the Highlands – *Dum . . . Dah-dum . . . Dah-dum . . . Dah-dum . . .* – saying hello to my godchildren. Of all the people I would see more often if I didn't work like a fool, the godkids would rank among the top five. If not four. Or three. They are excellent people, as are their father and mother. I turn up at their house like a guilty, custody-granted realparent with too many disreputable presents and mumbles of 'I know, it's been a year . . . I was thinking about you . . . And I was ill. And did you get my postcards?' And they behave like normal individuals who have been getting on with their lives. Apart from the *Dr Who*-watching, dog-walking and eating portions of our days, we spend a good amount of time talking nonsense, because we have all – in spite of, or because of, our educations – been encouraged into alternative thinking.

Dah-dah-dah-Dum . . . And the next train isn't the Glasgow train . . . it's now for Edinburgh . . . then it'll be the Glasgow train . . . No, Windermere next . . . Then Glasgow . . . *Dum. Dah-dum, Dah-dum . . .* That's not so bad. Always wanted the easy parts of travelling, the strolling, a bass line lolloping along in the background and the other layers lighting up, winking in, making music.

Among the godchildren's presents I hadn't included a bespoke story, partly because I wasn't sure if they might not have outgrown such things, and partly because building one for them would still have knocked me over – it was either dealing with the train journey to see them or dealing with the pages, I couldn't have done both. One of the children is, in fact, happily typing (on a typewriter) her own stories now and so I got read to, instead of the other way around. Her brother and I enjoyed ourselves immensely – and we're a tough crowd. And if this sounds twee, or middle-class, or dated, I would point out that both children are also computer-literate, that our fun cost us nothing, did us good and came from well-exercised minds that could have belonged to any class, colour or orientation. The stories made us happy, and why not have a corner in life that's gentle, where people give each other things they have made? And why not keep your head nimble and feed it, especially if you're young? Eventually, the world will nip in and give you a kicking, so you'll need all the imaginative resilience you can get. (We won't go into the fact that the child's stories are scarily good and I will have to kill, or at least hobble, her a bit to prevent competition. She has been warned.)

And here I can mention that there is nothing like writing for those you love. Building something out of words, an intensely personal medium – something for someone you respect, someone for whom you care – that's both a pleasure and a properly testing exercise. I have long argued that the writer's relationship with the putative reader should probably be one of loving respect: it's a way of maintaining a correct form of address. Having a literal someone out there for whom you would like to do more than your best, someone to please, can be helpful. There are risks, of course. Writing for children is splendid, but they will eventually grow up, things will, and should, move on. If you've ever tried writing for a lover, that can be intoxicating and wonderful, but it can also lead you into self-indulgence and, should the relationship founder, your deathless lines may end up all over the kitchen wall. Still, if you want to have a go . . . well, I wouldn't be able to stop you. Writing from love and for love – love of the words, love of your species, love of specific joys – that's a fine remedy for ills.

And it's a reminder – *Dum-dah-dum, da dah-dum dah-dum* – of a deep pleasure in being a writer: the permanent music it provides. Sometimes having the benefit of a free head full of words offers as clear and complex a melody as any track I'll ever play to cheer me. Sometimes the words are white noise, sometimes they can feel like being a kid again and simply happy, sometimes they're an excuse for nearly dancing on a railway platform, sometimes I get paid for trying to put them down on paper, sometimes they'll end up in a letter with a readership of one. And this is something we all have – it takes negative intervention (illness, fear, threat) to damage our music, muffle it. But it's still there, waiting, singing inside. Onwards.

XLIX

Today I can't speak. My body is clearly running through the dictionary of annoying ailments and, having dealt with the labyrinthitis, we seem to have staggered on to laryngitis, or a derivative thereof. I am hoping we won't be exploring the whole of L, or that we can at least skip Lassa Fever, which is often much more annoying than patients would like, even in cases where they can afford ribavirin.

You'll notice that I didn't write *I have lost my voice* – partly because, as long as I can write, I don't feel that my voice is lost; and partly because that is a phrase which always has a chilling edge for those of us who have spent decades trying to find, trap, tame and train whatever voice seemed available.

Being literally unhearable will frustrate me for a while, of course, but as I've spent all week watching grainy film of elderly care-home inmates occupying a space far beyond screaming, I know I have nothing to complain about. While I was starting to write, I spent a little over ten years working with various vulnerable groups in various facilities and watched the hard edge of Thatcher's reforms stealing a little more comfort and possibility from lives each day. It's impossible to forget the geriatric wards and homes where human beings sat and wept, pools of urine at their feet, robbed of all dignity, simply for being old and not wealthy.

I was working for an arts charity and would be sent in to talk with elderly people and collect reminiscences. (Sometimes we might even be allowed to do things that didn't involve only the past.) I was, at the very least, a kind of company, something to do. In the good places with good staff, the ones that were managing in spite of it all, we would share the stories of who people used to be and this helped to reinforce their presence, their reality as individuals. In the bad places, the worn-down places, the holding cells for the inconveniently-not-yet-dead, no one listened. No one paid any attention when inmates would simply yell in despair, so why on earth would staff want to hear about former careers, children raised, trams driven through the Blitz, losses, hopes? It would seem wrong to treat living members of one's own species with brutal indifference, so best to forget that they are members of one's own species – don't let them have a voice.

I specialised in working with people who were marginalised. After a while it became clear that society's margins are far more extensive than its comfy centre. If you want to stay out of them, avoid falling ill, having a disability, having an accident, having an abusive partner, being young and poor, old and poor, or unlucky. Above all, avoid being unlucky.

On the margins, voices are muted or ignored. One gentleman talked using a machine, but would sometimes use it to tell jokes, so the machine was put away in a cupboard. How would you like it if someone prevented you from speaking, because you were thought to have used your voice too frivolously? But if you have cerebral palsy, it's okay to remove your best means of expression. Just as it's okay to remove the benefits you need to live. The people we don't hear from can suffer without troubling us – we'll never be disturbed by the details of their pain. Now and then there will be a documentary that provokes comment, or someone will murder too many people too openly. Of course, we couldn't accept Dr Shipman's behaviour or anything like it. Then again, we can choose not to consider that when elderly residents are moved from one home to another there is always a saving – the move kills a predictable percentage. It's interesting to consider that caring for fewer people allows for savings and seems cruel, while making those savings in advance can mean there will be fewer people to care for and yet seems more civilised. I only know about this because it was explained to me once by a senior social worker. His voice was nicely modulated, reasonable, clear.

Sorry, that's perhaps a little dark when the sun is shining and Prince Philip is still officially recognised as a useful human being, despite having managed to be ninety. Beyond having to croak at people, all is well with me. And I have spent my last meetings with the Warwick University Creative Writing students as pleasantly as usual, but with a new addition. I had already mentioned the qualities of the eye of a bird of prey – both to the students and elsewhere in this blog – and this week I enlarged on my theme. We were joined one morning by two Harris hawks, a gyrfalcon, a barn owl and a white-faced scops owl. Shakespeare wrote both about the lover's eyes – which *will gaze an eagle blind* – and the poet's eye. His lovers write – they no sooner fall for the object of their affections than they are producing letters and poems and *words, words, words.* They look *from heaven to earth and earth to heaven* – they are hugely and as-never-before alive, expressive, observant, *soft and sensible.* They celebrate themselves and their love in their voices. If we are young, we will in some way come to this, if we are old it will never quite have left us. For me, the writer's and the raptor's eye are – like the poet's and the lover's eyes – intimately related and it is valuable for us to consider them.

I had long wanted to bring writers into the same room with the reality of that raptor's eye, rather than the metaphor: *Here is something so deeply and perfectly alive that it draws the eye, that it*

makes the observer happy – can you make your words do the same?
Here is a gaze about life and death, an utterly fixed purpose – does
your work have the same purpose, the same strength of knowing its
aim completely and completely committing to it? Here is something
shaped by its needs, made beautiful and simple by the necessities of
its life – is your work so beautiful, so uncluttered, is it powered by
the heart of your needs, the things it would be life for you to say
and death to stifle? Here is something that will meet your eye with
a force you will always remember, that is made to reach its aim –
can you meet your reader's eye with the same power, will you always
touch them? Here is an unshakeable focus, but around it there is
only flexibility, fluidity, the ability to deal with the vast variable
that is the sky – can you know the nature of your piece so well that
you cannot lose it and yet adapt to its needs and your own? In what
ways are you the bird? And in what ways is your writing, your voice,
the bird? Here is a relatively small thing, a living thing that may
come to your hand and be with you, but will also be still wild and
its own. Hold it too tight, it will struggle. Hold it too loosely and
you may lose it. If you treat it badly, it will object, it may leave you.
If you are calm, it may stay. If you are skilled, it may even work
with you, let you learn about each other. It is easy to love and easy
to be afraid of. It can change you, the way you stand. It inspires
respect.

Sometimes we are the falcon and sometimes we are the falconer. And sometimes we need beauty to feed us up and send us out into the world, to give us the strength to speak. And sometimes we can help others speak, too. The students are almost at the end of their course now, but before they graduate they'll be leading workshops, beginning to learn how to pass this on. And now they can think of birds, if that would help them – we all need our inspirations. Onwards.

L

I have a small blackboard in my study. On it, I carefully chalk all of the writing-related tasks I have not yet completed: essays, scripts, treatments, rewrites, short stories, letters, novel-planning, crying in a corner, talking to my kettle . . . There are days when I love this blackboard and its anal-retentive attention to detail: its tiny chalk-holding flange, its even tinier rubbing-out cloth; and there are also days when it feels like having a debt-collector in the room with me, smelling of broken legs and hardened hearts.

Having pretty much lost two months to illness, I am currently ignoring the board completely. I haven't allowed myself to approach it closely, never mind study its listed assignments, or consider how many others I am hiding from myself by simply keeping them in my head. Off the board and in my brain, I know they will come adrift from their deadlines and end up getting tangled in each other, but I don't care – a visible inventory would simply drive me back to the kitchen, where I would end up giving the kettle abuse. And actually my kettle's very nice.

Why do I have such a deep and intimate relationship with my kettle? Because for twenty-five years, give or take, I have been a person who knows they have something to write. I have written when nobody wanted to hear from me, I have written when I could earn as much as £30 in a year by my writing, I have written when I was tired from my day job, when I was filled with the terrifying elation of a new idea, when I was starting my first novel, when I was starting my sixth novel, when I was rewriting something apparently insoluble, when I was trying to prove myself employable and when I was just fooling about until I could see what might happen. In all of these circumstances and more, what was the common factor? The kettle. As soon it's inevitable that a writer must begin their first word, it becomes (almost) equally and conflictingly inevitable that the writer must do something else really quickly before scribbling breaks out. Hence the kettle: *Tell you what, I'll just go and make a fresh beverage – then I'll get down to things properly. Absolutely. Of course I will.*

Writers can generate industrial quantities of procrastination before their first sonnet is rejected, or their first novel-outline-plus-sample-chapter is exorcised, burned and its ashes buried at sea. *Are my pens facing north? Or magnetic north? What's that funny noise? Oh look, it's raining outside. My fingernails need cutting. I think my computer is going to break, better get it checked. Do I have toothache? Will I have toothache? I should call Whatshisname.* The possibilities lend new meaning to the words *eternity* and *purgatory*.

When I began writing, distractions were all low-tech. I had to worry about typewriter ribbons and correction fluid, for God's sake. There was no possibility of spending an apparently productive day making backup files, defragmenting already tidy hard drives, emailing, watching online movies of cats falling over, or playing virtual patience. (I once tried a more sophisticated computer game and, after many months, had managed to advance my character by one level and put him into a loop of crouching, rocking and saying, 'Oh, no.') Nevertheless, I could still burn away whole pre-Amstrad weekends in keeping busy, rather than writing. Ever rehung and filed your clothing along a colour gradient, or cleaned all your grouting with a toothbrush? I have.

R.L. Stevenson once said that he didn't like writing, he liked *having written.* And I think I know how he felt. The act of writing is delightful, once you've entered into the proceedings, it's simply that – like many other intimate, involving and tiring activities – writing creates nervousness, fumbling and an intense desire to run away before it can really take a hold.

I do love to write and I worked out relatively quickly that I should pre-empt as much of my delay and dismay as possible by removing sources of distraction and rendering myself as comfy as a Calvinist can be, prior to embarking on my opening sentence for the day. I then reached the point where I had to earn my living by writing, rather than the less-profitable avoiding-writing option. This means that, over the years, I have developed, abandoned and refined various preparatory manoeuvres to ease things along – the typist's equivalent of dinner and a tastefully naked European movie to follow. Before I could afford a comfy chair, I propped myself up with pillows and cushions. I made myself a cuppa, all ready in advance. I eliminated noise with nice music. I conditioned myself to associate pieces of music with having *already started to write* and went through – as time passed – more and less complicated routines of exercise, or meditation, or horrified staring. And there are, naturally, the time-honoured favourite forms of self-deception: *I'm not really starting, I'm just mucking about for a bit. I'm going to write this, even though it's not what I'm really meant to be doing and therefore a bit of fun. If I finish another page I can have a treat.*

Now, perhaps because I am old and tired, I may kick off by doing a bit of voice-work to wake myself up, I may embark on a new project by having a thorough wash and brush-up, or I may just tell myself: *Here we go, then.*

I am aware that there are writers who successfully avoid ever having to write at all. Whatever creative energies they may possess have been completely absorbed by displacement activities. These activities often include dressing, sounding and standing (if not drinking – in fact, usually drinking . . .) like an author, and so these individuals can seem far more convincing as artists of the well-turned phrase than many people who actually have been published. When I was starting to write, I found this type very confusing. Indoors, I was bewildered by both writing and not writing. I didn't know how to say what I wanted to, or if I really wanted me to, or if anyone else wanted me to. Out in the world, here were these amazing excuses to never bother about such things again. Their path was a temptation. But I did realise it also led to a horrible, horrible dead end.

I have, in my professional life, met numberless writers who seemed paralysed by their own desire to write, who had intelligent and reasonable excuses for not starting, not committing, not getting on with it, who could trump any arguments or suggestions I might make towards putting anything on paper. It is nice to win arguments, but not if it means you deny yourself the chance to do something beautiful and intensely alive. Win or lose, you have to be in the game to play it, and writing is a game which can deepen and enrich any player's experience, moment by moment. We can all feel we're not really up to it on any given day – and sometimes we're right, we should take a break. But not writing – that would be like not speaking, not touching, not kissing. Pauses are probably unavoidable, but perhaps use yours, enjoy them, shorten them until you can find their edge. We might look at it like this: kissing is good, but kissing after five or ten seconds of well-informed waiting – that can be better. Onwards.

LI

So. We have together gone through the process of researching a novel and then preparing to write, starting to write, continuing to write, finishing, losing the author's marbles, finding the author's marbles, rewriting, tweaking, discussing the cover of, hammering out the cover blurb for and generally the entire genesis of a novel. Next month the bloody thing – wearing its cover and blurb – will actually appear to annoy people in person. To those of you who have been around throughout, thank you for your company and support. (And a big hello to all those of you who think I'm a Left-Wing fanatic who should be shot as soon as possible. Somehow, the fact that you are of that opinion makes me delighted that you can manage to hold it of harmless old me.) Given that we've been trundling along for some considerable period now, I would imagine that a number of you have also completed projects. If this is the case, I hope they prosper.

I am now about to embark upon the round of promotional activities, which is always appreciated – if no one were taking an interest, that would be a very sad thing for the book – and yet which is also hideous. I will soon have my photograph taken by professionals who usually deal with attractive human beings, who can be safely enlarged across newspaper pages without causing public distress; we will both know that many things are very, very wrong with this picture. Still, I must try not to look as if I would rather slit my throat than be repeatedly humiliated in this manner. I must somehow stand at an angle that implies I have written something readers might like and smile a smile that makes me seem human, or at least not dangerous. Over time, I have got slightly better at this, but not much. Sometimes circumstances are kind, or I know the photographer, or we can chat about lenses, or light, or puppies, and pretend that the photos aren't happening. Sometimes occasions inform against me. For example, I was once snapped exhaustively in Paris quite close to the offices of *Vogue*. Parisian passers-by – who tend to be dapper, suave and socially engaged – made no secret of the fact that they were finding it very hard to work out why their arrondissement suddenly had a blighted gonk lurking in it for a photo-shoot, rather than the usual, achingly gorgeous succession of Brazilian lingerie models. For a long moment they would stare, then they would reflect and then they would make an internal statement which ran something along the lines of 'Ah . . . the Before picture'. Or, indeed, 'Ah . . . she must have been in a terrible accident and can no longer model lingerie, only surgical corsets and veils. *Quel dommage!*'

And then there are the interviews, during which – as a contractual and career-sustaining obligation – the author must be enthusiastic about his or her own work, must be coherent about his or her own working process, must not say anything that inadvertently damages or embarrasses a friend or loved one, must try to appear in some way interesting and must not mention anything inept or controversial, or comment upon anything to do with the Wonderful World of Literature that might blow up in his or her face later, causing untold woe. Given that I have broken all of these rules at one time or another, I'm kind of past saving. I do try to steer as sane and uncataclysmic a course as I can. This causes me stress, which causes me to make the mistakes that I am stressed about avoiding. There have been occasions when I have steadfastly and repeatedly shot myself in both feet and gone on to double-tap some additional pairs of shoes in the cupboard for good measure. There have been interviews when journalists have turned up determined to be nice, no matter what – even bringing gifts with them – and others have arrived and seemed entirely pleasant before putting together the type of knife-job I would think of as worthwhile only if I were anyone of whom anybody had actually heard. And then there was that time when an ex-boyfriend phoned up repeatedly with scathing comments upon my person until even the knife-wielder in receipt of his revelations became slightly uneasy. There is nothing like any kind of public exposure to make friends, enemies and total strangers act oddly around you. Sometimes, they give you free fruit. (Proper famous people get cars and suits and electrical goods, I know, but once-every-four-years-in-a-weekend-supplement people get fruit. Or maybe it's just me. I look as if I need fruit . . .) And sometimes I don't get any fruit at all.

When I first started writing, I used to read most of the interviews. I would think, 'I shall study this and find out useful stuff about me that I didn't realise and can put to work in my ongoing processes of personal improvement. It won't all just confuse and scare the crap out of me.' In fact, interviews have – over the years – informed me that I dress badly, look ill, have a dingy flat and illogical furniture, while creating an alternative persona for me, which is mildly useful as a way of being in public without getting threadbare, but which is bewildering as an artefact. I do have chums who are interviewed far more than me, and I have never learned anything about them from the press that I didn't know already, beyond random facts that might mean I can provide them with slightly more accurate Christmas presents. This isn't surprising – they are my friends, of course I know them better than someone they met for an hour in a hotel suite or a moderately quiet restaurant. But print seems so authoritative . . . If you're in any way unhappy with feeling as if your arse has been shoved out of a window for no good reason, then it's probably best to keep away from the thought of interviews, or their printed actuality, and to concentrate on being profoundly grateful that someone is helping you sell ten or eleven extra books.

Which is the point to remember: I am trying to assist my work. I did what I could to help it be alive – it came to me to be expressed, and I was grateful and I put the hours in as best I could. A number of other people at my publisher's have also put in their hours. I am mainly worrying about the next novel – but they are still working on this one. And now this novel has left me. It has slung its metaphorical haversack over its brave, small, metaphorical shoulders and is trotting off to do some Youth Hostelling in Indonesia without me. I'll worry, but there's no more I can do, beyond trying to get people to look out for it and maybe pat its head as it goes by and not murder it, slice it up and make it disappear into a series of oozing airline holdalls. Which brings us to the reviews. Onwards.

LII

Apologies for the unscheduled break from blogging. I wasn't waylaid by an endless stream of A-List book-launch activities, fervid searches for an unhackable phone and invitations from the *Big Brother* production team. I was simply ill. Again. Which gets tedious. I now have a specialist for whatever is wrong with my stomach and everyone telling me to rest in order to beat the post-viral/recurring-viral labyrinthitis. Picture me earlier this month in a small, boiling flat somewhere in Soho, lying down, throwing up, having panic attacks and listening to helicopters grind overhead to deal with full-blown or incipient riots. And crying if I had to do something complicated – like putting on my shoes, or trying to discuss my schedule with my editor. I was a bit tired. Writing a novel in eleven months instead of thirteen isn't a good thing. I console myself that writing two books a year gave Muriel Spark hallucinations. I'm not bloody surprised.

Meanwhile, we may want to discuss the fact that book launches are always fairly horrible, even setting illness aside. And this isn't just my opinion – I have checked with other writers, painters and creative sorts, including actors, who you would think were simply gagging for engagement with the wider public, and the feedback has been comfortingly similar. It seems that for many of us representing our work in the wider world always feels both disappointingly anticlimactic and weird. At a certain level you're aware that, even if you could call yourself an artist at other times, you are currently much more of a pimp. And, given that you're more than half way to pimping yourself . . . well, your job description gets rapidly less appetising.

At this point, all those of you who haven't been published will wish to shout at your screens/HTC's/iThings/looted BlackBerrys, 'Yes, but . . . you've got it now. You are published. You do earn your living. Shut up and stop moaning. I will be delighted when I am published. I will be dancing in the sodding street, thank you very much.' And I know how you feel. And I thought that, too. But I was wrong and it may be that you are wrong also. Perhaps.

When you're writing, when matters are actually going well and your work is being with you and you're with it – that's a cause for dancing in the street. When you've found someone insane enough to pay you – real cash money – to pay you for doing something you love, and the pressure of payment hasn't thrown you off . . . by all means why not have a go at something pavement-related and terpsichorean. When the first draft is finished, done, the final slope clambered up and you've got skinned knees and are exhausted, but you made it . . . dance away. Absolutely. When the final rewrite, the final twiddle, the dearGodatakeitawaybeforeIkillit stage has been passed and it's in the big, threatening envelope or, more likely, has been attached and emailed as per contractual blah-di-blahs – well, that's probably an excuse for naked living-room dancing. Or else, and do feel free, you may prefer something more al fresco, which could help you to get arrested and therefore start the whole publicity machine running, albeit a touch early. And when you open the big box of author copies and there it is – your book . . . Your shiny, genuine book, in person and in your hands . . . Dance while you can, I'd say.

But publication is funny – in the sense of being not remotely amusing and not really very much to do with you. Publication is what your publisher enjoys – if that special blend of moderate concern, review-checking, subscription-checking and moving on to what's next from whoever's next can be called enjoying. Publication is when something with which you've spent a lot of time definitively walks away and belongs to other people, who either get it, or don't get it, or write to you about it, or trash it in the press, or love it in the press (best to keep away from either) and it all feels . . . odd. On the one hand, you're thinking of what's next for you – or trying to – and seem strangely far away from the material you are suddenly being asked to discuss (quite possibly with an audience present), and on the other hand, here are all these strangers fossicking about in stuff that was quite recently only your stuff. Your book slept with you and travelled with you and woke with you and nagged you and delighted you and drove you crazy and tired you out. Now it's just another volume on a shelf – you hope – in a bookshop, much the same as all the others, and it belongs to everyone but you. You are the only person who can't pick it up and read it. In fact, why on earth would you ever want to? And how lovely, and yet really quite dispiriting, it is that people will read it – this thing it took you years to build – in a few days and then that's that. They'll read something else. You're over. The launching experience is, to be frank, mainly lonely. I don't say this to discourage you, not at all. I say this as an encouragement to get your fun in early – enjoy the parts that are real, that are about writing. Be glad and then more glad and then absolutely grateful if anyone, any human being, tells you that you gave them pleasure with your work. If you got one person through some hours in a good way, thank them for saying so and thank them again and thank providence for the opportunity to be of service – that's the only thing that really matters, or could be worthwhile. Truly. And try to defend the part of you that has to be kept soft and tender, the simply loving place from which you write. Keep it safe from the writing-related experiences which are not soft and tender or simple and loving at all.

So I will tell you, and then choose to forget, the launch day I spent mainly feeling lousy and oppressed and dizzy and worrying about a number of matters, including my inability to recover. I will forget about suiting up – because my suit knows what it's doing – and being steered out to a bookshop reading that felt very much like an absurd opportunity to celebrate the accumulated failures of my life. I will forget having to concentrate rather too hard on putting one word after another for an audience who had bothered to turn up and made an effort, and who were courteous and in no way responsible for my wanting to vomit and lie down. I will forget wanting to curl up and cry while signing books, when there is nothing wrong with signing books and it is very nice when people want them. I will forget about having dinner in a dizzyingly loud restaurant with three people I knew only slightly who were very kind, but who also just wanted to get on and have some good grub and a laugh – only there I was, the inconvenient spectre at my own feast. I will forget about being sick on or near my editor's shoes while he escorted me through a hot and weaving and vomiting Soho, within which I seemed simply more of the same, although not drunk and not stoned and not determined to party – just being led to my temporary home with instructions to cease trading forthwith and take a proper rest.

In four or five years it will all be faded and simply a story. And – if I'm lucky – around about then I'll be doing it again. But I hope better. I do hope for better. And for all of you also. Onwards.

LIII

As some of you may know, I've spent decades participating in literary events, many of which involve Q&A sessions. So I am used to audience queries that are just plain bonkers, or refer to dark conspiracies that mean enquirers will never themselves be published, or properly appreciated, while sneaky Illuminati and/or Lizardpeople like myself are given favourably termed contracts and buckets of baby mice on demand. I am also familiar with questions asked both in reality and in episodes of *Murder, She Wrote*: 'Do you write with a pen, or use a refurbished shuttle from a Portuguese handloom?', 'When do you first pick up your shuttle of a morning?', 'How long before you have to break off and eat some baby mice?' and the inevitable 'Where do you get your ideas from?'

Many of the above are now regarded as uncool and avoided by more savvy literary audiences, even though an attentive new writer might conceivably find something encouraging about X's yellow legal pads, or W's penchant for vellum, or N's fondness for scribbling on the backs of ginger lumberjacks. And if an audience is sitting there, reproachfully expectant once the Where From Question has been asked, then some kind of response probably should be forthcoming. I have known writers who routinely refuse to answer questions posed onstage, but unless they are genuinely being intruded upon, this tends to mean they come across like a date who kisses your ear and then slaps you for letting him. Not answering the Where From Question can leave a lingering sense that perhaps the typist under scrutiny acquires ideas under the counter from seedy back-street inspiration dens, or cheap foreign ideas, bred in conditions involving cruelty and inadequate hygiene. And then there's the *ideas provided by Satan at the cost of my mortal soul* option.

Am I happy about answering the Where From Question myself? Not hugely. This is partly because the area – though ill-defined – is hedged about with superstition. If I look at it too closely will it disappear? And it's partly because my answer will occur in a wider context which renders it absurd. I don't think it's any coincidence that the demonic bargain scenario began to lose currency just as authors lost their allotted role as people who performed, albeit minor, acts of creation and invention. It once seemed likely that human beings who could make something out of nothing were divinely inspired, or rattled by demons, or somehow Connected. This could make priests of poets – which isn't healthy for anyone – but it also gave respect to the craft and opened the possibility that imagining and creating might be human as well as divine. Then literary criticism – which has to involve research – remade the writer as a kind of self-obsessed photocopier, regurgitating cheap repros of reality, pinching bits of friends, lovers and acquaintances, then sewing them together and making the monstrous results limp off to people unsurprising little worlds. Fiction became autobiography. Or Commentary. Or Essay. Which is to say, not fiction at all: not powerful, mysterious, wonderful and overwhelming, but only something which can be fitted neatly into a PhD essay, or a review of the type that suggests the reviewer is privy to certain intimate facts about the character and circumstances of the author without which the reader will be lost. If the reader would be lost without those facts, of course, the piece of writing wouldn't work. Writing is about communication, not which parties you attend.

So now the tail wags the dog. Readers who love all kinds of fiction – including the most fantastic of fantasies – have to shut up about their passions for fear of being considered silly. Writers who spend their lives chasing ghosts, angels, demons, syllables and the shapes of things unknown aren't allowed to articulate how disturbing and fantastic and marvellous this process is. Meanwhile, the essays and the reviews flourish in the context they have constructed. It is very largely a dead context. It is a context many fine academics loathe. It is a context within which every mind is dreamless, has no whims, no thoughts of the past beyond accurate accounting, no hopes for the future, no intuitions about the present and, above all, no inspiration. Inspiration originally referred, as you will know, to the idea of being filled with divine spirit, some kind of transforming, burning Otherness, the sense of having an idea, a thought, a need, breathed straight into your lungs. I don't, as a writer and as a reader, ever want writers or readers to be locked away from the power and the beauty of that. Any individual might interpret it differently, but its absence would always be no fun at all. Its denial would be emotionally, psychologically and even morally debilitating. I'm not saying that creation is always Good – it's patently not. But without it, we can get very short on remedies for Bad very quickly, and the stories we tell ourselves shrink around us and reduce what we feel we can be.

To return to Q&As, there is now, quite naturally, an expectation that the Where From Question will be answered with something that refers to the author's personality and life, to people from whom he or she has stolen this or that, to a type of plagiarism from reality. This would, apart from anything else, be crushingly simplistic. Yes, the story does come through the author and is of the author. A tale of a murderous baker with one eye, as expressed by John Banville, might not at all resemble that expressed by Richard Curtis. The work will reflect the passions of the writer – it's unlikely that an author will commit to a novel about philately unless it really is something they want to be around for months. Then again, if an idea arrives and is insistent and involves stamp-collecting, then an enthusiasm for the sticky little buggers must be cultivated, because fantasy must be given the certainty of lived experience. (I know we live in an *X Factored* world of instant results, but an illusion of lived experience accessible to another is best created by hard work, not by living the experience – that bit's for you, not the reader.) The author's beliefs probably won't be transgressed – it's unlikely that I'll write about a woman who's scared of mice and wants only to cook for Her Man, and yet . . . if one arrived to be expressed, I'd have to. The process of personal commitment, exploration, loss, surprise and puzzlement fluctuates and coheres. Initial ideas are shaped and reshaped, sometimes consciously, sometimes – once again – in a rush of pressure which can seem external.

I have no meaningful clue about where my characters are from. Beyond those authors who are working through serious relationship issues via prose, I have never met anyone who could describe the roots of characters without also becoming quite vague. We all have our ways of developing character, but their sources remain blurry. I feel characters and their worlds are also potentially as engaging and visceral as your childhood's monsters, companionable toys and landscapes of adventure.

And this is where I'm supposed to deliver something technical, which will deliver your worlds and your characters to you. But how can I? The good news is, that's what you do. It's also the bad news, but not really – if we simply decide to be open to whatever might arrive, this will ensure that something does. No theft or patchwork necessary. Each piece of each piece will be bespoke, grown to fit its place and no other. And the joy of making something of nothing will be real. Along with – undoubt-edly – its uncertainty and its fears. When I hear, 'Yes, but . . . he must have been based on someone . . .', I am listening to someone afraid of letting go and seeing what will happen, someone afraid of making things up, of something simple, child-like, immeasurably influential and a gift. We are dealing with belief here: scary, exposing, generous, extraordinary belief – if you like, *professional* belief. If you believe your material is there for you, it will be. You have another option, but why take it? Letting what you need come and find you isn't easy, but it is lovely.

Onwards.

LIV

Once again, I must apologise for a long delay in blogging. Thank you if you're still around to read this. My ulcer and my slowly returning schedule decided to engage each other in not altogether positive ways. On the one hand, I have been able to get out and about a little, and that initially cheered me. I took part in Budleigh Salterton's literary festival, ate crab sandwiches and loosened my overcoat recklessly on the nudist beach. I was also allowed to present some excellent and charming people onstage at Cheltenham: James Rhodes, Mark Thomas and Richard Wiseman; and I had a chance to praise the work of Mervyn Peake in public. On the other hand, I spent more and more time lying down between excursions until gastric distress put paid to my gadding about entirely, and my days now navigate between Zantac and Gaviscon. I am the person you never want to casually ask, 'How are you?' I will tell you. At length.

There is, however, an aspect of this current self-inflicted woe which I have found intriguing. For reasons I can't pinpoint – exhaustion, drug interaction, stress – I am no longer really experiencing emotions. At its worst, this gave me the sensation of having died and being compelled to haunt myself, of floating three or four feet behind the action. I would hear sad news, I would learn bits of London were on fire, I would contemplate

228

difficult tasks that were looming, if not in progress, and I would be mildly aware of breathing in and out – nothing more. If I remembered past events they would seem unconvincing, no longer having emotional colour attached. Drama with any kind of involving content irritated me and I slumped down into evenings spent watching American TV series that operate under initials: *CSI*, *SVU*, *JAG*, *NCIS*, *OMG*, *BS*, and so forth.

As it happened, the only writing required of me during August and September was factual, but I was aware that the usual background mumble of fiction ideas was completely stilled. The encouraging fragments I had set down in my notebook were perfectly legible, but they had no meaning. Likewise for the scribbles in my computer Prose file . . . Every time I tried to look inwards there was a blank – not uncomfortable, or scary, only impenetrable. The fact that I was unable to register this as a cause for concern simply underlined the problem. No emotions. And no fiction.

This is hardly surprising, of course. I have spent more than two decades talking to writers about the importance of emotion in our work. In the absence of feelings with which to identify, readers can remain unengaged. A shot may ring out in the required manner, a man may even walk in with a gun – if we aren't somehow induced to care about the proceedings, he might as well walk in with a hamster or a bag of nuts. Fictional characters whose interior lives don't hum and gurgle with this or that emotional tone can't be expected to compete with the genuine and complex human beings against whom – at a certain level – they are constantly being measured. We expect readers to temporarily oust loved ones, pleasant memories, delightful antici-pations and present concerns for the sake of our inventions – an emotional reality in our work can make our demands seem much less unreasonable.

Part of what is frightening about setting out to write is the more or less acute awareness that somehow we must access or tinker with our own emotions in order to portray something workable for others. This doesn't mean, I sincerely hope, that we should weep along with Mrs Wiggins when we decide that her beloved guide dog must choke to death on a rat. But we do measure and remember and examine our feelings while we build our worlds and people them. The whole process can give the impression that it may expose us intimately. It needn't actually do any such thing. We're dealing with fiction here – unless the writer is a construct too postmodern to qualify for clothes and a mortgage, he or she will be out of place within it. Even if we include subtle blendings of autobiography and creation, effective writing will basically involve us in complex linguistic manipulations that we hope will provide the illusion of intimate exposure, or whatever other illusions we deem appropriate. We aren't *really* experiencing anything with the reader – we aren't there.

And our being harrowed or overjoyed whenever our characters have to would be a wearying distraction from all that multitasking. Readers – some of them reviewers and journalists – can sometimes assume that the writer has bled and sweated in the manner of his or her protagonists. This is gratifying in a way – it tends to mean that the piece has struck home to a degree. But writers mainly sweat and bleed in the manner of people trying to do something hideously difficult over and over until it's okay. Saying this in public can seem weirdly heartless, but it's true.

There are, naturally, times when I have cared for characters, but that care is primarily focused on portraying them in the way they deserve or, in collaborations, on defending them against odd direction, or poor performance.

I have no idea why my lack of emotion made creative writing impossible. Perhaps I lacked material from which to grow personalities and psychologies. Perhaps I believed I was no longer a safe pair of hands, given that I might not be able to give a toss about the quality of my work, or the well-being of my nascent people. Perhaps I was just very, very tired.

Embarrassingly, my emotions first re-emerged when I was told a disgustingly moving story about a compassionate horse and a child. (I know, I know . . .) Once I'd stopped weeping helplessly, I vaguely felt as if I vaguely felt. The situation is not yet quite as I would hope. Still, it wasn't too much of a shock – well it couldn't be, could it? – that my first short story in a long while nudged itself forward quietly as soon as my interior began to show one or two lights. The feeling at that point? Gratitude. Onwards.

LV

I feel I will disappoint regular readers if I don't mention that I spent this morning having an endoscopy and biopsy. This is good news. This is very good news. It means that my health has recovered to such an extent that my doctor and I can now explore my interior with vigour and the assistance of the most vile topical anaesthetic I have ever tasted. He said it was meant to taste of bananas, but wouldn't; and he did not lie. It would only have tasted of bananas if bananas tasted of arse. Sorry, but there it is. Or was. In my mouth. Had I been more media-savvy I would have asked for the whole Journey to the Centre of my Duodenum to be burned onto a DVD, and you could be viewing it now on the website or downloading it as a screensaver, but I decided simply to be happy that nothing untoward was found.

I declined the option of a sedative, because chemicals and I do not mix well. I also couldn't have spent the rest of today being smashed because I have a huge pile of work to get through: partly to pay for the Unbanana Experience and partly because work is arriving for assessment from the latest crop of Warwick Creative Writing students. Is it that time again?

As usual, I wonder where the new writers at Warwick get the courage to give work-in-progress to anyone, never mind someone who will comment upon it. I have also been moved to ponder just how any of us ever reaches the point at which it is possible to view our own work as clearly and dispassionately – we might even say diagnostically – as we could the work of some other writer.

It is hugely necessary, of course, that any writer should be able to examine what they produce in a creative, but critical manner. (When I write 'critical' I am remembering that it comes from the Greek word meaning 'to look at closely'.) We can't rewrite to any purpose without being able to find our faults and strengths, uncover passages and themes that could be expanded, dissect and then reconstruct our characters, tones, plots. But there are times – especially during our early days – when our attempts at exploration can seem as nasty and unhelpful as trying to shove a tiny camera down one's own throat. It's awkward. It's alarming. It hurts.

But we have to know what's there. We have to be able to look at our papery offspring as if they were not ours, to see them as horrified strangers might. And this is a clue to a way forward. If you've ever presented your real live children, or relatives, or loved ones to people whose opinion you respect, you'll be familiar with the personal unease this can provoke. *Oh, my God, I've produced the Antichrist – she's so rude. And loud. I am a bad parent. She is the bad seed.* Or else perhaps: *Oh, my God, he needs a haircut. I think his dishevelment is cute, but she doesn't. She doesn't understand. I must kill her. Or at least never speak to her again.* You need not present your work to others who are physically present – although it can provide a healthy pressure to improve – but you can always imagine doing so. This is often more convenient than announcing a flash-reading on Twitter at 3 a.m. and expecting anyone to turn up in order to help you with page sixteen.

Sometimes a change of medium will help. We all know that when we print out a piece which seemed acceptable onscreen we will usually find that it is somehow converted to inexcusable dross as soon as it hits the paper. But would reading the piece aloud help you, too? Would playing a tape of it back to yourself be informative? I have either internalised this process or always heard my writing in my head, and I've found it invaluable to switch from one form of voice to another. Would walking the piece through and changing direction at each piece of punctuation tell you something? What about running that otherwise pointless bit of software that tells you the key words of your piece, or picking out each verb, each noun, each adverb and adjective – is there something your piece is trying to tell you? Is it possible to let its true nature be announced?

Perhaps you have been advised to leave your work in a desk drawer for a week, six weeks, three years . . . That can work well, but what if you don't have the time? What if you're aiming for a deadline? In my opinion, as writers, we can and should be continually learning how our minds work and helping them to help us more. What do you respond to better: sight, sound, smell, touch? If you try picturing your work as a movie, does that help you? Can you summon up a detailed portrait photo of your protagonist, or an action shot, or a strip of snaps from a booth, maybe posing with their lover? Can you draw them? (If you can draw.) Does your text smell of anything – beyond a bitter lifetime of soured hope? If you trace your finger over your words, or write them out longhand, rather than using your computer, does anything new fire? I have sometimes played out scenes or sections of dialogue as comedy, then sci-fi, then tragedy, then sitcom. I don't change the words, I just see what happens if the tone is altered. Or is the tone indelibly there? Do I have enough information already on the page to make that kind of assault impossible?

And then, of course, we can ask ourselves whose opinion we most respect and if they would like what we have done so far. (It will be informative if you discover that your own opinion is all that matters . . .) We may actually hand unfinished work to an editor, or a group, but I think it's important to be able to take this power into ourselves, too. It's perfectly possible to sit and imagine a wise chum, or a dear pal, or Antonin Artaud, or Captain Ahab, or Captain Scarlet, or Captain Haddock – whoever works for you – and to ask ourselves how satisfactory they would find our efforts.

If nothing has done the trick for you yet, don't despair – it simply means that you have more investigations to pursue and a very real opportunity to discover what kind of author you are, with what kind of mind. Best of luck. Onwards.

LVI

Happy New Year to you all. 2011 has gone away at last and I can now solemnly reflect that it didn't actually kill me. Beyond that, I have nothing good to say about it. Last year began with my being ill, kept on with my being iller, then I was unwell, followed by being poorly, with a tiny interlude of infirmity. Only in December did my bone marrow perk up, while my ulcer healed and the *H. pylori* admitted defeat. I finally had both the energy to cook a large curry and the ability to eat it. Despite having been advised by a friend to 'Maybe go easy on the curry . . .', I made up for eighteen spice-free months by downing nothing but curry for the best part of a week. *Because I'm like that*.

Of course, my health troubles could have been much worse and much more permanent. Any of you out there facing long-term or serious medical difficulties have my fullest sympathy. I am aware that offering sympathy is cheap, largely unhelpful and often irritating. I am aware that the NHS is increasingly unable to assist the sick, so sympathy may be all you're getting. And I am aware that my own situation was not assisted by – as mentioned above – my personality, *because I'm like that*. As a properly guilty Scot, I am more than willing to accept responsibility for the inadequacies of the Versailles Treaty, the burning of the library at Alexandria and Ed Miliband's suits – well, maybe not the suits – so it's hardly surprising that I would feel my imperfect health was entirely my fault. It wasn't. But my nature did play its part.

At some point during 1986 I made the decision to be a writer and to do so absolutely. Rather than having a go, or trying, or tiptoeing forward, I decided to write as well as I could. This was, in a way, an extreme decision and an open invitation to risk, because if I really threw everything I had into writing and got nowhere, then I would be definitively No Good At It. I hadn't worked out that going halfway into writing (or any art, or anything else worthwhile) wouldn't be safe, it would be a guarantee of failure. The joy and fear and work involved in writing have to be real and full to have meaning and to achieve anything. I didn't know that, I was simply feeling useless in the midst of Margaret Thatcher's recession with no proper job I could go to. So I wrote. I really wrote. And I was lucky. I got published – and therefore found a way of life and a profession and a love I could never have anticipated. The same drive that leads me into foolishness with curry means that I committed to an art and craft, and that it could commit to me.

It also means that – for better or worse – I can't let a sentence rest. I'll batter at words and syllables until they're at least not offensive to me. The drive is what makes me do my best. My best may not be great and certainly isn't to everyone's taste, but it is still my best, and why would I want to waste so much of my time over anything else? The artists I truly admire and am inspired by all harness the healthier aspects of perfectionism to keep learning and growing and to do good work. I know a pianist who will unashamedly obsess over a single moment in a two-hour concert. He's a relatively young man, but he already hears in a way that I can't. He has made himself somebody different, some-body more than he was. *Because he's like that.*

I know a painter who has spent decades producing extraordinary work and who is still attentive to every hair: hungry for light, colour, exposure to new work, to photography, to the seen world and its suggestions of the unseen. He has made himself a master craftsman and is still learning, still looking at the world more than I can. *Because he's like that.*

I know an actor who never fails to move me and who – I am happy to say – once consented to perform something I had written. He inserted an *um* where there had been no *um* and that's the kind of thing I notice and usually – silently – deplore. But this was a good *um*. Because he understands timing and music – among other things – his *um* decision was perfect, was inevitable, was lovely. Again, he's a person who never stops paying attention, is helplessly committed to staying interested and improving in his profession. He can generate levels of focus I cannot. *Because he's like that.* In short, all these people have positively harnessed their drive.

Which is great for art, but may be difficult to balance with other considerations. I can get hung up on a syllable, but completely miss the early symptoms of illness. I can forget to follow up on doctors after they've taken tests, or to check the side-effects of medications. I self-maintain very badly, while travelling and working beyond what is reasonable, skipping meals, skipping sleep and generally ignoring things that just don't seem as interesting as my work. I slap down advice in this column about tending yourself sensibly as a writer, feeding your inspirations, taking time out to have fun. I can look at newer writers and see that they need encouragement and kindness as well as discipline and interior fury. And yet I am often discourteous, if not threatening, as I continue to be a dreadful self-employer. *Because I'm like that.*

But this isn't a bad thing. Although I learn very slowly and change more slowly still, I have one very beautiful thing in my favour – I write, I do something creative. This means that when all is darkness, it isn't. It can't be. The way of life I have chosen allows me to take – sometimes quickly, sometimes not – any negative element and use it, change it at some level. I don't at all subscribe to the idea that the ardent typist should dress in mourning and cultivate fake doom – that's a form of self-harm and a waste of energy. Life will inevitably have its bleak spots without our help. Meanwhile, it can be cheering to consider that, if we survive, we'll maybe get a sonnet on divorce, or a character with toothache, a novel that can be properly lyrical about grief, or a joke about colitis. There may be times when we end up just sticking our tongues out at reality and times when we can connect with the human condition as we never have before, maybe both. We may even have the unlooked-for pleasure of being useful to someone else who draws strength from what we've built. Above all, the pure act of writing – the truth that it is still there for you, and you for it – is a wonder. And it need have nothing to do with the details of your life. Within it, you can be away from everything and saying out new dreams, just because you can, because human beings do sing for other human beings and make unnecessary beauties. Onwards.

Introduction to the Essays

Before we begin these essays, I thought it would be appropriate to tell a story. It was, like all my useful stories, told to me by someone else. I have found it sustaining and hope that you may, too.

My grandfather, who was an amateur boxer for some years, would sit up with me into the night and tell me about his early life, his work in the steel industry and his exploits in the ring. He told me wonderful truths and magnificent lies, his voice purring in his chest while he did so. I knew him as a huge, apparently invincible and yet deeply gentle man. Until I was four or five, he could extend his arm straight out and I would swing on it, as if he were a tree, or some other wonderful thing filled with the forces of nature and indomitable life. He was one of the few people whom I have loved beyond my capacity for affection, someone therefore who always made me larger and better than I was.

One evening we were together, everyone else asleep, and he told me about his first competitive boxing match. He said that it was the only fight he'd ever lost and that he knew why – he'd been scared. I found this difficult to imagine, but there was something very young and small in the way he spoke about himself, climbing on to the canvas square and facing someone bigger and stronger and faster than he believed himself to be. I was a nervous child and understood, or thought I did, exactly how he must have felt. I was frightened by almost every door I had to open, by strangers and apparently more assured acquaintances, by most available knowns and unknowns. I wasn't aware then that my grandpop's father had been violent, that his home had been uneasy when he was young and small, and that perhaps part of his pursuit of physical excellence and power was intended to help him defend what he loved. He may have intended never to be scared again.

My grandfather made sure I was physically confident, taught me self-defence at such an early age that it was just another game, at such an early age that it became instinctive. He took steps to keep me safe, even without him. My grandfather worried that I had trouble with figures and so he taught me how to play cribbage, a card game which is rather more complex than it seems and which demands a grasp of basic arithmetic. He took steps to make me numerate and, as he did so, to illustrate how charlatans and tricksters might seek to prey on me, with and without the aid of pasteboard. And my grandfather advised that I should be very, very careful before I granted any gentleman the honour of touching me above the knee. He wanted me to know what I was worth.

And my grandfather understood that I was fearful, often terrified. When he told me about that first fight, he explained why he lost. 'When you're scared, they don't beat you – you beat yourself.' He gave me that insight. I refer to it elsewhere in this book, but I don't say that it took me decades to realise what he meant.

I wouldn't suggest that living one's life as if it were a constant combat would be wise, and I try not to do so myself. I do know, from repeated experience, that I can defeat myself with fear at a moment's notice. I can encompass the combat and its ugly end in a breath. Procrastination, half-heartedness, cowardice – they are all fruits of my fear and have robbed me, sometimes daily, sometimes hourly, of many joys. Caution is wise; I've found that paralysis is less rewarding.

I have no personal advice to offer anyone, beyond mentioning to friends that if they're asking me for guidance, then they're already in more trouble than they know. (I'm always good for a cheap laugh.) But if I am talking to a writer, or if I am trying to encourage myself, I find more and more that being without fear seems the key, the solution to most problems. I feel it is both practical and beautiful to demonstrate that of ourselves which dreams, and to do so in security and freedom. Our nightmares are fearful enough: our dreams, I think, must be better and louder and unafraid.

Insomnia

Perhaps because I was born in the middle of the night I never have really associated the hours of darkness with wasting my time in sleep – more with being up and about and ready, I sometimes think much more ready than I manage to be in the day. Insomnia started early for me, but it wasn't about *not sleeping*, it was about being full of other things, being too delighted to let go and drop away. I'm told that when I was little I would go to bed quite obediently, but then for a while I would sing – small person in under the blankets and singing, happy to elongate the day. And perhaps fond of music, I suppose, I'm not sure. I had no work to engage me, no social calendar, no pressing concerns, I only wanted to be me, with my own restless skin, just following along behind my thinking.

This was around the time when I can recall my parents tucking me in and then edging out of my room with 'I'll just leave the door open a bit, so it won't be dark.' This meant that I suffered from nightlight envy. Other kids had nightlights that glowed fondly, or revolved endearing pictures around their bedroom walls, that played tunes, even. I had *the door open a bit*. This, very obviously, was going to let the monsters in. And also provide just enough illumination for me to be stricken by the sight of them as they pounced. I've slept with my head underneath the covers ever since. Sheets are impervious to monsters, everybody knows that.

By the time I went to school, my twin causes of sleeplessness – overexcitement and monsters – were already well established. I was a pupil in the same institution for thirteen years – primary, junior, secondary – and until I became an occasionally carefree senior, my education seemed based around a core curriculum of shouting. The primary-school shouting was especially intense. To be sure, I was usually much too spineless and translucent to be shouted at myself, but there were always the wholesale excoriations of our class as a nest of imbeciles and ne'er-do-wells to be endured and I never did know when some unforeseen regulation might not be personally transgressed, or my inability to handle sums or swimming or shoelaces might become finally intolerable. Sunday nights – already full of the chill and flinching that were a natural part of Monday morning – became ill-fitting and pushed me into a habit of wakefulness. When I finally did drift off, I would dream of uncompleted homework and werewolves and shame.

But the stronger push was always from varieties of elation. I could read before I went to school and – as soon as narratives didn't simply involve the variously hapless animals of Blackberry Farm – I would be found and held by book after book. I wouldn't be able to stop reading: all comfortable and uninterrupted, and what could be wrong about staying in this or that beautiful world until three in the morning? I knew that I'd wake up tired, I knew that I'd feel queasy if I had to run about in gym or if – since my school was obsessed with the moral and physical benefits of Scottish country dancing – I were required to disport myself through a gauntlet of Dashing White Sergeants and reels. And shouting. But I'd also worked out that the world was full of books, that centuries and continents of books were heaped around me, enticing and funny and scary and hypnotising and over-whelming books, and how could I possibly read them all – never mind the new books mushrooming up on every side – if I didn't keep putting in the hours?

And more overwhelming still was the unmistakeable drive towards writing. It wasn't at all that I believed I could do better than any of the authors by whom I was surrounded, it was only that writing my own words was the most overwhelming experience of all. Given the horrible standard of my early scribbling – ramblings through a pseudo-Celtic mythical kingdom, mildly satirical songs for the school magazine, years of utterly inexcusable poetry – I can be entirely certain that no one else would have been overwhelmed by anything other than nausea in its clumsy, purple, self-important presence. But it made me elated and, after dinner and schoolwork and dog-walking and the rest, even if I'd put the light out and laid myself down for definite repose, little ideas and scraps and nonsenses would tickle in and start to shake me. They would make the nights too bright to resist. I remember once, long after school and university, being in possession of my first laptop – I'd pottered out to the kitchen and left it by itself in a darkening room and when I walked back in with a coffee, it was there and shining: this word-holding thing just quietly glowing like a window into somewhere else and better and more wonderful and I remember thinking, 'Yes, that's how a good page would look if you could really see it, that's how it always did look in my head.' It's a light that I hope will always wake me.

But, of course, not being a creature of moderation, as soon as I was able to earn my living by writing and nothing but, I and my ergonomically disastrous laptops – I burned through one every couple of years – would work too hard and too long and too late into the lovely and undisturbed nights, finally being paid to do what grown-ups had told me not to. So I got ill. My spine – like every other human's – is still mainly designed for activity, hunter-gathering, swinging in trees. It grew tired of unnatural compressions, poor posture, self-employed stress and carrying the staring weight of the brain to which I had retreated. I developed a herniated disc. Six months of misdiagnosis and increasingly desperate alternative therapies only harmed me further. Finally, an unwise business trip to London meant I folded up in my publisher's offices and was shipped to an A&E – as it happened, on my birthday. After an afternoon of 'If you'll just hold still . . . oh, and happy birthday . . . press the button if you feel claustrophobic . . . and I see from the form it's your birthday', I was X-rayed and MRI'd and diagnosed with both the dodgy disc and muscle-wasting. I emerged with one week's pain relief, a neck collar and the temporary ability to flag down cabs, no matter what.

Immobility and muscle-wasting and pain, pain and immobility and more muscle-wasting – I spent a decade in that loop. Waiting lists, physio, a diminishing income. The first time my range of movement was assessed I wanted to cry – I could barely lift my arms. I was wearing slip-on shoes, buying my groceries one tin at a time. And there was no sleep. I would pass the nights watching sci-fi and stand-up comedy. There was no light left in the darkness, only the thought that going to bed exhausted me, that this was my life now, that kissing hurt. And I was angry – I'd given my life to a vocation and been rewarded with this – a pain that made even typing almost intolerable.

And I hope I will never forget that slowly, slowly friends and strangers suggested remedies and tiny advances were made, and that gently the pain of unaccustomed exercise could replace the pain of being me and the fear of getting worse again, being knocked back into more days of lying down. I was offered places to stay and recuperate, advice, concern – the world was bleak, but also generous. And I did recover. A few years ago I could be in New York and arrange to meet a friend across on the other side of Central Park and I could amble over in twenty minutes and then have to waste time in coffee shops. I'd planned that my journey would take an hour. When I'd last been there, it had.

Naturally, I promised myself that I would be sensible thereafter and never overdo things again. I would take breaks and holidays. I bought a special chair to support me, I practised Tai Chi almost every day, I took vitamins and went for long walks, lots of long, long walks. I tried to remember to be grateful for mobility, for the mercy and simplicity of comfort, and to make up for being antisocial and bad-tempered on so many, many occasions when the pain was too bad and too boring to mention.

But I'm me – I love what I do, I love to sit up late in my wonderful chair and drink too much caffeine and make something mildly dramatic out of endless typing – the all-night sessions, the two- and three-day sessions, only interrupted by baths and black-and-white movies. It now seems traditional that I'll finish my novels in an all-out dash, running just ahead of them and hoping I won't fall. I spent last year bundled up in a New England barn conversion, supplied with Diet Coke and Jimi Hendrix, grinding the hours away between summer storms that whitened the whole sky, that flashed me into somewhere else, drenched me in warm rain when I stood out on the deck. I write, God help me, very much according to the model set out by Honoré de Balzac – a man who habitually woke at midnight, who lived through love letters rather than love, who killed himself with black coffee and overwork.

Which means that, as I write this, I am recovering – I hope – from months of viral labyrinthitis. It's a condition which produces a kind of profound seasickness and anxiety, which leaves you clinging to your spinning and ducking bed while savage possibilities rage over you, every thought you shouldn't have: loss and permanent ill health and hurts to those you love. For the last few months sleep has been either unobtainable or a long, hot succession of nightmares, often with the illusion of having woken, but being paralysed while yet more fears unfold. And it's my own fault. In the last ten years I've taken precisely two holidays – during one of which I had to work. I should know better. I should do better. I have to do better.

I write at night, because it's the proper time for dreaming – emails and essays during the day, journalism, correspondence, payment of bills – but I wait for the sun to weaken and set before I can find, as old William says, that '. . . imagination bodies forth the forms of things unknown . . . and gives to airy nothing a local habitation and a name'. Unfortunate when the forms are monsters, their names familiar – 'What if I don't get better? What if I fall even further behind? What if the work is failing and I can't see it? What if he doesn't love me? What if I don't love him well? What if my life won't work? What if, as usual, the little joys are wasted and go wrong?' Everyone has their 3 a.m. tribunal of mistakes made and damages received and threats that are more or less credible, but all insist on being heard. It's perhaps why, when we care for each other, we so often ask, 'How did you sleep?' – we know what a terrible place the edge of sleep can be. It is perhaps one of the quieter reasons for making love, or rather for being each other's companions in our beds – we try to be present when the people we need most have to drop into the other little death, and we like to feel them there for us when we surface badly, when we are afraid and pulling the sheet up over our faces will make no difference, will not save us.

And we wish each other 'Sweet dreams'. Of course we do. And, sometimes stupidly and sometimes sensibly, I will spend my professional life and night after night attempting to build dreams for other people and for myself, trying to sing and elongate the day. Trying to make the words that shine, the way so many other people's words have always done for me.

To Save Our Lives

Let me begin by saying that I gave up. Not completely, but mainly, I gave up. For those of you who haven't worked this out, or those of you who were thinking quietly. Yes. I gave up.

I worked in the arts with marginalised people in marginalised communities from 1987 until around about 1995. I worked with people who were disabled, or less able, or disadvantaged because of physical conditions, injuries, illnesses, age, various types of imprisonment and, of course, the biggest and bitterest prison of all – poverty. And then I gave up. Not completely, but I don't now run between ten and twenty workshops a week, I don't build up long-term relationships of trust with individuals and groups and I don't bring people who have no access to the arts access to the arts, not really. I'm relying on other people to do that. I now earn exponentially more than I did and am more comfortable and work less. This is something I thought we had to address. So I have.

Whatever my position, it would always be an honour to address a room full of people who have an interest in the area where health and well-being and the arts meet, which, in my opinion, is the whole area. Or it could be, or it should. But I no longer do what you do. I cheer on from the sidelines and I try to help when I can. But I am, to a degree, a dirty rotten sell-out and if you want to view me in that way, I won't object. I got out of community arts work because it was sort of killing me and I had seen people working with others on automatic pilot and not doing right by their craft, or themselves, or their clients, and I didn't want to end up being someone else phoning it in when maybe I was providing the only session this or that (perhaps fragile) person would get. I didn't want something that could have changed their lives to simply be a way of passing a dull and patronising afternoon, because of me. I think I had good reasons for leaving, in that regard.

I also had a very selfish reason for leaving – I wanted to do my own work. I had seen, in ways I could never have imagined, how the arts could enrich lives, alter behaviours, sing to the wider world on behalf of its practitioners and make beauty, and I wanted that for me. I wanted to mainline creativity for myself and I couldn't deny that desire any longer. So I left. But I don't think what I learned has ever left me and I'll talk today about what I know of working in the arts with others and how it relates to health and well-being. This is something which is obviously particularly relevant at a time of immense hardship for many, when every sustaining possibility is needed, when the basic medical care and support systems that will keep people alive, or in lives worth living, are being more and less gently removed. This is a time when something like arts activity can seem a ridiculous luxury if it's for non-paying, non-middle-class people and when the arts themselves – the allegedly self-indulgent, inexplicable, elitist, expensive, irrelevant arts – are perhaps less valued than they have been for generations.

Let's begin at my beginning. Perhaps some of you will identify. I had an interest in theatre – it had lit me, had sustained me through a small-town childhood and adolescence. I remember watching a TV production of Chekhov's *Three Sisters*, knowing nothing of the man or his life, but understanding when the characters said 'To Moscow, to Moscow' that I knew exactly how they felt. Chekhov articulated the horror of being trapped in a dead end and out of context, of being a permanent stranger. He had therefore spoken on my behalf. He had also let me know that I wasn't alone, other people felt like that – like Chekhov, whose brother remembered him saying, 'In my childhood I had no childhood.' Chekhov grew up in the Crimean backwater of Taganrog, not Moscow – it took him a while to reach Moscow, to reach himself. On the 7th January 1889, when he was just shy of his twenty-ninth birthday, he wrote to his friend Suvorin:

> Write a story about a young man, the son of a serf, a former shop-minder, chorister, schoolboy and student who was brought up to fawn upon rank, to kiss priests' hands and to worship others' thoughts . . . write how this man squeezes the slave out of himself, drop by drop, and then wakes up one fine morning to discover that in his veins flows not the blood of a slave, but of a real human being . . .

As I say, when I saw *Three Sisters* I didn't know about Chekhov's life, I didn't know he had a bumpy childhood like mine, I didn't know he worked with prisoners and the poor, I didn't know anything other than what he made, the product of simple, joyful, human creativity – his writing. But it started to squeeze the slave out of my blood, drop by drop.

And I read – all I could get – and then I went to university, because a grant made that financially possible for me. It wouldn't have mattered how many exams I passed, I wouldn't have got there without a grant. Beyond university, I started to work with community groups and special-needs groups, partly because I couldn't do anything else, partly because I was looking for something and I didn't know what, but it somehow seemed the proper course for me to write and to search in the company of other people. On the one hand, I was completely busking it. I was working with groups of radically mixed ability, in unsuitable spaces, inventing everything from scratch. Very few people were working with non-literate people to produce writing – I had to make up how we did that, relying on the fact that written words are simply a high-status record of what someone would say in their absence. I hoped that if we worked out how to catch what people wanted to say and how to finish it in a way that was pleasing to them, we could proceed happily. And so we did. I was making a tiny amount of money out of long hours. Simply earning a living until I found out my proper direction was pretty much all I had as a plan, but then I saw – I saw face after face changing after one session, ten sessions, twenty sessions – I saw the slave leaving the blood. I laughed more than I ever had. And I cried. We all laughed and cried. I found out about people. I was no longer alone. I found out what happens when, for example, I watch *Three Sisters*, when I touch art and art touches me. That's when I get something beautiful and new in my life. I feel no longer alone, I have more strength to be myself and I see there may be other possibilities beyond the here and now. I receive a gift within which is a kind of hope about human nature – it's not naïve, but it's not the unreality of reality TV, not a cheap and nasty opportunity to feel good about ourselves because other people are manifestly more dysfunctional than we are, more stupid, more greedy, more sex-obsessed, more shoddy. Fully functional art doesn't show us that – a toxic stasis, a warning to not leave the house – it shows us what we truly are and could be, good or bad. Art is about motion, strategies, rehearsals of new futures. It's a power. And think – of course you've thought – if you're not just receiving the end product, accepting the gift from the artist, joining in humanity with someone who may be in many ways alien to you – from another culture, another country, another time, who may be dead – what if you make that art? What if others suddenly can know a part of you, a deep and intimate part of you, the dreams you make? What if you light them and are useful, bring them in to what might previously have been an alien experience? What if you change their lives? How could that possibly not be a joy in your life and change you? How could that possibly not improve, for example, your health and well-being?

I began with mercenary and confused motives, running drama workshops, leading writing workshops, improvising from nothing – and I found a wonder, a purity: people making things for other people, being useful and getting well – not markets, not an industry, not egos, not much – just beauties, at very little expense, over and over and over.

Which means, incidentally, that I have very little patience for the kind of writer who sits in cafés wearing black pullovers while not writing and finding everything *really difficult*. Writing can be tricky and lonely, yes, but good Lord, it isn't *really difficult*. It's nothing but jam and gravy and good luck to be able to do this, to be able to be, in my case, a professional writer. It's a high-quality job.

And it's important. Being with people in art, helping it happen – that's important. I know we're not supposed to say so, but I am. It matters. When the chiropodist interrupts your reminiscence group – apparently just on principle – or someone hasn't taken their medication in the mental-health group and you remember your public-liability insurance might not be up to date, or someone has a fit and you're by yourself to cope and no one told you anybody might have fits. Or someone is dying, dying before your eyes. Or someone is beautiful inside and has shown you this repeatedly and wonderfully, but they live in hell. Or when someone quits a project, or when the funding is cut, or when a group doesn't come together. Or when it all goes well and you make the movie, or you put on the musical, or the exhibition, or unveil the mosaic, or you print off the magazine, or the anthology, or the comic book and maybe you think, 'Is this just self-indulgent, is this just having a laugh, just playing?' When you forget how everyone has grown and changed – yourself included . . . On all those occasions, it is probably wise to step back for a moment and remember: the arts are important. Practically and politically and personally and in general they are important.

When we make art, art to which we commit ourselves, art which isn't simply a commercial artefact, a pose, a gesture towards a concept, when we go all out and really create, we do a number of remarkable things. We take on a little of what we usually set aside for the divine – the troubles and delights which spring from overturning entropy and bringing something out of nothing. We excel. We offer something of ourselves, or from ourselves, to others. We allow and encourage a miracle – one human being can enter the thoughts and the life of another. We can be the other: the king, the foreigner, the wino, the superstar, the debu-tante, the murderer, we can experience a little of the large, strange, wonderful, horrible thing which is human experience.

What we make can reveal us to ourselves as greater than we were and help us practise addressing the world with courage and – because it is practical to involve such a thing – with love. As the listener, the viewer, the reader, the recipient of art, once again we are, of course, encouraged to be greater.

The proverb tells us we should walk a mile in a person's shoes before we judge them. And if we've spent a whole novel in their thoughts, if we've heard their heart in music, if we've seen as they do how light falls, if we've breathed with them as they speak, felt the way they dance under our skins? Then I believe it is very difficult not to grant others at least dignity, at least that. In the arts, I feel we are in the dignity business.

And now let me mention a man who was a lawyer – which doesn't sound especially artistic. He was also an incredible writer.

Lawyers can be artists with words – they believe in the power of their medium, as artists do. This man changed the world by inventing a word. He was called Raphael Lemkin and he invented the word genocide. He put it in Webster's dictionary, defined it, so it couldn't be ignored and it could be made illegal. The failures of multiple governments to live up to his hopes and his passion and his law – he isn't responsible for them. Lemkin worked himself to death, to try and save lives – with a word. And he thought a great deal about genocide: how it starts, for example. He realised that murder isn't the first step. Cultural annihilation comes first – what he called 'barbarity' and 'vandalism'. Barbarity was 'the premeditated destruction of national, racial, religious and social collectivities'. Vandalism was 'destruction of works of art and culture, being the expression of the particular genius of these collectivities'. To put it another way: before I can oppress you, hurt you, kill you, I have to silence you. I have to silence your dreams, I have to destroy them, in order to weaken and demoralise you, make you deaf and invisible to yourself, and to let myself forget your humanity, to rehearse the silence into which you'll disappear.

In the world now we have many silences, many rehearsals, more or less catastrophic. If you work in art, automatically you're working against that. When you sit in that draughty library, that weird-smelling community hall, when you wait for the latecomers to turn up again, work round that guy who's always drunk, again, wish that the Zumba class would keep a lid on it next door again – you are part of something literally life-saving.

Although things are a little more complicated than that. Art can be weakened, altered for the worse, often by people with good intentions. Here's the late Ray Bradbury writing in the *New York Post* on censorship. I'll begin where he mentions a school's anthology.

Some five years back, the editors of yet another anthology for school readers put together a volume with some 400 (count 'em) short stories in it. How do you cram 400 short stories by Twain, Irving, Poe, Maupassant and Bierce into one book?

Simplicity itself. Skin, debone, demarrow, scarify, melt, render down and destroy. Every adjective that counted, every verb that moved, every metaphor that weighed more than a mosquito – out! Every simile that would have made a sub-moron's mouth twitch – gone! Any aside that explained the two-bit philosophy of a first-rate writer – lost!

Every story, slenderized, starved, bluepenciled, leeched and bled white, resembled every other story. Twain read like Poe read like Shakespeare read like Dostoevsky read like – in the finale – Edgar Guest. Every word of more than three syllables had been razored. Every image that demanded so much as one instant's attention – shot dead.

Do you begin to get the damned and incredible picture?

The point is obvious. There is more than one way to burn a book. And the world is full of people running about with lit matches. Every minority, be it Baptist/Unitarian, Irish/Italian/Octogenarian/Zen Buddhist, Zionist/Seventh-day Adventist, Women's Lib/Republican, Mattachine/Four Square Gospel feels it has the will, the right, the duty to pour the kerosene, light the fuse. Every dimwit editor who sees himself as the source of all dreary blancmange plain porridge unleavened literature, licks his guillotine and eyes the neck of any author who dares to speak above a whisper or write above a nursery rhyme.

Or there's the school's version – I'm not kidding about this – of a Philip Larkin line, which goes, 'They tuck you up, your mum and dad.' Which is sort of sweet. But I found the original version more helpful.

And art can be completely stripped of its humanity. By that point, I wouldn't really call it art, but it has some of the characteristics of art – it still has power and can be influential and toxic. As Vonnegut mentioned, Nazi Germany trained a population to be blind to the dignity and humanity of some others. A diet of soft porn, cheap sentimentality and hate proved effective. Radio Mille Collines pedalled fear, poisonous pop music and a sense of unhinged communal power – it helped to push Rwanda into the abyss. All over the world, cultures have sickened and grown sickening and rehearsed dark times so effectively they have been able to come to pass. Lemkin predicted the pattern – those who wish to be powerful deny those they seek to victimise a voice. The victims' art is suppressed, no one is to see or hear from them, to feel with them, to find their dignity, be touched by their humanity. They are unpeople. And into the space their signs of life once filled – fakery, lies, expressions of loathing and fear and nothing else above a whisper.

In our own country we currently have mostly mild rehearsals, little injuries. We might say that it's easier to take away disability benefits when we don't really see that many disabled actors, when we apparently don't have famous disabled poets, when housebound people stay that way. We might find it's easier to steal a generation's education when our young people only come to notice if they're rioting, or being arrested. There's a mass of experimental evidence – try reading Stanley Milgram and Philip Zimbardo for a start – that shows human beings do care about each other generally, but the further away we are, the less well our caring functions. We have to use our imaginations to enter into the suffering of strangers and we need practice to do that. A diet of constructed reality, gossip and porn won't really cut it. When I bang on – and I often do – about wanting more and better from my media and my so-called arts, I am being elitist. I don't see why elitism is only acceptable if we're talking about sport, or fashion. I am being elitist, I think, with good reason.

Trying our absolute best as artists helps us grow better and stronger in what we do, it improves our craft. Doing our best with others – not thinking, *it's just a community group, it's just kids, it's just nutters, it's just a bunch of window-lickers* – doing our best, committing to make what they want possible so that maybe for the first time ever they can say what they want and get what they want – I think that's artistically and morally and practically the only way to go. Making a decision to do that means everyone grows and the end product is powerful and the slave leaves everybody's blood. And producing art in which humans are shown to be human keeps us all safe. It steers a panicky, self-obsessed, easily led, fearful and fragile species towards the light.

At this point when I delivered this piece as a lecture, I read a young person's poem, a young writer's poem. It had perhaps some imperfections, but also had a good heart. It spoke of impossible journeys, of flying and soaring, of travelling the world in absolute freedom, bathing in experience and opening oneself into a full life. In this it shared characteristics with a significant proportion of writing by authors who are in some way threatened or confined. They remade the world as a better place.

The poet was an amateur, a child called Avraham Koplowicz and his poem, through the imperfect medium of translation, was his voice. It still is his voice. It is the shape of his breath in his lungs, the music his mind arranged for his own delight and for that of others, for the invisible, unencountered other that artists can't help but anticipate in a kind of permanent hope. Artists always do seem to wish and reach out towards a future time and place. Even when the promise of those things is frail beyond measuring, they produce art, they make the beginnings of better worlds.

I don't know if Avraham would ever have become a fully fledged poet, I only know that he wrote himself a dream of escape from inside the Jewish ghetto at Lodz. The ghetto was sealed by the

Nazis on April 30th, 1940. On the 4th of September 1942 the last consignment of its living children was transported to Chelmno Extermination Camp where, like all of the previous consignments of human beings – men, women and children – they were gassed to death using carbon monoxide fed into specially converted Renault trucks. I came across his poem in Yad Vashem. I read that he hoped to reach twenty and to set out upon adventures.

Now, as it happens, the ghetto at Lodz was very well documented, both by the Nazis and its own Jewish authority: we know the names and addresses of almost all those imprisoned there and their countries of origin and dates of death. Avraham, for example, was born in Lodz in 1930. We know that in a little over 1 and a half square miles the ghetto was forced to contain up to 250,000 Jews and 5,000 Roma; we know about the soup kitchens, the ghetto newspaper, the morale-boosting activities; the typhus outbreaks, the forced deportations, the break up of families onto transports. We know that around 43,500 people died in the ghetto of starvation and despair and that around 800 Jews were left alive there when it was liberated by the Soviets. We can subtract, if we'd like, the number 800 from the larger number 255,000. We can consider how many thousands suffered and passed through to further suffering and death.

Good journalism, good non-fiction writing, the proper and fastidious presentation of fact can help us to understand what is incomprehensible: 100 dead, 1,000 dead, 100,000 dead, 200,000. I believe that to understand many deaths we have to understand one, the absence of one life. When we read lost authors we breathe on behalf of someone who no longer does, we navigate the frailties and strengths of their minds and hearts. In a minute way, we bring them back. We can begin to understand a little of what was lost with them. We do not need to have known the dead to mourn them, to mourn a life turned to silence, a loss of our shared delights.

I mention these things although I cannot reproduce the poem here. Commercial considerations and the current owners of the rights to reproduce Avraham's work have combined to produce a new kind of silence. I would encourage you to seek out Avraham Koplowicz's work if you can, but you can't find it here.

Let me say that the song Avraham sang is now a part of me and that I carry it with me and promise you that it has made me different, stayed with me for over twenty years. I believe our creations, our fictions, our arts can give dignity and understanding and cry for help. Why? Because they offer the articulated potential, the spoken dreams, the unmistakeable beauty and the possibilities of the immense, human interior reality inside that Other, inside all those human beings who are not myself, yourselves. Art lets its creators become powerful because they build something out of nothing – they overturn the basic laws of physics and they remind us of the truth that we are all more than what we seem, and that what each of us holds is irreplaceable.

And now I can tell you the anecdotes – you'll have yours, I have mine – about the lady who came to a writing group who seemed to be listless and in some way mentally impaired – she'd been in a residential institution for many years – and after a couple of weeks it turned out that she was mostly bored and had hidden inside her deafness to observe and let the world that patronised and bullied her pass by. She had a great interest in current events. Her family finally found out who she was – when she was in her sixties. Or the schoolboy who suddenly found he could write about the death of his mother, write beautifully about the terrible day when she was taken away, when policemen called him 'Mr' for the first time, when her head was angled up to the sky as they carried her out. I've remembered his story for more than eighteen years and how his hands shook when he read it and how he hadn't just written it, he'd crafted it, he'd gone beyond the statement of facts. Or I could tell you about all the people who rehearsed who they wanted to be in art and then were bigger, more alive, more themselves. Or I could tell you about the group from a day centre – people who were all non-literate, had difficulties walking and even talking, quite a vulnerable small group, but we worked out how to write as a group and how to rewrite and they ended up producing a lot of poems – one of them, 'Troon, Troon, Troon', about the Glasgow taxi drivers' outing once a year in decorated cabs to Troon – where the cab drivers would play football – and this trip was a nice gesture, a day out, for sick kids and adults with special needs, which might seem to be the same kind of people, but isn't really, and they were grateful for the attention and it was a day out, but some of them had been going to Troon for decades . . . to watch cab drivers play football on the beach. Troon, Troon, Troon. And I got a male and a female professional author to read out the poems at an event in the Strathclyde Regional Council Buildings. The writer's group had T-shirts made and they sat and listened while their work was read and they were happy about it. And the audience of council officials and social workers and community education workers sat and they smiled at the beginning of the event in the way that people do when there's going to be a kids' concert, or someone's dog is going to do a trick. And I watched the audience as the reading went on and many of the smiles faded, not all of them, some people were moved and pleased, but a lot of those smiles faded, disappeared. There was one poem, for instance, from Murray about how he'd like to be allowed to get on and off buses without help – it might take him a while, but he was a man now and it was only right. And there was one poem about how at night owls hide in the sky . . . and slowly those smiles went away. The poems were not necessarily good news for the people who were supposed to provide services for the vulnerable and those with special needs, because the work was human and articulate and it came from real human beings who deserved the best. But they couldn't have the best. The poets in my group were meant to be grateful for not much and to shut up. They weren't meant to make anyone feel guilty, or uncomfortable, or as if not enough was being done. Troon, Troon, Troon. It was an interesting afternoon.

And here is where I tell you that eventually I worked out two contracts to use as an arts worker. Neither was legally binding, but I wanted to use them to make things clear before I started work. The first contract, manifesto, mission statement, if you insist, I gave to the people who were in charge of the venue, or the centre, or the school, or wherever. Those in authority. That contract – to sum up – said *I know you will tell me that you've asked for arts activity and that you'll be happy when it happens, but this is to warn you that after a while that activity may mean your clients say more and want more. They will get into the habit of expressing themselves and having opinions about what you do. They will probably get more focused and happier and livelier and probably there will be an end product that could make you look good, but docility and silence will be in shorter supply. If you don't want this, do not let me in. If the end product that you get is controversial, or weird, or involves a bit of commitment when you can't make one, or just leads to boisterousness which you deplore and then you come in and call a halt, you will have made me hurt people. You will have let me open people up and get them to trust me and to trust they will be heard. If you then demand silence, you will hurt them. And I can't have that.*

Obviously, the contract didn't always help and wasn't even always read. And, among other things, I learned that bullies are really self-obsessed. Care staff who've abused patients believe that's the first and main and only thing that clients will want to write about, or talk about. Very often people just want to be free to say what they like – the further away from themselves and reality, the better. Often people just want to produce art, joy, expressions of themselves and their humanity – it's only a coincidence that their work makes you feel really shitty about having hit them that time, or held their head under water just for that moment, or yelled at them to say their address when the group was actually dealing with questions they could answer and couldn't get wrong, and could learn from, like *What makes you happy?*

And how much you learn about the human condition when you ask someone what makes them happy and they don't know. Or when you take a party to a museum for some general inspiration and you can't get them beyond the foyer because the foyer is the most wonderful thing that anyone has ever seen – just the foyer. Prisons come in all shapes and sizes and many are invisible.

Of course, apart from anything else, all of this makes a nonsense of the generally held opinion that if you really want to do art, really enter in, then you have to be mad or ill, or get mad or ill. And suffering is elevating – unless it's happening to someone powerful in which case it's a tragedy – and art without suffering is impossible, and watch out because there's a price to be paid for every joy and a penalty for every step towards freedom.

Well, in my opinion, suffering makes you suffer. That's why they call it suffering. You may be able to turn it into a gift, and art can help you do that, but it's still suffering. You wouldn't wish it on a friend, why wish it on an artist?

And if that kind of thinking isn't a prison, then I don't know what is. Working in the arts is insecure, low-income and therefore stressful. It's like many kinds of self-employment. That takes a toll. But doing what we do is also such a wonder, such a privilege – the chance to be paid at all at any point for doing something which is a vocation, which sings in us, that's not a recipe for madness and ill health. People like me, we may go over the score a bit and get ill from overwork. I'm an overwork kind of person. Give me a box of tamarinds – you can buy them in Chinatown by the shoeboxful – and I'll eat the box because they're lovely. A box full of tamarinds has a horrible effect on the digestive system – but I never learn. I just like them. My work is lovely, too. So I do it too much and sometimes get ill. This doesn't alter the fact that jobs in the arts are real jobs: safe, clean and satisfying jobs. They're a significant part of the economy, they're not all fantasy and fairy dust, they're flexible, they're open to people with all kinds of levels of ability and disability and in all kinds of circumstances, and they provide proof of dignity and humanity and daily pleasure – if we keep our wits about us – for those who produce the art and those who receive it. There is nothing wrong with that. But, of course, all that dignity and humanity, demanding that everyone should be allowed to fulfil their potential, that we should pay attention, that goods and services should probably be more equally divided, that we should help . . . well, for some people that can be worrying. And some of those people are influential. So we are taught that artists are mad and bad and dangerous to know.

And sometimes we do like to act as if that's true. Why not, if you can get away with it. Doubly why not if you've been ignored most of your life. But it isn't true. What is true is that art is about other people. If I refer to my own particular profession, fiction is always about people other than the reader. By agreeing to read it, we agree to collaborate with the minds and the voices of the authors and their characters, to let them put their words into our mouths, our minds – one of the most intimate intrusions possible. In the case of the novel, we may sustain this intrusion for days, if not weeks. We do this because we tacitly acknowledge that others' thoughts can be as important as our own and because they address us, uniquely, with the 'uncritical respect that you give to friends and relatives', if not lovers. We believe in the people authors make. Whoever they are, we care about them, understand they are important, help to make them important, suspend our disbelief and take them into our imaginations and this is enjoyable and feels very natural and is, I believe, an exercise which can begin to make it harder to murder, or torture, or harm other people, even other people that we don't know. I think it also makes it more difficult for us to stand by while such murders and tortures and harms are committed.

Why do so many campaigns suggest we send postcards to prisoners, why on earth would this be effective? Because postcards make the prisoners feel not alone, but also because they help the warders to imagine them as human and to know they are not alone – they are, in fact, observed. The arts send all kinds of postcards into all kinds of prisons.

Particularly now – and I've written about this elsewhere – we, as people who advocate using the arts to work with people, get asked variations on the question that goes 'Baby who needs an incubator, or a creative writing class – you only have the money for one – are you seriously saying that you'd pick the creative writing class?' And I would answer and have answered and always will answer – No. The baby gets the money every time and the writer who'd have led the workshops will make do for now.

But.

If the baby isn't here, if it isn't my baby, if it's a foreign baby, or a baby from another religion, if it's a baby I know nothing about and with which I have nothing in common? Then an individual piece of art – a poem, a painting, a story, a sculpture, a film, a photo, a song, a whatever – might be what helps me understand I have to find the money for the incubator. It can make it more important. The practice of entering imaginatively into someone else's way of seeing and being, the practice of entering into others' dreams, of seeing the world differently, that can mean I then change the world. Maybe we all chip in a fiver and we buy an incubator, maybe the minister doesn't get the new gazebo and there's suddenly more in the budget – who knows?

Why should we care about work that exercises our imagination? Because without imagination we cannot believe in a time when a seemingly permanent injustice will have been removed, we cannot plan its removal. We cannot imagine health, solutions, recoveries, reliefs, or the pains of others. We cannot call up those elements of the past which nourish us and make us ourselves, we cannot *have* a future, because nothing, in reality, exists other than the endless, inescapable now – tyranny demands an eternal, unrelieved present tense, a forgetting of our own interior lives and those of all others, our cooperation in the process of our own removal, thought by thought.

Why else would an oppressive regime and really, I would have to say, any government with an eye to its own survival become at least unsettled by the widespread use and demonstration of imagination amongst a population it seeks to control?

Because if we have imagination, apart from anything else, we can fit actions together with consequences – even if those consequences are being intentionally obscured. So let's move on to consequences . . .

The second contract? I gave that, or read that, to the people I worked with. And in it I promised that whatever they wanted to do – once we'd worked that out – I would try to make that happen to the limit of my abilities and available resources. I promised that what we made would be about them and about what they wanted and who they were. I promised that the material they intended to be private would stay private and what they wanted public would get out there. I promised we'd work in a safe place and said that would be about all of us making it safe and then we'd begin.

And I don't think that was a bad contract. I believe – obviously – that I was bringing something good to the people I worked with and that arts activity can be good.

But. I knew – eventually knew very well – that I couldn't

always rely on management teams, or parents, or care workers or whoever to back up my promises, or not be alarmed by even the smallest demands from clients. I tried to learn how to read bad institutions and avoid them.

But then again that meant that the worst places where people were the unhappiest wouldn't get any interventions. So I had to compromise and do what I could. I couldn't often decide that nothing would be worse than opening a hope that couldn't be fulfilled, because I had no idea what an individual might find sustaining. I know that for me a single session with a great teacher, a single phrase in a book, a single story told me, has made all the difference at key times – what if no one bothered to tell me the story, or give me the book, or offer me the single session?

It is truly remarkable what imagination and its practice can help us endure, when enduring or ceasing to be are our only options. Take the case of Talha Ahsan – Talha is a British subject and resident who was arrested on the 19th July 2006 and who has been held without trial ever since, awaiting extradition under the terms of the increasingly notorious Extradition Act 2003. The US requested his arrest and the UK authorities obliged, although he has no case to answer in the UK. The Extradition Act doesn't require the provision of prima-facie evidence. It seems that evidence gathered during Baber Ahmad's interrogation – interrogation described in the High Court as 'grave abuse, tantamount to torture' – may have helped form the case against Talha. Ahmad was later awarded £60,000 compensation by the Metropolitan Police and also has no case to answer in the UK. He also remains in custody awaiting extradition to the US.

Talha is a poet. I know him through his poetry and because I write to him and he writes back. We've never met. He has allowed me to imagine him. Talha is very close to being extradited now and if he is and he's found guilty of whatever charges he has to answer, then he'll be kept in solitary confinement for the rest of his life. I'll read you two sections from one of his letters to me. 'The ECHR judgement of 10th April was disappointing, but I am philosophical, I believe nothing occurs in this world except for a great wisdom. I am content and grateful for these experiences in making me a better person . . ..'

Talha is a very spiritual person – he welcomes the peace of prison for contemplation and follows the tradition of imprisoned religious men and women. He may also be stronger because he can create. He can, in a way, transcend his prison – he can write . . .

> Sometimes I like to imagine I am an Ottoman prince condemned to spend the rest of his days confined in his palace by a rival sibling who has usurped the throne. Having exhausted myself with the odalisques in my seraglio with endless games of battleships and hungry hippos, I shrug off the jeunesse dorée of my entourage and stroll the gardens in my finery with a mournful and dishevelled manner. I no longer mind the impertinence of the peacocks ignoring my presence. When I reach the walls I hear the common folk bemoaning my brother's rule and praying for my return.
>
> And that's it. My situation's one big art happening. Some may see influences of the surrealists or Kafka. Ultimately it's a farce and on the way I hope it raises a few laughs.

Over more than twenty-five years I have read writers with limited mobility, writers who were confined, who were imprisoned in various ways, and many of them – like Avraham, like Talha – sustain themselves with flights of fancy and by practising the arts of livingness, however constrained. An older lady, sitting in the one room of her care-home, the one room she still lived in, the one room she would very probably die in, learned to focus all her interest in her window. She had trained herself to find her view – the tiniest details of plants, birds, passers-by – a universe of interest. She was not diminished by being diminished and passed that truth on.

As I've said, people like Talha seem to me to be strong people. It seems to me that they are strengthened by art and an access to art. Still, I think, we need to bear in mind how much art can wake us – how it can remind us of feelings, or needs and wants – and of what makes us happy. What if someone wakes and comes to themselves and they're in a lousy care-home, where the air is full of ammonia and the cries of the distressed, and human beings sit surrounded by their own urine, the remains of inedible food. (I'm not exaggerating. There are many such places and I have seen some of them.) What about the places where our forgotten are warehoused before they die? Do we go in there? If we can't make things better? Is the fact of our company enough of a benefit when we will eventually leave and perhaps not be replaced? Should we enliven awareness when we may be helping human beings see how dreadful their surroundings are, how bad things have become, how little time they have left?

These are difficult questions to answer. I think we can only answer each case as it arises and do what we can to help each other. I think our lives should be about doing what we can to help each other. We all will need help eventually – life is hard and ends badly. No one gets out alive. This makes the kindness that arts can bring – and every other kindness – of great importance.

I tried to work within good institutions. I tried to provide continuity and lasting end-products and to make links between different groups that might become self-sustaining. I tried to bring work to light that might help people see the marginalised as human and might help them press for better care and altered priorities. But in the end I did go away. And in many cases I wasn't replaced. I like to think that I did more good than harm, but I wonder if I could have made the work undertaken more lasting. I think we do have to be vigilant in this area. We have to keep the people we work with safe and make sure the gifts we can reveal for them have no price.

And, while I'm being depressing, I'd like to address the other side of imagination, the dark. Human beings imagined Talha's confinement before it began. They chose not to imagine the suffering of someone detained without trial, or rather to imagine him as being unimportant in his suffering. Human beings thought of adapting a truck's exhaust, so it could gas children. Human beings imagined the benefits of possessing a nuclear bomb before they made it. (Although some of the scientists who invented it then had time to imagine the consequences of its use and protested against it ever being deployed.) Right now, human beings on every continent are imagining the refinement of tortures, the imposition of fear, the subordination and destruction of people they cannot accept as being people. Human beings are creating the fictions which make their crimes seem justified, acts of self-defence. You know the kind of thing, you've heard them before, the lies that rehearse extinction, that seek to justify: *all aboriginals are animals, rapists and drunks; Chile is under threat from a mass, Left-Wing conspiracy; all Negroes are lazy and ignorant degenerates; women are essentially immoral and worthless, they cannot be educated, seen in public, or allowed to work; the cockroaches must be exterminated before they exterminate us: the civilised world is being bled dry by a secret Jewish cabal; all immigrants are criminals and freeloaders who contribute nothing to the countries which receive them; all Muslim philosophy is essentially violent, all Christian philosophy is essentially violent; and on and on and on . . .* Imagination is a power, it can be used in many ways. It isn't inherently good. All the more reason then to exercise it loudly and often in good ways when we can.

But we may be confronted by that other puzzle: *How can it be that bad people who do bad things are also artists, have an interest in the arts?* Hitler painted dull watercolours, Eichmann played the violin. Radovan Karadzic, responsible for thousands of deaths in Omarska, Keraterm, Susica, Prijedor, Srebrenica, and on and on and on, described himself as a poet. He likened the shelling of Sarajevo to poetry. Issie Sagawa, student of literature, shot Renée Hartevelt while she was reading aloud from Schiller and then ate parts of her body raw. In at least one later interview he took pains to mention that he hadn't done this simply in order to write a book about it later. He did write a book about it later. Several.

But think of it another way. If a sociopath isn't cured by art, should we be surprised by that? Would listening to Wagner have cured Hitler's dental problems? No. And we wouldn't have expected it to. Showing someone a painting won't heal their broken leg. But it may sustain them. We know that all manner of dictators were and are very happy to be sustained by music, art, theatre and, indeed, they often appropriate it with enthusiasm. This is because dictators are also human. They are terrible, they are monsters, but also human – art is uncomfortable when it reminds us of this, we would prefer to be more savage than they are to destroy their savagery. And humans can derive joy from art. There are many illnesses and disorders it won't cure, can't cure, but naturally the powerful and wicked can steal art to enjoy. And they can choose to deny its joys to others. They understand art's power enough to limit access. Which is a clue – the inhumane who want us to join them in their inhumanity know they should keep arts from us, know they should separate us from our own and others' dignity. As previously established.

I find it odd that we can view the arts as being weak when every massive, heavily armed dictatorship has always taken care to battle poems, plays, paintings. It's interesting to note that a rather bland tapestry reproduction of Picasso's *Guernica* in the UN building was covered with a tasteful blue cloth while Colin

Powell and others talked us into invading Iraq. Public pronouncements were usually made with the tapestry as a backdrop. But not this time. A watered-down version of a dead man's painting, a highly abstract image of civilian casualties – it was making everyone uncomfortable. Just a picture.

The arts have power. They can do almost immeasurable good if we let them and keep them healthy, and they don't have to cost a lot. Through lower drug costs, more active lives, better mental health, better physical health, employment opportunities, saleable artefacts – they can in many ways be said to earn their keep.

And let's return to the question of awareness, increased awareness in hard times. Yes, awareness is not always a welcome gift. But if the opposite is numbness, a reduced livingness, a death in life, then I think we can still choose it. And I think, as artists and people who work with new artists and with arts in the community, we can consider the work of Viktor Frankl, psychiatrist and Holocaust survivor, someone who specialised in the prevention of suicide. He believed that the key to feeling that life had purpose lay in finding its meaning, embracing even the worst in order to meet it with the strength, the fact, of your continued living. At one point he was on a work party in Auschwitz. He was in darkness, fear, hunger and cold and he was thinking of his wife. The dawn was coming and he was imagining the reality of his wife, from whom he had of course been separated and who had been, of course, murdered by people for whom she was not human.

In *Man's Search for Meaning* he writes:

A thought transfixed me: for the first time in my life I saw the truth as it is set into song by so many poets, proclaimed as the final wisdom by so many thinkers. The truth – that love is the ultimate and the highest goal to which man can aspire. Then I grasped the meaning of the greatest secret that human poetry and human thought and belief have to impart: The salvation of man is through love and in love. I understood how a man who has nothing left in this world still may know bliss, be it only for a brief moment, in the contemplation of his beloved.

And I know that in my life the truth is that I have been allowed to do something that I love. Doing this allows me to love better and more, to know what makes me happy and to be alive in more and better ways. It also happens to be how I earn my living, and I was given all that possibility by the art of others and by the example of artists around me and of the human beings around me who chose and choose to live in a creative manner. I cannot do anything other than offer that to others whenever I can. I try to make art that people can like, that has a regard for human dignity at its heart, and if I have an opportunity like this I try to explain why that kind of thing is important. And sometimes I still get to work with others.

I would encourage you in every possible way to love what you do and to pass it on. We all meet our ends, happily or sadly and sooner or later, but in this way of helping each other, in this manifestation of joy and hope and kindness, we also have a kind of immortality. And we need never be entirely alone.

Does That Make Sense?

Approaches to the Creative Writing workshop

I am in a stuffy room in a poorly maintained building which is, like so many poorly maintained buildings, intended to be a community resource. I am sitting in a rectangle of shabby desks and seats with a group of visually impaired young people – they are making a video about being visually impaired. Their choice. The filming has been completed, we are at the end of another very long day, full of unexpected technical challenges and small triumphs – we are now all tired, hot and battering at the long prose poem which will make up our narration. Their choice. It isn't quite right. It needs one more word, which – if we're being technical – has to be an amphibrach. We aren't being technical. We're writing. We are spending a good deal of time saying *du-DA-du* – which feels right. It could be built out of one, or two, or three words, we don't know and we wouldn't mind which – the rhythm is the thing. The sense and the rhythm – we need them both. We have the rest of the sentence, the rest of the piece . . . we tap the rhythm. We repeat the rhythm. We think the rhythm. We sit. We continue to be tired and hot. And then, here comes the word. We can almost feel it – there is a sense, in fact, of it falling, beautifully and effectively, into the head of a dark-haired young man who, as it happens, hasn't been too committed to the wordy side of the project. It then emerges, as we might say, wearing his voice. It is confident and his and itself and ours and the perfect word, the one that sits well in the sentence and in our spines. It is *regardless.*

Regardless opens and echoes and is impressive – as if it had walked out of paradise and spoken its name for the first time, only to us. It is operating at that level of significance. As I said, impressive. It is one word with a kick which increases our respect for a whole language and for ourselves. It is both important and – apologies in advance – *fucking beautiful.* We have just made something *fucking beautiful* – the writer who found it, the rest of the writers who found the rest of the words, all of us, we have made beauty. And soon we will give it to other people, this very fine thing which is of us, but not us, like some magnificent bird we have coaxed inside to fly on our behalf. We are silent for a while and then very over-excited.

When a workshop works, you remember. When a workshop works, you learn. When a workshop works, you leave it with faith in the efficacy of your craft and yourself as a practitioner, in its ability to transcend itself, in humanity's ability to transcend itself. But how often do workshops really work?

I have spent the last thirty years giving writing workshops. That is to say, I have spent three decades trying to use a communal, public instrument to help people perfect what is an individual and private, sometimes very private, craft. I have studied the form, attended workshops, heard about others, read about still more. My own workshops have taken place in settings from the oppressively tranquil to the moderately unwise, with participants ranging from highly experienced authors to tentative newcomers. Participants have included university students, non-literate groups, people with special needs, people with degenerative illnesses, prison inmates, the visually impaired, children, residents in elderly care and psychiatric facilities, adults in community groups and passers-by at arts events. In short, I have worked with a relatively wide spectrum of those who, for whatever reason, have chosen to spend time examining their own and others' voices, who have an interest – no matter how small – in something which develops their expressions of themselves and their worlds and helps them find new ways of seeing and being. I have worked with those who wish, or hope, or intend to be heard. I remain uneasy with the workshop as a tool. It can undoubtedly be useful, but in its most widely accepted form it is almost completely unfit for its stated purpose and in any form it can invite laziness, calcified thinking and emotional abuse. In a climate which makes the 'teaching' of creative writing a low-cost source of revenue for a variety of organisations and institutions I am increasingly concerned that bad workshop practice and bad workshops are becoming the cornerstone of an industry which takes aspiring writers' money while rendering them less able to be writers, or to enjoy the benefits of what we might call a writer's mentality.

If we are writers, workshops are expected of us – often by people who are not writers and who do not understand what we do and how we do it. Worse still, we may be set mildly or wildly inappropriate tasks by those who think they do understand what we do and who will never take the trouble to find out they are wrong. But we may also not understand how best to use workshops, perhaps because we are busy and/or tired and/or scared and/or fundamentally interested in our own work rather than that of others. Perhaps we may have stopped trying to explore and expand what we do, perhaps it may never have occurred to us that we should. We may simply be earning money by delivering something which is, after all, expected of us, which fills timetables and makes libraries and community centres look slightly dynamic, something which is believed to be useful so strongly that whether it serves much purpose at all, whether it is in actuality destructive, has become irrelevant. This situation seems less than ideal.

What follows will mainly consist of questions which I hope will help us examine ourselves, our craft and the workshop as a medium in a constructive manner. I believe that if I have as clear a grasp as possible of my relationship with writing and myself as a writer and if I understand my aims and as much as I can about my workshop participants, then I have a chance of giving workshops that work. I believe a process of long-term interrogation can help us be better writers and give better workshops.

I will not be suggesting exercises. Exercises in general, games, snappy mnemonics, PowerPoint presentations, flipchart-bothering and the whole battery of workshop and masterclass strategies and gimmicks will only ever be as effective as the intentions and intelligence behind them. I would rather spend this time looking at what's behind them. I believe this will represent the best use of our time. This is no more than my opinion – but for what it's worth, it is very firmly held.

What do you believe writing is?

I know, this is a ludicrously huge question, but we can't avoid answering it – even our ignoring it will be a kind of answer. Regularly asking this question means that, in the preparation of any workshop, we can learn more about our relationship with our craft, how our emphases are altering, if we really know as much as we think, and enough to allow us to distil our knowledge in ways that others can grasp. Do we seek to disguise our ignorance and bluff our way, to coast along with what we know already, or to push our understanding? I would suggest the last.

I currently believe that writing is a way of life, that it is a massively demanding discipline, that it is an almost irresistible source of enrichment, expression and change. I think it is possible and useful to use the workshop to show how writing can inform all other activities – including the workshop – and how all other activities can feed the writing. This means that I will often tend to deconstruct the workshop process as it progresses.

I believe writing is personal – personal to you and personal to me. This belief, like all my beliefs, affects how I run workshops: they can't just be about an end product, or simply examining the utility and qualities of voices, tenses, constructions. My understanding would be that writing touches writers – professional and amateur – so deeply that, for example, issues of safety and intimacy need to be addressed from the outset, for the sake of the workshop and as a note for future writing. I think it's legitimate and sensible to discuss workshop practice within the workshop, to ask people to be aware of whether they feel unsettled, manipulated, confused. I hope to allow participants to be both comfortable and happy to report anything that seems amiss, to warn them of bad practice they may encounter in the future – either from their own poor self-employment or from others, including myself. I feel that creating a place of safety from which to write is hugely useful for any writer. This means that I will discuss issues of confidence, doubt, fear, and means that the workshop must be manifestly safe. Threats and negative intrusions can't come from me or from others, or must be swiftly dealt with if they do.

To choose a small example, I make a point of asking, 'Does that make sense?', when I have explained something to a group and I need to know if they have understood it. This seems to be the least threatening way of checking if we can all go forward. The wording of every question and comment directed to the group is important. I have witnessed more than enough encounters during which care assistants gatecrash sessions to bellow at participants, 'What's your address?' For some group members, this is a humiliating question and something easy to get wrong. It is also irrelevant. Writing is usually and most interestingly about the questions only the writer can answer, our privileged knowledge, the certainty and creativity of ourselves. Writing isn't about those questions with which others bully you, although it may sometimes be a response to them. I have bitten my lip while tutors have fired off, 'Do you understand?' at students so often and so violently that their communal IQ has withered and the session has simply clotted into an exercise in self-defence. Just as ungenerous writing tends to be less effective, ungenerous workshops tend to communicate information poorly.

Any workshop leader can only bring groups to levels of intimacy with which they are comfortable, but I have certainly run and observed workshops where participants have wept, where depths of experience have been shared – just as much as rooms have become helpless with laughter, or have pottered amicably. If emotional release is necessary, then I feel a tutor has to find a way of welcoming it, rather than locking it down – always with the emphasis on safety. This takes a degree of watchfulness, confidence and concentration, but is worthwhile.

What kind of person are you?

Without plunging off into chasms of self-analysis, I would hope I can assume that – if you are a writer – you have some level of personal awareness.

(If you are not a writer, I would rather you didn't give writing workshops. Then again, if you fully commit yourself to the process of your workshops, you may become a writer . . . Allow me to assume that you are.)

As a writer, like any person behaving creatively, you will draw upon yourself to produce work. Again, it's realistic to acknowledge this in others when we offer workshops. The fact that our work comes from ourselves (whether it is in any way autobiographical or not) is part of why revealing it to others can be so nerve-racking and why it is so deeply pleasant and positive if we can build something beautiful and realise it is appreciated beyond ourselves. We have to bear this in mind when we construct our workshops and help participants to engage without feeling over-exposed. Safe opportunities for sharing work, safe opportunities for creating work in real time and succeeding are to be maximised.

More prosaically, we do have to consider if we ourselves are shy, funny, anxious with crowds, likely to forget things, if we work better with a flipchart or with notes, if we enjoy improvising. Perhaps ask an honest friend what your social manner is generally like. Consider how best you explain things, your presentational weaknesses and strengths. Taking a mixed bag of exercises out of books and then presenting them in a manner alien to our natures is possible, but more targeted preparation might mean everyone can actually be comfortable together. And, of course, do find out if you're generally audible and specifically audible for any given venue or participant. There's no reason for you to turn into a game-show host, but if you are at ease and confident with the material you are presenting, then your writers will have the opportunity to relax and take part, rather than being unconvinced by your content and worrying if you're going to drop something, or faint. High percentages of your writers will need you to have faith in them before they can – you won't be able to offer them this if you give every appearance of having no faith in yourself. If you are incurably rattled by groups, you may want to find one-to-one work, to act as a mentor, or to team up with another writer. Workshops are a huge source of income, but if they're unbearable for you, then they won't do you – or the people who attend them – much good.

If you are the kind of person who wants to make cash by rolling out the boilerplate workshop – *everyone reads their work out and comments while you occasionally throw in something that sounds definitive or, better yet, make no effort at all and simply bounce back something like **and what do you think about that?**, thus making no actual effort at all* – then I'm very surprised that you're still reading this and I dislike you. Sorry, but I do. Everyone deserves better – always. Even you.

What is your attitude to your participating writers?

If we honestly ask ourselves this question the results can be interesting. It's very easy – particularly after we are established in workshopping – to find that our initial response might wear down to something along the lines of: *I think they are narcissistic, untalented people who stand between me and my own writing. There is no helping them and therefore I need not particularly try to be of assistance. They make me tired.* Although it may seem counter-intuitive, the best remedy for tiredness, staleness and misanthropic revulsion within workshops is increased effort and increased knowledge of your participants. If you can feel that your workshop is somewhere you can go in order to explore and expand your work, while others journey with you, then – no matter how desperately you want time to write – it won't feel like a waste of your energies. If you take an interest in your group, your group will duly become interesting. If you can bring, in a reasonable and practical manner, your own doubts, troubles and vulnerabilities as a writer to the workshop, this not only encourages others to share and address their own, it also allows you to look at the nature of character. What interests us in people? We identify with emotions, past experiences, weaknesses and quirks. We have our own; our characters should have theirs. This area alone can produce a month's worth of discussions, study of pieces, objects, music, film segments and exercises.

If you approach a group with a convincingly magisterial air, intent upon setting them tasks that will burn up their allotted session time and keep them quiet, they may never complain. If you assume they will have roughly the same problems as most writers at their stage of development, you may not be wrong. If you give them the same old notes on page layout, application of grammar, dialogue, how to use the *Writers' & Artists' Yearbook*, they may not storm your desk and hit you. If you mainly kick back and offer them literary anecdotes and name-dropping, they may not throw up in your face. Equally, they may not come back, they may not tell their friends they've had a great workshop, they may not fill in the feedback forms with enthusiasm, they may not help you to get more gigs and earn more money, they may not offer you the pleasure of seeing them discover themselves as writers or of their company as you grow and learn together. Behaving altruistically is, very quickly, its own reward – spending an hour in a room with twenty happy people is infinitely nicer than sixty minutes spent trapped with some strangers you're conning, or scared of, or who are clearly tolerating you, but largely dismayed.

There are, naturally, grotesque and tedious people in the world and occasionally some of them are moved to take writing workshops and you will have to deal with them. They will be relatively rare and usually surrounded by the kind of slightly nervous and almost unreasonably pleasant and patient people who are more commonly workshop participants. Treating people with respect allows them to respect you, themselves and what they are doing. If you are a writer, it is probably good practice to respect writers.

And, in all seriousness, in every workshop – as in every short story, every poem, every novel – you have an opportunity to change your participants' lives. Your workshops can change how they write and who they are. This isn't me being grandiose: I'm stating a not unreasonable aim, which can inspire us. We may rarely succeed spectacularly or on a massive scale, but it is relatively easy to help someone become positively different, more themselves, more articulate, more fulfilled by adjusting their interior and exterior voices. Why wouldn't it be? Our voices are hugely important to our identities, deeply embedded in our personalities and our bodies. When we make our voices stronger, more flexible and more articulate, we can set up a cascade of positive effects. Equally, when we fail in a workshop, or behave badly, we can do actual and unpleasantly intimate harm. At this level, the writing workshop isn't about being published. Given the current state of publishing it would be an agonising activity if it was. Writing and the writing workshop are about being more deeply alive. And that goes for the tutor, too. There are few things more wonderful than seeing someone come into focus, surprise themselves, sing out who they are, through writing. All writers get wearied at times, get stale – seeing writing at work in others reminds us of why we love it, reconfirms its power.

Under certain circumstances, having an attitude of respect for your participants may mean you have to withdraw from a workshop or an institution, if forces beyond your control mean that participants or their work are poorly treated, that their privacy can't be guaranteed, that the expectations and enthusiasms you raise will actually open them to abuse or disappointment. Although I would always want writers' work to be confidential if they wish it to be, working within prisons and psychiatric hospitals may mean that their material must be open to others. All we can do is point out this lack of privacy to our writers, or choose to avoid working in these contexts.

Do you know the abilities, wants and needs of your participants?

Sometimes you won't. In fact, very often you won't.

It would be great to read work in advance, to vet the participants in advance, to read potted biographies. This will almost never be arranged and, if it is, the additional work involved will probably be unpaid. Sometimes you will build up knowledge of a group organically over a number of weeks, months, even years. Sometimes you will enter into an existing community of writers and have to bear in mind that you are both an invited expert and a guest. But, on many occasions, you will walk in cold to an unsuitably arranged room filled with mysteries and this one hour, or two hours, or day will be all you have. Which is where time management, good planning and a depth of understanding of what writers might require – of what support you yourself might have wanted at various stages – will help you.

In some contexts – usually where you are working with the most vulnerable participants possible: children, those with special needs – you will usually have very little prior information and may be dealing with staff who cannot answer your advance enquiries helpfully. You may not even know how many people you will have in your group. This is where your self-knowledge, your wider interrogation of what you believe writing to be and how best to examine it, and a small amount of practical consideration will help you.

I'll deal with the practical points first. If you are going to work with the young and vulnerable you will, of course, get a CRB check, and if you are working with the public at all – even apparently sane and healthy adults – you will have as much public liability insurance as you can afford. This is sensible and easy to ensure, and the Society of Authors and a number of other providers can help you with this.

If you are working with people who have health or mental difficulties, or both, you need to know what these difficulties are and you need enough people with you to deal with any problems. If you are working in a prison or a secure mental hospital, you need someone from the institution with you at all times and you need to know where the panic button is. It is impossible to overestimate how easily and quickly you will, in fact, find yourself alone in a room where almost anything might happen. You may be surrounded by people, all of whom may have potentially fatal fits at any time, or who may be experiencing a radically different reality from yours. Should your workshop have proved successful last week, or should you simply have failed to kill anyone on your last visit, today you may find your space packed with all manner of participants, abilities and potential risks. In a way, this is a vote of confidence. It is also something to avoid. People who work with the vulnerable or potentially unpredictable can become blasé – we shouldn't. Be safe and be safe and be safe, and also always ensure that you and your writers are going to be safe. Apart from anything else, we shouldn't reinforce the Hollywood/*Dead Poets Society* model for artistic endeavour – every group does not require a death, or even a minor injury. What we do is about life and, even if some of us insist on suffering for our pleasures, writing is actually quite hard enough work to satisfy, without additional impositions of misery.

In what might be seen as a more conventional workshop context it is still worthwhile trying to ensure that the room you are placed in will be fit for the purpose, that any equipment you aren't bringing with you will actually be provided and will work and that you won't be disturbed. This may mean your initial interactions with your employer can seem fussy, anal-retentive or irritating. Remember that you want your workshop to have the best chance of success and, as you respect yourself and will respect your participants, you probably need others to have some respect, too. Be diplomatic and understanding, but also firm. Of course, something will usually go wrong, despite all manner of good intentions – mechanisms will break, fire alarms will go off, animals will intrude, latecomers will come late . . . It is perhaps best to always arrive knowing that, should you be left with nothing to work with beyond yourself, you could still deliver a useful and meaningful workshop.

What is your workshop?

The answer to this question will partly be a product of what you have learned from the preceding questions. Your idea of writing, its qualities and strengths, your understanding of yourself as a writer and your relationship with your own writing, your attitude towards and knowledge of the writers in your workshop will all interact to produce pathways and responses.

My understanding would be that the best possible use I can make of time with a writer would be to read their work in advance and to give them fastidiously detailed notes – I use a numbered key so that as many notes can be packed into the text as possible, with the minimum negative emotional impact. The numbers in the key not only identify problems, they also give general notes about possible sources of problems and therefore show a way forward. The key is revised on a yearly basis. The aim with any writer I see over several sessions would be for their work to transcend the key, to become so individual (and articulate) that there are no quibbles, or that the points queried need to be individually described. These notes – or anything else the writer wishes – are then discussed in individual sessions of about an hour.

This is the most effective way that a writer can learn, in depth, from their own writing and so progress.

This is how a writer learns to write.

This is how I remember how I am learning to write.

This is the service I am most rarely asked to provide.

Outside some university programmes and Arvon courses, truly effective help for writers is thin on the ground. Worse still, truly ineffective help appears to be epidemic.

Which brings me to the classic writers' workshop format – the one that is expected of us, within which writers present their work-in-progress in a group, the group discusses and everyone goes home. It is almost impossible to describe how many things are wrong with this. But I will try.

The work is being presented at too early a stage – exactly when the individual writer should be taking control of the piece, it is being opened to a barrage of opinions. These opinions are very often simply statements of what other writers would have done if they were writing the piece, and are therefore mainly useless.

These opinions are very often as bewildered, and bewildering, as any you might expect from people who don't yet know how to do something effectively and yet who are being forced to discuss it. Unless the tutor exercises such iron control that the group is no longer really operating as a group – Richard Ford is notoriously good at maintaining purity-of-workshop focus – then this workshop format will consist of the metaphorically blind leading the metaphorically deaf up a very unpleasant creek.

Those who are socially dominant prosper in groups – even if their writing is appalling – because groups are about groups, not about writing. Those whose work is already individual, which falls at either end of the possible bell-curve, and is quite likely to be of quality, will often feel that they are unusual within the group. Because they are. These participants are as likely to have their confidence destroyed by a workshop as they are to find their egos inappropriately distorted by premature praise.

Writing consists of a multitude of individual decisions, massive and complex control of language in depth and considerable personal responsibility – the classic workshop can accustom writers to avoiding decisions, or averaging out solutions to possibly irrelevant problems with texts which they should be learning how to master. And in a scrum of opinion, play and risk become silenced or stunted. Meanwhile, workshop exercises which set subjects remove a huge part of the writer's responsibility – subject choice. They remove opportunities for writers to learn what their inspirations feel like, how they develop, how they can be encouraged. The workshop process can infantilise writers: having abandoned responsibility for subject and craft, the writer cannot progress without the workshop. An art that is supremely independent, adaptable and low-cost has been rendered feeble and expensive.

A good and authoritative tutor can offset some or all of the workshop's failings to some extent, and a good group of writers can police itself and be intelligently supportive without a tutor, but still we are faced with the unalterable fact that no text can ever be examined closely enough using this format. It might do for a spot of light 'Have you read and understood?' This could be of use to undergraduates taking an English degree, but it does not adequately address writers' requirements. Writers need *other people* to read and understand – the difference may seem small, but it is vast enough to hold the work of a lifetime. Unless we are willing to extend sessions over periods of days, and can rely on immense patience from all concerned in examining others' work and immense tolerance when their own is subjected to scrutiny, we simply cannot use the standard workshop to look at texts in anything other than a cursory way. Although the standard format is favoured by higher-education institutions and English departments, it frequently offers a weekly time-filling farce and we should not indulge it.

What do we put in its place?

Everything else.

That sounds flippant, but I mean it quite literally, and writers given half a chance already do break away from the form as often and imaginatively as they can. If we accept that the aim of the writing workshop is simply and purely to help writers to write better, then every possible source of inspiration and stimulation is opened to us. Yes, there are times when there will be a flipchart and when we may look at passages of text. But it may often be infinitely more effective to, for example, stimulate voice by working literally with voice, to take the one potential positive aspect of the standard workshop – the act of reading our work aloud to an audience – and to develop writers' ability to present their work, while releasing and exploring their voices. If a group is tentative, perhaps it might benefit from looking at relaxation techniques, guided visualisations, ways of maintaining comfortable mental states. If we want to look at character, surely we should look at drama, we may talk to actors and directors, we may wish to perform ourselves, or to interact with our characters and their development in a variety of situations. If they go on to be anything like full-time writers, the people who attend our workshops are going to be savagely self-employed. Shouldn't the writing workshop address methods of sustaining personal enthusiasm and inspiration? This might take the form of field trips, interacting with animals, with articulate professionals in other fields, with as many manifestations of beauty as we can encounter. Any workshop will have limitations – and in a recession there may be many – but we needn't insist that everyone (including the tutor) would benefit from a three-week trip to Buenos Aires. Part of the joy of writing is the ability it gives writers to inhabit the moment in whatever circumstances. It may be that our workshop helps the infirm elderly to look out of their windows and see more, feel more, express the complexity and dignity of their experience. A group might simply eat together, go to a concert, take a walk, or be offered texts, films, music, images that they may not have encountered – or that they have not encountered as that group. It may be that a group occasionally writes as a group in real time, works full tilt on the challenges of a sentence in the relative safety of communal effort, but with a chance of examining the detailed choices and issues within the writing process. Just as writers may relax and really enjoy reading other authors' work aloud, it can be exhilarating to enjoy the act of writing as a group – it can offer a strangely intimate appreciation of language as an entity outwith any individual author.

Used imaginatively, the workshop can address both vaguely tedious but necessary points – how to compose a covering letter, how to find an agent – but can also engage with the kind of powerful metaphors that can alter and permanently strengthen someone's craft. I fully intend to run a workshop using horses at some point. Horses are powerful, beautiful, frightening animals, which magnify the rider's emotional state, yet which respond readily to moderate discipline and carry the rider where they wish to go. They are useful as a metaphor for writers who also know about horses, so why not make them available to other writers?

The workshop can create the icons, the good-luck charms, the positive habits, the strength to carry writers through. The workshop can help writers to appreciate that inspiration and support are ubiquitous; it can challenge and nourish both tutors and participants and make mature, independent and confident voices ready to move beyond it. The workshop should aim to make itself redundant, not to render writers dependent.

And all of this does take effort. It is more difficult and does take more planning and negotiation than doling out photocopies of work and sitting in a circle while not quite addressing our work, or each other, as we grow older but not wiser. I would argue that any effort expended tends to be more than repaid. A positive and open approach to group work allows the energy of the group to be released and harnessed, rather than ignored or wasted.

Have you addressed all the necessary technical issues?

This is the tedious bit – but it does reflect another layer of respect for yourself, your participants and the people who are paying your wages. I feel that the buck stops with us. We may not be in our own building, the disasters playing out before our horrified writers may have nothing to with us and everything to do with the shelter for dysfunctional leopards across the road, but we should try our utmost to control those elements that we can, for everyone's convenience and comfort.

It will take a while to get the feel of how long it takes you to deal with the points you wish to address in any session – and groups vary massively in their ability to grasp concepts and move on. It may be fine to spend two hours on a small area. Or it may mean you have lost control and not provided the session as advertised. Try not to overrun massively – even if people are enjoying themselves, they have lives and buses to catch and want to feel their experience has come to a proper conclusion, rather than ended with treats they couldn't share because they were running for a train.

And I take this opportunity to say that I am prone to overrun.

It is now possible to give groups satisfying and impressive multimedia experiences. This probably does mean that you have to familiarise yourself with a variety of technologies, and the ideal would probably be to travel with your own equipment. Even this will not save you from unsatisfactory power supplies, lack of tables, poor sightlines, inadequate blackouts, lost batteries and the unforeseen. Try to foresee the unforeseen.

Do try to establish realistically what the context for your workshop will be. If you are working in one place for any length of time it's best to come in with something amounting to a contract, or bullet points giving people an idea of what you will provide, possible pitfalls and the support that you will need. I feel that the group should always be protected. If they write a musical, it should be possible for it to be produced, not just put on a shelf. If they express opinions, it should be possible for them to be received and taken seriously. If they produce work, it should be possible for it to be shared and celebrated. If they can be published at some level, or helped towards editors and agents, then this shouldn't be (although it usually will be) dealt with as a series of scrambled favours out of hours. Generally, if you have misgivings about individuals and institutions it's best to walk away, rather than betray your group and/or yourself later.

Are you genuinely achieving your aims?

Any writer should be able to look at their work and offer it the benefit of serious criticism – the same should apply to our workshops. Writers attending workshops can be kind and may be unfamiliar with how much they could get out of a workshop – their comments may not be accurate. It is best if we check regularly to see if we are continuing to develop our ideas, or if we are stagnating. Perhaps in some areas we have found pretty much the best way we can deal with this or that set of points, but maybe with a different type of group we might come in differently; maybe there are still improvements to make; maybe our opinions have changed slightly and we are not reflecting that fact. When was the last time we tried an entirely new workshop? What have we learned from the last year of workshops that we can use and take forward? Are we improving, or are we complacent? Are we working within institutions and organisations that stimulate our work, or that encourage despair? The despair may not be our fault, but shouldn't we try – if we can – to move somewhere that can mean we have joy in our work again? As our writing progresses, has our use of workshops kept pace? Are we serving our own needs effectively when we workshop? These questions shouldn't be accusatory, they are merely a way of ensuring a level of professional contentment for ourselves and as good a workshop experience as possible for others.

In closing, I would thank the students of the 2009/10 MA in Creative Writing at Warwick University who asked me for a workshop on workshops, from which much of the material for this essay came.

And I will offer one last question.

When is the last time you gave a workshop and knew something special had happened, that you would never forget it, that a life had been changed?

We may always fail a little, sometimes more than a little, but I believe that if we commit ourselves to the pursuit of writing's qualities and their transmission, to the care of our craft, then we will do no harm and may do a great deal of good.

When a workshop works, you remember. When a workshop works, you learn. When a workshop works, you leave it with faith in the efficacy of your craft and yourself as its practitioner, in its ability to transcend itself, in humanity's ability to transcend itself. It's something to aim for.

Character-Building

It would hardly be fair if a reader was asked to expend mental energy and invest their interest in a fiction inhabited by characters who seemed unfeasible and frankly less interesting than the genuine, human people they could be meeting and interacting with, if they weren't suffering through this or that dreadful book. Hopefully, the effect of a finished character will be convincing, involving, idiosyncratic, natural – in short, *real*. There are, of course, schools of thought which maintain that providing fully formed characters is just pandering to the reader.

It is.

And it should be.

We, as writers, are intimately intruding upon the reader. We set our words inside their minds. Whatever else the reader could have been doing with themselves – the daydreams, plans, happy memories, erotic fantasies, all the fun a person can have with their own head – we want them to leave that and read us instead, listen to our voices, our stories, meet our people. It's not unlikely that, in addition, the reader will have paid for our work, or at least have gone to the trouble of stealing it from a shop, finding a library that still contains books, or picking up our volume from where it would otherwise have been languishing, perhaps under a vandalised bench, or stuffed down the back of something with a back. The reader deserves our best attentions; without them we would simply be indulging in extraordinarily florid episodes of self-love. We need the reader. The reader needs to be convinced. So we should surely try to offer them illusions that convince.

As readers ourselves, we can appreciate these illusions as something wonderful: an opportunity to do the impossible, to see through another's eyes, experience another's world. Perhaps because of this very sense of wonder, the process of creating characters can seem mysterious, if not a little miraculous, even to those who have already begun to write. Consideration of any working narrative makes it clear that a character's identity and psychology will almost invariably influence tone, voice, imagery, the whole fabric of a piece, so it's clear that the stakes are very high, that a grasp of character is essential for an effective writer. Nevertheless accessing, exploring and then making a character manifest can appear to be an overwhelmingly difficult task. It need not be, but a number of misconceptions and misunderstandings may stand in our way.

Personal experience may, for example, be suggested as a handy source of authenticity, perhaps because of the tediously repeated 'advice' imposed upon new authors: 'Write about what you know.' Many people are still unacquainted with the unabridged version of this advice: 'Write about what you know. I am an idiot and have never heard of research, its challenges, serendipities and joys. I lack imagination and therefore cannot imagine that you may not. Do not be free, do not explore the boundaries of your possible talent, do not – for pity's sake – grow beyond the limits of your everyday life and its most superficial details. Do not go wherever you wish to, whether that's the surface of your kitchen table or the surface of the moon. Please allow me – because I'm insisting – to tell you what to think.'

Rather better advice – should it be absolutely necessary to offer any – might well be: 'Write about what interests you. Write about what excites you. Write about what speaks to you. Write about what obsesses you. Write about what you need to. Write about what outrages you. Write about what alarms you, but won't leave you be. Write about what you love. Write about what you feel you may come to love. Write about what you can come to know.' All suggestions that can be useful when we begin to work with characters.

A few readers – and a percentage of journalists and academics – believe that a character's reality comes from a type of theft. They feel that the writer must wander about, stealing the attributes of relatives, friends, lovers and so forth and then passing them off as inventions, or – indeed – parading them about as comments on relatives, friends, lovers and so forth. Of course, there are such things as *romans-à-clef* and they are a very good reason for never marrying a writer. Then again, the fact that they have a special, French name might suggest that they are in some way unusual and that there is a method of building fictional personalities which does not rely on a variety of body-snatching, followed by some more or less ugly sewing and patching, à la Victor Frankenstein. As writers, we must all make our own personal decisions about how safe the secrets of those close to us will be, how private others' privacy will stay, whether we want to keep our relatives, friends, lovers and so forth, treat them well and not utilise them as subject matter.

We may also consider how merciless we will be with the material of our own lives. I would suggest it might be a good thing if – forgive me for being frank – the choices we make don't mean we eventually become soulless and rapacious shells, pumping all and sundry for sordid incidents, the centre of our personalities and experience translated into no more than *material*. There's a fine line between paying attention, being stimulated and inspired by reality, and simply using it as something to cut and paste. Naturally, whether any of us is always absolutely on the right side of that line is sometimes questionable. There may well be days when you catch yourself staring inappropriately, *noticing*.

And then there's non-fiction – but we're not dealing with that here.

Fiction or non-fiction, I would hope that *being a writer* never overrides *being human*. I would hope, in fact, that writing is a vocation which can enhance our humanity and sensitivity and our ability to celebrate and explore what it is to be human and in this world. I have made what I regard as ethical choices in this area, which I like to think are comfortable for me and those around me. But I have to say that choosing to work imaginatively, rather than recycling and/or distorting fact, was primarily an instinctive and practical act, because *it is both easier and more fun to make things up.*

Endlessly paddling in the lukewarm pool of your own self is not necessarily as exhilarating as reaching out and trying to be someone else, someone who has never existed, someone who almost seems to summon you to help them be expressed. (This reaching out coincidentally allows the writer to take advantage of what I might call a meditative absence of self, should he or she wish to.) And even the most devoted narcissist might do well to consider whether the undiluted joys of their interior landscape really are absolutely all a discerning reader could wish for from a piece of prose. Abandoning oneself as subject and simply gathering together scraps of existing people has its own perils. People who exist are already grubby with very specific emotional and intellectual associations. They either tempt the writer in towards the setting those real individuals would usually require, or add a huge amount of alteration work before the task of assembling a whole, coherent, organic narrative can even begin – trying to trim and tailor them to fit a narrative which should be developing its own alphabet of associations, imagery, incident, its own life. I repeat: *it is both easier and more fun to make things up.*

And making things up allows us to take advantage of our love of fantasy and a powerful and fluent energy that we may not have accessed since childhood. It makes use of our desire to have more than we can, our delight in playing and play-acting.

But how do we make our dreams available to others, how do we make them articulate, how do we create the illusions that seem true? In answer, I will try to look at my process (which may be useless to you), but also look at the principles that underlie it.

First, I think it is necessary to spend some time examining how you relate to real people – something I would assume you have been doing since an early age, something familiar, something about which you can feel relatively confident. How do you remember someone? What is it that you respond to most strongly? Do you remember faces, voices, postures, scents, mannerisms of speech? To give me an idea of your invented character, you can use the skills and areas of speciality you already have. I, for example, remember people by smell. It is hugely important to me that I ask myself what the character smells like, or can smell. This is a powerful way into their experience for me, even if I ultimately don't use it. So perhaps it will be useful to think about how you understand people, what sense you usually use, what senses you neglect, and how to bring them all into play.

Second. What do you already have? Presumably you didn't just wake up this morning thinking, 'I need a character.' It's rather more likely that you had a sense of them doing something, or that you had a fragment of plot that involved someone, a line of dialogue that someone said, an impression of a face, an action . . . the possibilities really are pretty much endless. Even if you *have* just decided to build someone from scratch, the investigative process you can go through will be the same. It's not complicated. You simply ask questions. You can even just repeat the one question 'Why?' if you can think of nothing else. Beyond the very early tipping point, answers will suggest questions that will produce further answers. Any question can generate more information, even if it's a negative. With nothing established you'll have to make at least one decision to get rolling – for example, 'Is this an adult or a child?' 'Is this a man or a woman?' 'Does he have red hair?' You'll notice he's now male – according to me – although we don't know if he's old or young, a post-operative transsexual or, indeed, a man trapped in the body of a middle-aged lady. If we add 'Why?' even to something as bland as 'Yes, he has red hair', then you can begin to link information into more coherent chains, rather than just having a list.

'Why?'

'Because his dad has red hair.'

'Why?'

'He doesn't know.'

'So he looks like his dad?'

'Yes.'

'Has he done this for a long time, or a short time?'

'A long time – he's forty-six.'

'Does he like that?'

'No.'

'Does he like looking like his dad?'

'No.'

'Does he look like his mum, too?'

'His mum's dead.'

'Did that make him sad?'

'It made him happy.'

These are not complicated questions, they haven't taken long and they are already suggesting certain options that are more and less likely, avenues to pursue. If we already knew, for example, that this gentleman was our protagonist and would be involved in a violent incident with a number of youths, we could add this in. Half an hour spent asking questions is rarely wasted, often enjoyable, sometimes frustrating. If you are thoroughly stuck, of course, stop and try again later, and/or try some of the other approaches I will suggest. Even if you are stuck, you will have the distinct impression that you are bombarding somebody awkward with questions and they are being uncooperative – that's a step forward in itself. You are thinking of the character as a person who needs to be found, not as an extension of your own mind. It is useful to believe this. Without actually buying them clothes, or insisting they have a place set for meals.

The question game can also be played with, for preference, two other people. If they are writers, too, then they'll be able to take part fully – this will mean that person A can be asked questions by persons B & C, then B can be asked them by A & C, then C can be asked them by A & B. It is very important that whoever is being asked questions answers *I* rather than *he* or *she*. This is a simple, but very effective, way of bringing the character closer to the speaker. There are many variations on this game – you can alter the positions of interrogators and interrogatees; you can be still or move . . . With two people asking questions, the pace tends to keep steady and the person being questioned will find that they are slipping easily into decisions that simply feel right. They are getting into character, in fact. And do pay attention to the words and phrases used when answers are given – which is why doing this out loud is so useful – as you will find they become coloured with the character's voice almost automatically. With one person asking, the pressure to come up with questions can be too great and there can be awkward pauses. Three or more interrogators can leave the interrogatee feeling harassed. This game – if we were actors – would be called *Hot Seating*.

It's not surprising that we can learn from actors and their games. Actors have to go onstage wearing more or less well-written constructs and actually make them walk and talk while paying members of the public look on. Actors do what we do at our leisure and with opportunities for rewrites, only with observers and in real time. So look out for books by actors about their craft, for interviews with actors, books of games, or books by voice specialists like Cicely Berry, who deal with the way language translates into physicality. I'm not going to give you specific titles because that's a great big area of discovery you can enjoy for yourself.

Third. Let's get back to you. Take a little time to consider what you think of human beings. Do you trust them? Are they all self-serving? Are they lost in a big wilderness? How do you see the world? Are working-class people thick? Are upper-class people thick? Are all women manipulative? Does your character agree with your opinions? It's unlikely that you'll write a story with a narrative thread in which you can't believe, or with which you can't be comfortable. It's very unlikely that you'll even try, unless you're being held at gunpoint, or being paid a huge amount of persuasive money. I don't think all people are self-serving, nor do I feel women are especially sly. Threats of mutilation and death might temporarily force me to change my mind, but my fiction will generally reflect my worldview. Still, if my character has other opinions, even repellent opinions, I will have to allow him or her to be true to themselves, to be real. The character may not even agree with my gender – they may arrive and be male and connected with a plot that can best be told from the 1st Person. This means I will have to write 'I' and mean a man. I may even have to be a man who thinks everyone is self-serving and hates and distrusts women – so be it. I probably need to be grateful that he's already well defined enough to be rattling at my boundaries – he is a challenge, not a threat.

Fourth. You may not like your character as he or she emerges, but make sure that this doesn't mean you neglect him or her. The best idea would probably be to love your character – that means you'll allow them to be whoever they are. Remember, you don't own them. They simply came to you to be expressed. If you object to them too strongly, they'll go somewhere else. Again, this is partly nonsense, but it can be a useful way to think. Let characters outrage you, surprise you, bewilder you, if they have to – these are all indications that they are taking on independent life. And if they are going to convince the reader, that's exactly what they'll need.

Fifth. Back to games and questions. We are used to knowing people and to knowing ourselves. If someone asks us, 'How old are you?', we can answer, 'Twenty-one' rather than 'About twenty'. Try to push for detail. Equally, if your character is being stead-fastly vague, that's an interesting clue. 'About twenty' may not mean that you haven't focused in well enough yet, it may indicate that your character is shifty/sensitive about their age for some reason. Nevertheless, having specific details to hand does, in real life, tend to imply that you know either yourself or someone else. So look for details. When you ask for them, they'll tend to appear.

'Why does Paul have that scar on his forehead?'

'He doesn't ever say.'

'He was bitten by a terrapin – he has dreams about terrapins.'

'He doesn't ever say, but as I am his author I know that he was bitten by a terrapin and will seek them out and punish them for ever.'

There are all manner of possibilities. Watch out for blurs, evasions, instances when you behave as you wouldn't when describing someone you knew well, or had special access to, or who was yourself. Remember that as a writer you have the ulti-mate Access All Areas pass – that's great fun, but also a great responsibility – you're building all the areas. If there are blank patches, fill them in. You can also spend many profitable hours asking questions of what you have for a plot and what you have for a setting – how do they relate to your character? How does your character affect them? And, naturally, there may well be other characters around. Where do they fit in? How do they interrelate? Whose psychology will influence your images and symbols, your way of saying what you have to say?

You may want to take your character as an invisible passenger on journeys, or as a companion in real events. You may enter his or her world by literally going to places that he or she would enjoy, know well or be interested in. Or you may find out about those other places – and other times, for that matter – and then slowly ask enough questions to know how she or he would behave in them, as if you have both gone there. You may, in fact, lay that extra place setting at dinner, if it seems necessary. Remember to have fun with this. It's not unlikely that to others, you're going to seem slightly obsessive, if not unhinged from time to time – you might as well enjoy it.

Sixth. Remember that you are making up one other person, a piece at a time. Your character is not all people of their type, they are not a crowd, they are not a generalisation, they are themselves. They are going to be consistent with their own emotions and thoughts, actions and experiences. Don't pressure yourself with thoughts along the lines of 'Oh my God, I've never been a Russian submariner in the 1970s – I'll get it all wrong.' You're only making ONE Russian submariner. Or several, but one at a time. They only have to make sense *as themselves*. Find the details, ask questions, find more details, do your research, hold your breath under water, eat borscht, learn how to sing 'Korobushka', whatever it takes. Then you will be in the happy position of being able to *forget* the research you don't need and limit what you say, with the help of your character's concerns and the incidents of the plot. But you will know that you aren't going to go wrong. You will write like someone who knows who they are writing about – that sense of confidence will infuse what you produce and will relax and persuade your reader.

Seventh. Learn more about people. By this I don't mean that

you should hollow out everyone you meet like a human melon-baller, whenever they give you the chance. I mean listen to people, look at them, read about them in anthropology, or sociology, or – heaven help us – psychology books, if you want to. Above all, be in the world. You'll discover that if you're out there taking part, you'll remember what you can be inspired by later without making notes, because it will be memorable. Inspiration is memorable.

Eighth. I have left this late, because it may make you nervous, but it's close to being the most important point. KNOW HOW YOUR CHARACTER FEELS. We identify with others because of their emotions. We know that people are important because their feelings trigger feelings in us. When do we know we know someone? When we know about their feelings. What will make your character seem real? Having real, credible feelings. And yet, in order to give a character feelings, we have to reach back and compare notes with our own feelings. We measure them against the only scale we have – ourselves. This means we can feel exposed – very intimately exposed. All manner of writers, myself included, will take all kinds of measures and make all kinds of excuses for why their character does not have feelings. This is because we are trying to run away from writing. We are trying to be there on the page, but not really. We have to bear in mind that all the reader has to do is read us – they see everything. There never has been anywhere to hide and never will be. If we try to hide and try to hide our characters, the reader will notice. Noticing is what the reader does. So we must stand and be seen. We wouldn't be there if we weren't going to be seen – pretending otherwise, or avoiding the issue, just wastes time. Allow your characters to feel. They won't be your feelings, this is not a commitment that is any more intimate than any other; this is just the last stage in knowing your character and allowing him or her to live. Let it happen. Your character may be doubtful and confused (bear in mind that characters sometimes echo their authors, they are our children for a while, after all) – that doesn't mean that they have no thoughts or feelings. Being confused means you have more than one thought or feeling and you swing between them – that's why you're confused. If your character is confused, the reader needs to know the positions between which the character is swinging. That's how a reader knows the character is confused, rather than the author.

Let me in, as a reader, and I will add to the person you made, care for them, love them. I will take them far, far away from you and enjoy them as if you had never existed. If you do your job well, you will be invisible – which is the opposite of exposed.

Ninth. HAVE NO FEAR.

In fact, you may well be afraid during your progress towards the finished piece. That's reasonable and normal. If you're not, you may not care enough about your work and its quality. But, if you allow it to stay with you, fear will muffle you, make you anxious and self-conscious and stilted. Fear will make you hide. It will stop you writing. If you can examine what you are afraid of and find out why, then you either have new inspiration or a new task to complete. 'I can't write about terrapins – and yet I want to – and yet they scare me.' Then maybe write about someone who is scared of terrapins, or maybe wait a while, or maybe write about what scares you about terrapins – or maybe find out why you're wasting your time forcing yourself to do unpleasant things and setting yourself up to fail.

'I'm afraid this story is no use.'

Then make it better.

'I'm afraid this isn't interesting.'

Then make it interesting.

'This bit's rubbish.'

Then rewrite it. You get the idea.

If you can lead yourself firmly but kindly onwards, you and your writing will benefit. In short, the creation of character relies on many very simple and familiar processes: asking questions, daydreaming, meeting people and getting to know them, being human. These are brought together and allowed to interact and interrelate until they form something which is hopefully complex and apparently capable of genuine, compelling life. The complexity comes from simple elements and the writer's understanding of how they work together and change each other. With luck and application, the whole is greater than the sum of its parts, and something that has been fastidious, obsessional, painstaking and occasionally frustrating will seem – to your readers – effortless, inevitable, even beautiful. We can at least aspire to that and see how far we get.

Proof of Life

T his is a voice. My voice. And yours also. Together, we are speaking in your head, ghosting in your mouth, firing in your mind: meanings, resonances, memories, the newness and familiarity of words. These are sounds that need never exist beyond the privacy of thought, sounds I might never be able to make as neatly as this in person, but here they are singing, nonetheless. You let them sing.

And clearly this is also writing: not quite literature – an essay. This is marks on paper. For me, this is currently marks on a screen: dark little fiddles walking out in lines across blank space, a code we may both agree to break, understanding in conveniently different ways. But, above all, this is voice.

At this point, I have to relax. I don't find it easy to relax. I usually suspect that if I give way to relaxation I will become in some way dangerous. In my present context, this belief is unhelpful and so I ignore it. I lie face down and concentrate. When I inhale – as instructed – my stomach presses snugly into the padded mat beneath me. My torso is used to this process now and enjoys it. When I exhale – as instructed – I almostsoundlessly open my mouth as if I am saying 'Aw'. My mouth enjoys this. I imagine myself as a thing which lives at belly height, which draws in and pushes out breath – my proof of life. I enjoy this.

Although we often use the language of the spoken word to describe its written counterpart – *tone, rhythm, melody, musicality* and so forth – I have long been surprised by how little attention is given to the reality of voice in writers' lives. There are clear connections between an individual's voice on the page, the voice in which they carry on their own interior narratives and the voice with which they address the world. Improve someone's mastery of one voice and the others also strengthen as they grow, adapt and change. Undermine or muffle one and the others will also suffer. It puzzles me that these interrelations are rarely discussed or explored amongst writers, even though writing is difficult, even though I know I'm not the only one looking for any and every assistance, all possible paths to improvement. The literary and academic worlds seem to prefer a model of writing within which dignified thinkers move letters about on pages – no sound, no breath, no sweat. This appears beguilingly safe, but may constitute a form of suffocation.

The impact of audible failure for a writer can be huge. An author's ability to read work effectively to an audience has always been commercially useful, but it can also lend a sense of genuine power and confidence. It can root work in the face-to-face reality of human communication. When a reading goes wrong, listeners may not be able to forgive either the writer or their poorly delivered writing. And at a very personal level, hearing one's own words falter out loud in the real world, knowing them to be badly offered and badly received, can be devastating. One whole element – an increasingly required element – of the author's life can become a succession of perceived narrow escapes and outright humiliations. The sound of one's own voice may become more or less definitely linked with nerve-racked acts of public self-destruction. Who wouldn't want to avoid that? What author, what human being, wouldn't be interested in establishing a virtuous cycle within which the thought, the spoken and the written word might be able to nourish and support each other?

Who wouldn't be interested in sounding like themselves, but in deeper and more effective ways?

Why wouldn't finding your voice help you find your voice?

I am breathing in and out. No thinking. No stress. Relax the head, neck, throat – which, of course, immediately tense when I give them my attention, which is a kind of thinking and I shouldn't think too much here, I should trust . . . So I try to ignore the stresses. I let myself untie myself while I keep on with the in and out and being soft, being a soft thing, and being here and being now.

When we speak to each other, we have to be here and we have to be now. The transaction is uncomplicated. And within it – horrifyingly, beautifully – there is nowhere to hide.

In 1983 I was a Theatre Studies and Drama student. Which is to say, I was hiding. I had embarked upon a three-year course which would be not quite theatrical enough to produce a performer and not quite academic enough to make me feel pressured in any real way. I had committed myself to remaining uncommitted. I didn't even turn up to my own graduation.

I was already a nascent writer, had many of the tribe's characteristics: good at English and a small range of clevernesses, often sharper on the page than in person, a loner, and with a growing disconnection between thought and emotion, the body and the skull.

Not that I didn't have passion. I had fallen in love with words – books lit my childhood, were a kind of blessing. And I adored words when spoken in others, could be moved by the theatre as by nothing else. The sense of words in my own mouth – they never reached much further into my body than that – was fascinating, but I was mainly bewildered by my love and I also knew that if I once genuinely tried to express it, then I would probably fail. I didn't want to fail.

I was not unaware that, by avoiding failure, I had guaranteed it, boxed myself in. And then something happened: a moment of true education. A voice specialist was brought in to take our class one day. I hated her on sight for no tangible reason, beyond the facts that she was offensively comfortable in her own skin and far too audible. I was generally neither. The specialist stood us in a line and gave each of us one word from a complete sentence. We then had to say our words in order, say the sentence. And we did try. But the sentence fought us at every syllable and won. We sounded dreadful: unintelligible and powerless.

I had already decided this was a waste of time – like poncing about in a leotard had been, like talking to chairs, like spending weeks prodding at my already sparse interior marbles in order to say a total of ten words during a production of *Marat/Sade* in a suitably barmy way. I was angry – because I was scared. Here and now was something else I couldn't do. And yet I did want to be here and now. I enjoyed the security of being given words to say and things to do – being stared at by an audience felt like a relieving lack of responsibility. And in everyday life – unpredictable everyday life – people did speak to each other and this seemed a rather fundamental skill to lack. I wanted to do and be better, but I felt, as on many other occasions, like a balled-up mumble with feet.

The specialist then told us that for the duration of the workshop we would be working with our words – one word each. Three hours, if I remember correctly, for one word. My word was *the*.

Yeah.

I duly and with bad grace said, shouted and whispered *the*, lay on the floor with *the*, ran with *the*, ran away from *the*, reinvented *the* as a sodding movement – *oh, spare me.* I progressed from furious, to hopeless and then calm.

The.

And finally we lined back up and said our words again – same words – but now the sentence lived and owned us and we owned it and were friends and we were together very beautiful. We sounded good. My voice had just proved it could sound good. And I had learned, entirely against my will, that simply establishing a real relationship with the definite article would probably take me a week. I moved from hating the voice specialist – whose name I regret I now cannot remember – to being in awe of her mystical skills and signing up for what I think were two available extra sessions, along with a few of my equally keen companions. In those sessions I got a tiny idea of the way a voice can lodge in the chest, or the face, or the throat, or the stomach: its sensitivity to confusion and stress. My voice seemed to me like some ridiculously wilful and delicate animal: scare it and it would disappear, feed it and it could make a sense that could even exist without my intellect's interference. And here I was in a place of safety, feeding it words that I already loved and trusted, words that can baffle you one moment and slot in under your feet to lift you up the next. I was given a piece of Shakespeare writing for Burbage: an author tailor-making a part for a time and a voice, but building to last. Giving the words the small thing that was my full attention – including my physical attention – snapped them into a response, an immediacy that any writer would long to create. In under the layers of meaning was a continuity of breath across centuries, of dense and demanding lines still governing the *in* and the *out* long after their author's death, their original performer's death, the so many other performers' rising and falling and fading away.

And relax the shoulders. My teacher sets her hand down over my spine – inoutbreathing – presses on the out. There seems to be an inherent mercy about the gesture.

Suddenly – the voice work causes these inrushes of emotion – I remember a friend, someone I love, and seeing and knowing that he was hurt. I set my hand down over his spine. Moving before I could think, I touched him.

Here I am.

I was perhaps trying to read whatever damage had occurred. Perhaps.

Here you are.

I was trying to comfort his breath. Pats, rubs, caresses to the back – they are a common way to reassure.

Inoutbreathing. Feeling it.

Feeling what?

Don't analyse.

Remembering.

I am remembering affection, helpless affection and being not alone.

I am remembering that in being not alone I am helped and perhaps helpful.

This is what happens – these sudden bursts of hot information.

Allow it.

And let it go.

Inoutbreathing.

I'm in the playground and seven, maybe eight. I was, until this second, as usual the mutterer. My nickname has been Muttley for a while, after the incoherent cartoon dog. I am the hunched-over kid in the corner, troubled parents at home, academic, indecisive. But now I have lost my temper. I don't even know why. To be truthful, there isn't much of a reason why. But I am yelling. This noise is ripping out of me, starting from my feet, mouth wider than it ever has been and someone – bully, taunter, accidental irritation – is standing staring at me. I have shouted them to a stop. The sound I am making is changing them, is putting me in charge. I haven't a clue what to do with being in charge: it has, after all, never happened before. Behind me, a schoolmistress appears – my din is carrying, and has drawn her in. I know her – she used to teach me in Primary Four, making my life an even more strangled misery than I would have constructed for myself. I am distantly aware that she would like to be angry with me again, but can't quite work out how. There is no room for her anger because of mine, and I am no longer the girl she expected me to be.

I like this. I like the way she is almost scared.

For the rest of my school life I am never as loud as this again.

But I take to public speaking – competitions and debates – unlikely, but true. I paint myself into a corner and then have to make a noise.

And inoutbreathing as my teacher – Ros Steen – good teacher – proper teacher – briskly rubs down along my side ribs when I exhale. I have the mild sensation of sinking into the floor. I am feeling rich-headed and warm.

Even the first time we did this, I wasn't scared. A good teacher – proper teacher – makes the scary things seem normal and necessary, small enough to breathe in and then blow away.

I seem light, like Muttley flying: like a plump, round-shouldered dog, lifted up by his daydreams and a madly spinning tail, a triumph of hope over physics.

Ros Steen is head of the Royal Conservatoire's Centre for Voice in Performance. She teaches, researches and lectures internationally, writes on voice and acts as a voice consultant for theatre, film and television. She is, in fact, Professor Ros Steen, MA, DSD, IPA, FRSAMD. I'm glad I didn't know this when I first met Ros – seeing so many letters after her name would have scared me. In fact, my ignorance gave me focus and permitted me to approach someone who was, in many ways, out of my league.

I simply knew that I needed to *really deal with my voice*.

I hadn't a clue what *really deal with* and *my voice* might mean.

Everyone I'd asked about my *really dealing* had told me – *Ros Steen will help*.

They were right.

My short-term goal was to prepare myself properly to perform a one-person show, 'Words', at the Edinburgh Festival in 2009.

In 'Words' I had written a script which dealt with being a writer and what it could mean. It seemed to me that the performance should be unmediated: no set, no lectern, no mike – just me and (hopefully) an audience and the words. This was intended to be a proof that, with no visible means of support, even someone as inept as me could be communicative, could live more and better by communicating, could try to jump the papery gap between the pages and the reader.

This was more than enough to be going on with, but I knew that work on my physical voice would affect my other voices and that I couldn't predict how. After the displacement of a cervical vertebra and more than ten years of upper back pain, stress and muscle-wasting, my voice had weakened and shrunk. The pain was finally gone and I wanted my sound back and more than back – I wanted unpredictable change. I wanted – it has to be said – to *find my voice*. Terrible, self-indulgent phrase. Then again, you're nowhere and no one without a voice. And yet, from your first cry onwards – they're glad you're alive, but want you to *be quiet* – the force of imposed silences builds to hide you from yourself. Power has an audible scale: men should be louder than women, adults louder than children, the rich louder than the poor, the accepted louder than the outcasts. And, in our current media, the frightening and stupid should be louder than everyone.

Ros wasn't the first practitioner I'd asked to address my vocal difficulties. When I stumbled away from university and into the life of a jobbing arts worker and evening scribbler, I made a living by leading workshops. Ultimately I was giving two or three workshops a day – permanently travelling to a succession of different bacterial micro-climates, in hospitals, day-care centres, elderly care-homes, prisons. I succumbed to a succession of respiratory and sinus infections and still had to keep talking and talking and talking. I also gave lectures to social workers, care workers and community care workers, pointedly without notes: *Here I am, with no visible means of support, to prove that working with words can make you more coherent. I am shy and easily folded, but I am also standing up while you stare at me and making this noise.* The various pressures – to be coherent, to be brave, to be functional while tired, energetic while ill – were wearing me down. I found it difficult to apply what little I'd taken on board at university when it came to speaking. I vaguely knew how to deal with theatre spaces, but was only ever in a range of dry-aired and often mayhem-filled rooms. By the end of most days, my throat was sore. Right at the beginning of what I always feel uncomfortable referring to as my career, I was deep in the joy of discovering writing's power – for myself and in others, in so many side-lined and patronised others. But I was also literally losing my voice.

So I went to a Lady Who Taught Elocution. (Why are so many practitioners in this area women? We'll get to that . . .) I was given taxing sentences about rugged rocks and ragged rascals and taken right back to my school days and the speech and drama lessons which were supposed to render me confident and plain-speaking, but which mainly folded me even tighter. At school there had been more rocks and rascals and colours of leather and Peter Piper getting on my wick while I jammed – can this be true? – a plastic prop between my front teeth to keep my jaws open. The prop made me feel crippled, a muscle-spasmed cause for concern.

I didn't sound like that first school speech specialist and I didn't want to. I remember her saying once, with puzzled distaste, something along the lines of, 'You seem to like your voice the way it is . . .' This didn't seem helpful, or relaxing. And I do remember her name, I'm just not going to pass it on.

When I submitted myself – shamefaced, or more accurately tongue-tied – to the Lady Who Taught Elocution, I paid money I barely had to practise the same old tongue-twisters. I said things no one would ever say, or want to.

I also had to read out passages from various books. One week, I was presented with a section from some Russian novel. It was a remarkably featureless description of a corridor. I could do nothing with it. The elocutionist asked me what sense I found most stimulating. Although I had never formally considered this, I was immediately able to answer that smell was my key sense. For example, I recognise people more by smell than sight. She asked me what the paragraph smelled like. When I focused on the piece, I discovered that it did indeed have a real and complex smell: wet plaster, neglect, old cabbage . . . If I held on to that information, I could then read the words as if they had an emotional and visual depth, which I couldn't find by simply poking them with my intellect. I may not have liked her teaching style, but this was gold. If I reverse-engineered the process with the Russian paragraph, if I tried analysing my own writing in terms of my senses and clarity of voice, then I might be able to increase my efficacy as a writer. I also noticed that a very minimal improvement in my ability to say one word after another led to a much larger improvement in my willingness to take risks on the page, to push the prose forward to its next stage. I walked away from my lessons and their expense with advice to avoid dairy produce for the sake of my sinuses and to set down a saucer of water in rooms for the sake of lubricated speaking. As if my voice were a thirsty pet. Mainly, I was still aware that I wasn't in charge of the sounds I was making, or even happily out of control.

Keep relaxing, sinking, inoutbreathing.

On the out-breath, Ros presses at the base of my spine, buttocks – suitably ridiculous word – thighs. More emotional history unreels lightly in the background – all those leg-trembling childhood days, wanting to run – adult tensions – an adolescent accident: the Leabrook Methodist Chapel Christmas party when I was thirteen and over-excited and fell from standing to sitting in less than a thought – incredible pain at the time and my grandmother worried by the way my face changed when I landed. Gran invited half the chapel to visit me as I sat in the bath and soaked my, as it turned out, broken arse – heads round the door and good lucks, for God's sake . . . Then from my late twenties onwards I have the pain that comes from owning a sacrum that healed oddly and now tends to the left. Like me. And then there's typing, hunching, compressing – my body gathering its strength to kick out a disc and make me stop, reassess.

And is it a coincidence that all the people who have tried to work with my voice have been women, that lists of recommendations have only comprised women? Is this because women are quieter, quietened, more in need?

My maternal grandmother – she of the Leabrook Methodists – was loud and awkward, wore above-the-knee skirts in her sixties, had been a flapper, owned a laugh so loud it could fill a theatre, would be up on stage to volunteer in any and every end-of-the-pier show. She was tempestuous – with her own mother, her own daughter and with her second husband: the grandpop I knew. To be frank, she could be suddenly and inexplicably scalding with anyone. Her first husband and, as they say, the love of her life, died suddenly soon after their marriage. She broke and then healed oddly and definitely tended to the left. I increasingly suspect that I resemble her.

My mother was much quieter, a murmuring soft presence, a storyteller by stealth, low phrases slipping in, a hand around mine, all those soundless hugs. While I was growing up she was unconversational, shy and nervy – a woman in a punishing marriage, a woman with an RP accent in post-industrial Dundee, a woman who'd been brought up by her grandparents who had remained very Welsh, although they lived near Birmingham. She had developed a North Welsh accent as a child. She went RP during her teacher training – 'You can't sound like that, people will laugh.' Now she's happily long divorced, happily back in the Midlands and – seven years after her move – is garrulous, expansive, confabulating, dramatic, a musical presence. Something of her always dances, the way she did on good days when I was a kid: simply dancing for the joy of it. She won a gold medal for both ballroom and Latin when she was younger and single, when she was at home.

She kept that quiet.

These days, it's louder. One word at a time she has returned to herself, come back to full, and fully audible, life.

And I think of all those women I've met who can't quite say, 'Yes.' They make do with a little gasped inhalation and a nod, as if stating a preference might in some way expose or betray them. And 'No' doesn't even seem to arise, only the words that compromise, avoid it.

And why, when I do stand-up comedy – apparently when any woman does stand-up comedy – is 'You've got a big mouth' the most common heckle? The standard unimaginative heckle for guys is, 'You're shit.' But we get 'You've got a big mouth.' The simple act of talking while female is apparently, for some audiences, wrong, wrong, wrong. The standard female comeback is, of course, tediously simple, 'No, love, I don't have a big mouth

– you just have a tiny cock.' Which is also, in a way, wrong, wrong, wrong. But also, in way, right, right, right.

I remember telling this to Cicely Berry – grand, scary, famous Cicely Berry, who haunted my student days with her authoritative books and the tail end of the RSC's golden years: productions that woke up the lines and made them happen *here, in this moment, new.* She's slightly frail now, if still wiry, and perhaps mildly deaf, although there is every chance that simply being in the same room with her made me crumple internally and therefore lapse into mumbling – back to Muttley again. When I quoted, 'You've got a big mouth', the air changed around her and someone who might have been mistaken for a little old lady tensed and thrummed with a deep and righteous fury. It's her belief that we speak to save our lives. I do not disagree. Preventing someone from speaking is therefore a kind of murder – and too often a rehearsal for the real thing. Try telling Dame Cicely she's *got a big mouth* – things would not go well with you, I feel.

Almost at the end of this stage in the preparation. Ros rubs down and presses on my stockinged feet – I have to breathe right into my feet – inoutbreathing – plumb my depth.

When I started out with Ros I remembered how good it is to talk in stockinged feet, bared feet, to root into something solid and see where it leads. The old-style elocutionists favour shoes, restraint. When I write, I prefer to have bare feet, and when I speak, also. How could I have forgotten that?

It became clear that when I performed my show, I should have bare feet. This would hopefully connect me to the ground and one of my voices to another – the one in my head to the one that should reach to my feet, plumb my depth, see what's in there. This sounds like the sort of arty gibberish that usually leaves me nauseous. Even so, it makes sense. It feels like making sense.

It also meant I would spend a number of gigs wondering what

I'd stepped on and if I was bleeding, asking stage managers and all manner of men who knew where brooms were kept if they would mind just sweeping the stage, please. This became one of the ways to know how the technical parts of an evening would go – was the Stage Manager/Technician/Person with Keys to the Lighting Box understanding about my feet? Understanding: lighting cues would be on time and probably intuitively tweaked for the venue. Not Understanding: I couldn't rely on anything being lit as I'd expected and should sweep the stage myself, if I could find a broom.

I would usually unwind after a performance by washing in whatever facilities were available. My feet would almost always be happily filthy, as if I'd been playing outside. Remembering my mother dancing barefoot – Steeleye Span on the telly – 'All Around My Hat' – difficult for dancing . . .

I don't dance, not really. Can't remember when I stopped playing outside, stopped shouting, discovered I can't scream.

Remembering that evening in Edinburgh – nice gig, nice crowd. Other comedy gigs had gone well before, but this was different – this time I sounded like myself. I was saying what I wanted to, the way I wanted to. My voice found me. And we shouted and said bad words and had a laugh. We played outside.

The show had an early outing in a Glasgow arts centre. Our start was slightly delayed: people had difficulty finding their way through the building, and outside someone was threatening to commit suicide by jumping off a roof. At the time, I only knew about the first of those problems. I was inside trying to be the opposite of killing myself.

As it worked out, the guy didn't jump. Only talked about jumping – the story of it being enough.

The day was oppressively hot and the space I'd been given was additionally warmed by vast areas of window. I and the audience broiled. At about fifty minutes in, the script tries to illustrate the power of language and so, as planned, I talked about toothache in a slightly hypnotic way. A woman at the front – latecomer and therefore less heat-exhausted – dropped immediately into manifest dental torment. I was both delighted it had worked and worried she wouldn't emerge from her pain.

Fortunately, she did – the words that told her she was well again convinced as fully as the ones that had disturbed her. Somewhere, as I rolled on to my conclusion, I was aware that: a) I never find positive words as convincing as negative ones myself, and b) I needed significant public liability insurance. What if I proved that language is indeed hugely influential by getting myself sued, courtesy of an audience member, plagued by a phantom molar?

Inoutbreathing. If my problem is partly a story, a narrative of fears and accidents – fall from a horse, ill-advised lifting, the stresses of self-employment, the stresses of stress – then how can its physical symptoms be cured? What if I can't find the story to talk myself out of my box?

After the toothache comes the metaphorical sugar. The audience is asked to imagine somebody they love, the details of what and why they love, why they smile when they think of their love. They are asked to tell themselves the story of their love. And, simply because they have been asked to, they do so. How remarkable this is – a room moving, because you have made noises at it. Then, together, we write I LOVE YOU on the air with our fingers – sounds corny – is corny – but it works. And means that I get to look up at a house full of smiles: in Toronto, Richmond Virginia, Galway, Bath, Hebden Bridge . . . all those smiles. And one afternoon in Edinburgh a couple imagine, write and then look at each other, link their respective fingers, smile again. They were in the same story, each telling the other.

This is a version of an exercise I sometimes use in workshops. Think of your love, focus and then write I LOVE YOU. Feel the pleasant impact of that in your body, your arm, your hand, your face. Now look at the words. To you, they may be a distillation of everything, the sum of your best joys. To your reader, they are a cliché. One of your principal problems as a writer is how to give your reader their version of that pleasant impact using only words – no meeting, no touching, only those little lines of marks.

Inoutbreathing and Ros talking me through my part in this and hers – the story of where we are, our here and now. She lifts my legs by the ankles as I try to be limp, to be soft and easy – inoutbreathing – and she shakes me looser.

I am aware of the weight transferring down to my pelvis, of the energy there, the fact that a part of the voice is from the hips, in the way that our movement comes from the hips: where a boxer's punch would start from, or a dancer's step. And this is a sexual energy, something which shouldn't be absent from voice, ashamed, locked in, locked out.

One of my principal problems as a person: I have never been able to say, 'I love you.' I was in my forties before I could write it, if it contained any personal meaning. Love – a word too horribly itself: starts with a push, your tongue pressing forward into everywhere that's not yourself – it's only your teeth that save you – and then a sudden opening, openness, the shape of surprise, shadow of a kiss, softness, plumbing the depth of yourself from your lips to the pit of your stomach (the soles of your feet if you'd like, if you can manage) and then the gentlest of endings, your mouth tensed around a final sound, this kind of close-by-the-ear and private thrum.

L - O - V - E

I know the theory.

But I never said it. Not to relatives, friends, not for the sake of an emotion that should perhaps be shouted, painted on hoardings, turned into operas and neon and fireworks and banners dragged out behind biplanes in the traditional manner. The more important it was that I should mention my affection, the quieter I became.

So I never told my grandmother I loved her, not even when she would rage at nothing, batter out insults and strange, urgent anxieties and end by yelling at the room – wiry little woman, fierce – 'You don't love me! None of you love me!' At these times none of us, myself included, would do the simple thing, the proper thing and say, 'I love you. You're loved. Of course you're loved. You're prickly and crazy, all temperament and elbows, but you are loved.' My grandmother, who was addicted to chocolate Brazil nuts and *True Romance* magazines: the doctors and nurses and star-crossed youngsters and troubled but noble souls finding each other and declaring declarations of startling and voluminous devotion. My grandmother, who could Charleston and Black Bottom – not prettily, but with enough style to fill any room. My grandmother who'd sit in bed reading happy endings, while my grandpop quietly brought her a hot-water bottle and tea, kissed her, both of them aware that her first husband stayed in her dreams for the whole of her life, a comforting torment. And her daughter and grand-daughter lived far away in Scotland and she was only really happy when we were back in the same room – so she could shout at us all at once.

She was always scared that her second husband would slip away on her like the first and leave her alone. He didn't. She was the one who left first; suffering a massive stroke one night, she dropped rapidly into a coma, unspeaking. Grandpop had been trained in first aid. He knew what was wrong, but when he called my mother he just said, 'I can't wake her up.' In our family, we never do tell each other much.

My eyes have been closed until this point, I have been bobbing somewhere inside myself, but this is when – inoutbreathing – I have to come back, roll on to my side and tuck briefly, gently, into a foetal curl, eyes opening before I roll again, tuck my feet under myself and slowly stand, unwind upwards in a slow curve: set the hips in place, the small of the back, and higher and higher still and the shoulders – widen the shoulders, imagine them broad and opening and – inoutbreathing – the neck and head last, the heaviest and worriedest thing left till last. Imagine your skull rising on its vertebrae and a sense of it floating, aspiring beyond itself.

Strangers have been uncoiling me into a standing position ever since my ill-fated total of two sessions at Music and Movement – another attempt to fit me into a confident shape: one leotard amongst many in a chilly Scottish church hall. And I actually was asked to be a tree. I never have wanted to be a tree.

I've never told my mother I love her – my truly wonderful, dancing mother. I am sure she knows I do, but she's never heard it.

Almost forty years later and for the first time, I do want to be me. I want to be me standing. It's all right for me to do that, to take up space.

Be myself, have my voice, see how that goes. I want to say what I have to, when I have to. This is about more than just writing, this is about my whole life.

I never told my grandfather I loved him. Not even when I was almost certain I was seeing him for the last time, when I was saying goodbye at the end of our last time. I write 'almost certain' because it will make me feel better – as if a small doubt prevented me from being decently expressive. In fact, I knew: *say it now or you'll never be able to.* I didn't.

But I loved him. I loved all of him and perhaps not especially his voice, but certainly I very much loved his voice. For many years I would only see him for two weeks in each year and the rest of the time we'd make do with telephone calls: a chat with Gran and the receiver handed over to Grandpop: a relatively shy and taciturn man. All the same, the sound of him would feel like sitting on his lap with my ear at his chest – *this is the dent where the cannonball hit me* – and listening to his beautiful, big lies. And he told me the truths of him, too: what he got up to and when, bits of philosophy, self-defence tips, tales from wild days in London when he slept with a knife under his pillow, boxed and fought dirty, took dancing lessons for his footwork. *If you're scared, they don't beat you – you beat yourself.* Even now, the thought of his voice can bring me close inside the smell of Lifebuoy soap and Swarfega – that's him fresh in from work and washed. He was a chargehand tool-setter and the workshop's Safety Man. And he favoured powerful aftershaves: Old Spice, or Hai Karate, the taste of Player's Navy Cut under that and the sharp tang of the workshop – metal and ingenuity and dangers. I'd drink him in – *inoutbreathing* – and listen to his heart beat. He was a soft-hearted man, that's what failed him in the end. And I'd be lost in his baritone and tender purring. He had a quiet Black Country accent – not Brummy, not the same in any way. It's an eccentric and playful way of speaking, it savours vowels and is fancifully gentle. And, when he was happy, he'd purr.

Late on Saturday nights we would sit together – my grandmother gone to bed – lights off and some harmless old horror movie on the telly. He would be in his big leather recliner and I would be perched on a cushion between his slippered feet. I'd hook my arms up, one over each of his knees, and lean my back against his chair. And we would be fine and soft and easy and he would purr enough for both of us: big man, muscular, former card-sharp, former middleweight and quite possibly bare-knuckle boxer, featherlight dancer, hair Brylcreemed back like a gangster, knew how to pose with a cigarette in a photograph, make that classic 1950s movie-star shape. And he was mine, my safest place, my best place. And I never said.

Too late now.

He never said he loved me, either. He wasn't the type. But I knew that he did. It was certain as holding our hands together and putting them both in his overcoat pocket: as warm and comfortable as that. And as wonderful as him calling me *Tiger*. Nobody calls me Tiger, why would they? And no one will say it in his voice.

Standing. Upright. Breathing as if I never have and arms wheeling in the manner suggested. It's oddly tiring and also intoxicating to breathe at your full tilt. The first time I did this I was eventually unable to stop myself laughing. Facing a professor and laughing, giddy. Ros didn't mind, she understood.

She moves us on to the next stage of the process: the move from interior to exterior, breathing as if for observers, an audience, reaching towards the people I want to . . . what? Touch? Change? Contact? All these possibilities.

I recall again the passage from Last Words of the Executed *by Robert K. Elder, which describes a mass execution of Native Americans: thirty-eight men singing and dancing to comfort each other before the end, trying to hold hands and shouting out their names and 'I'm here! I'm here!' Proof of life.*

Alfred Wolfsohn was born in Berlin in 1896. He was a loner whose mother sang to him. A law student, he was conscripted into the German army and fought in the trenches during World War One. He was both horrified and changed by the sounds of men in agony around him, human beings screaming their last. The life in their cries was extraordinary to him – that the dying should sound more alive than the living seemed somehow wrong. He returned home in some ways broken and then healed oddly – he gave up the law and began to study singing. Dissatisfaction with his teachers led him to begin shaping his own theory of voice – at its heart the belief that we should express ourselves fully, physically and emotionally, throughout life, rather than only becoming entirely ourselves when we are dying, beyond help. Wolfsohn began to teach, blending inspirations from literature, art, psychology and horror. When Hitler's National Socialists came to power, they brought in new horrors with hideously effective propaganda – distorted voices, lying voices, sounds of the not-quite-living to summon up pandemic death. Wolfsohn, a Jew, fled Germany for London and devoted his energies to uncovering another way of speaking and of being. He continued his teaching until only days before he died in 1962, working with singers and actors, including Roy Hart.

Hart was a South African loner and fee-free student at RADA. He felt his life and career were transformed by meeting and working with Wolfsohn, although RADA didn't exactly smile on Wolfsohn's influence. Hart became Wolfsohn's most passionate supporter, acting and teaching himself, working with psychiatrists, actors and singers. Hart went on to found the Roy Hart Theatre and, although he died in a car crash in 1975, the theatre continues to explore Wolfsohn's ideas. Roy Hart's diary says of Wolfsohn, 'He accepted me just the way I was.'

An original member of the Roy Hart Theatre, Nadine George, went on to found the Voice Studio International, which is based in London. Ros Steen has been deeply influenced by working with Nadine George.

Which is a long way of saying the faith that a voice can, and should, do good to its owner and to the wider world is now, as far as I can make it, a part of how I breathe. I owe this to three generations of work and thinking. This fits well with the blurry suspicion I have always had that if my written voice gets me attention, then I should write at least some of the time to focus that attention on harms that should be prevented, or undone. I play with my shoes off and get paid for it, I'm allowed to be heard. Part of being heard should, I feel, be about speaking for the silenced. Not that fiction doesn't do that, too – it is a sustaining and world-shifting thing itself – but sometimes it's necessary to point out that it's hard to enjoy a story when there's screaming going on.

This is where we pause. I sit. I sip water. Ros asks me if I want to talk about anything. Sometimes I can articulate what's going on: physical sensations, thoughts, feelings, flashbacks, how the process seems to be feeding back into the novel, or the show. Sometimes there's simply this joy.

Here I am.

It is often remarkable to fnd a joy in that.

We'll go through to the piano next.

Not the least unsettling sentence – 'And now we'll go through to the piano.'

But it's okay. I don't mind. It'll be fine.

I remember our initial session – awing and oohing and ahing – and it seemed that the top of my head would fly off, that I'd fall over, that some great big something was waking up inside my chest.

Who'd have thought.

Alfred Wolfsohn, for one. Ros, for another.

It is 2001. I'm in Canada and waiting to do a reading as part of a Canadian literary festival. I enjoy readings and I am amongst friends. The only person I don't know here is Michael David Kwan, author of *Things That Must Not Be Forgotten*, an autobiography based on his childhood during the Japanese occupation of China. He is the first reader, slightly nervous. We are all looking forward to dinner after the event, getting to know Michael. He seems a delicate, courteous man, a gentle presence. Michael is introduced and walks out beyond the curtain into the pleasant little theatre in Victoria, Vancouver Island. We other readers sit on the stage, but behind the curtain in a warm, muzzy dark. We listen. Michael tells the audience that he's nervous and they make a small, sympathetic murmur. They sound nice. He begins to read a passage where he is playing in a tree and a Japanese soldier spots him. It is suddenly clear that the soldier may mistake him for a spy and shoot him. He may never get to tell us the story of a long, full life. He feels the wings of death flutter over him. And here Michael breaks off, says that he isn't well and then we hear him fall and his head crack off the wood of the stage.

There are doctors in the audience who rush down as we hear Michael give a last breath, ragged and awful. We have never heard anyone die before, but we all know what this is, what this means. This is dying.

We listen through the curtain. There is nothing we can do, we can't even seem to leave. The doctors perform CPR and fresh breath rushes in. Michael gasps like a man rescued from water.

Then he sinks again, is brought back, sinks . . . We hear Michael David Kwan die twice and come back to life three times.

Once he's stable, he is rushed out past us to the hospital, where he will later die and no coming back, only gone and silent.

At the piano, I sing scales.
Singing scales seems to suggest something irrelevant, indulgent: crinolines and embroidery next.

But our scales are to do with not being gone and not being silent.
We start with the scale of C Major as a kind of support. The
sound live and different every time.

The reading was, of course, cancelled. All of us, audience and
writers milling in the foyer, thinking of people we'd like to call,
to be with, picturing their frailty and our own.

We work according to a division of the voice into four qualities –
two 'male' and two 'female', the deep and the high. Intellectually,
these make minimal sense to me, but while I'm singing they feel
completely identifiable, suggest wholly different ways of telling stories
in themselves and in combination with each other. I'm forty-six and
clearly I know very little about myself or anyone else, about how we
might sing and what would be lost if we were gone. And we will
be gone. We all go.

Dying. Grandpop always called it *shortness of breath.* 'Know what
he died of? *Shortness of breath.*'
   I wasn't there when my grandfather died. I was too late. My
plane landed at about the time he left me. He was lying in a hospital
bed with his brother beside him. He knew I was on my way.
   The night before I'd been sitting in a restaurant – business
dinner – and suddenly the room had swayed and I had smelt his
perfumes, been rocked. I don't believe in supernatural phenomena,
but if I'd had any sense I'd have gone to the airport then, there
might have been a flight.
   But I think I was also afraid to face him, worried that I wouldn't
know what I should say.
   Inexcusable.

Now the singing will focus on one quality, will initially draw my
voice up higher than I can reach, into my head and then beyond

me, into high air. Then we'll turn and descend through squeaks, to horrible sharps and then into my range and lower and lower and finally down to the place where I'm exhaling from the depth of me, no music left.

The first time I did this – me emptying my lungs – I thought of Michael David Kwan and the sound of his death. I knew I was listening to the way that I would die, the first sound that I wouldn't hear, the end of my breath. I didn't feel sad, more lonely and maybe tired.

All my life, I have seen and felt and heard words as they have rehearsed and defined and conjured the energies that save and illuminate lives. They have saved mine. Over and over. I had a good education, I had a huge well-stocked library I could walk to when I was a kid, a house full of books, a mother who taught me how to read before I even got to school. Child of a single working mother, I was able to attend university because I received a grant.

Now I live in a country where mastery of language will become increasingly difficult to attain. Education is constricting, libraries are closing, the paths into words are being blockaded on all sides. There may never be book-burnings in Britain – if you've stolen the books already, there'll be no need for public bonfires. For many it will be harder, if not impossible, to break open the codes that tell our story to ourselves, that march out, letter after letter, to speak in our absence, record us, translate us, claim our rights, celebrate our joys. Slipping into the minds and mouths and hearts of others may soon be something only certain people are allowed to do.

And – perhaps unsurprisingly – voice work has never been part of a national curriculum, freely available to all. Public speakers, lawyers, captains of industry and politicians may be coached in persuasion, some school kids may be driven to abandon their accents, but the exploration of voice could do so much more for so many more. Depending on their training and career paths, actors will always have to at least maintain their voices, and by now it will be obvious that I feel writers should, too, but expressive citizens, informed and informative consumers, an articulate electorate – what would happen if our voices unleashed that? What if, on the page and in the air, we found muscular, living freedom, freely expressed?

In my most recent session I worked through the usual process and reached the point of my ascending and then descending through the scale. This time we were exercising an aspect of the Female Voice. I exhausted all the low sounds I could make, sank into simply exhaling. As Ros continued to play lower and lower notes, I breathed out more and more deeply each time until I heard it again – the truth of my departing breath. But this time I didn't feel this was like dying.

No, I was producing these huge sighs, almost racking: jaws open, letting a purpose rise from the heels and punch out.

This time it felt like fury.

It felt like love and being broken and healing oddly, or perhaps not healing at all, staying raw and as alive as I had ever been and proving it, racing it out.

Afterwards, I sat and Ros left the usual space for me to talk about what seemed to be happening.

What seems to be happening?

I am alive.

And I am writing this in a time when there's a great deal that's being broken and taken away, a great pressure towards silence, the closing of unsuitable mouths. But there are so many mouths, so many new and fast and clever ways for them to speak, and there is so much passion to spur on their inventions. All over the world, we may be able to read the start of a story where people with nothing to lose start writing and speaking and screaming so unstoppably that they become different people and make a different world.

This could be a story where we decide to be the opposite of killing ourselves, where we do not kill others.

I hope so.

I hope we can learn to listen, as well as sing.

I know this is a voice. My voice. And yours also. Together we are here and now, alive in this – loud as we like and everything possible – alive in this.

To remove this would be the most severe and crippling form of censorship – to unwrite the books before they are written, to silence the mind and to steal the words that could say, 'I love you', 'I'm dying', 'This has to stop.'

But here I am.

Here you are.

Here we are.

And as long as we have this, any story can be changed, invented, repeated until it can make itself true. We can remember that we are ourselves and that being ourselves requires freedom, imagination, dignity, the chance to speak.

Here I am.

Here you are.

Here we are.

Words

A One-Person Show

In the beginning was . . . a small person, inclined to mumble. In the beginning was . . . the lips the teeth the tip of the tongue and the thought of the shape of the taste of an idea. In the beginning was . . .

It's the 23rd January 2008, and I am London. You know London – colourful cockney characters, the West End dazzle, entirely reliable bankers with little hats . . .

It's the 23rd January 2008 and it's 4 a.m. London is shut. In the whole of Chinatown there's just me and this lady who's sitting in a doorway smoking crack, and because I believe you can only survive London by pretending you're in a novel – by Dickens – I greet her as if she is a perky urchin.

'Good morning, crack-whore.'

'Morning, lady.'

And that is the most sensible conversation I have had in hours – because last night I won a book prize and for ever after journalists have been asking me, 'How do you feel?'

Journalists are very emotional people – they always want to know: 'How do you feel?'

'Tell me, when your entire family was sucked into that combine harvester and their remaining bloody fragments were eaten by particularly ugly dogs – How did you feel?'

Me, I don't know what I feel, and meanwhile I am being distracted by the other question they keep asking, which is: 'What're you going to do with the money, Al?'

And I have this incredible urge to say, 'Spend it on Pringles and sex.'

Which isn't true, but I have a story going round and round at the back of my head repeating and repeating, so eventually I will believe it's true. And say it, possibly on live television.

And meanwhile why don't I feel anything? I just won a prize. If I can't be happy for myself, I can be happy for my words – they just won a prize . . . Does this mean it's like a bad marriage now, and we lie there side by side in the dark after making paragraphs and maybe I'm embarrassed, because at that vital moment I shouted out the name of another book . . .

Has it come to this?

So – okay – I'll try to remember when it all started: me and the words. What was, for instance, my first word?

And I know that. My first word was *no*. Sign of a Calvinist childhood. 'No.' People kept saying it to me – *No* – Oh, but I was saying it back.

'*No*. I say *no* to your *no*. I am a small but incredibly determined person and when I am grown up I may even say yes – probably to weird stuff that I'll regret later – but I'm gonna say it, anyway. I am going to be a *positive Scot*.

'Yeah . . . On second thoughts, my second word won't be *yes* . . . I think it'll be *UP*.'

It was, that was my first word – *up*. Anyone I saw who was taller than me – which was everyone – I would go to them and say, 'UP.'

'No.'

'Up.'

'No.'

'U-uuu-UP!'

I was a frustrated child. And, of course, because of going to

340

be a novelist – I was troubled. You have no idea how difficult it is being a four-year-old girl who wants to dress only in black. There is no Mothercare Goth Range. I checked. To be more interesting, I tried affecting a limp. So people would look at me and say, 'Aw, she does really well for a little girl with a limp.'

'Yes. Yes, I do. I'm incredibly brave.'

I considered running away. But I wouldn't have got far, what with my appalling limp. So I was trapped in Dundee. Born there. That's sort of like being born in the late 1750s, but without the fun of cholera and public executions. Dundee. The City of *The Dandy* – they made it there – and *The Beano* and *Just Seventeen* . . . And *The People's Friend*. How best might I summarise the typical *People's Friend* letter . . . ?

'*Dear People's Friend, I have been knitting a husband since 1953. I now lack only one ball of flesh-tone Sirdar 4-ply wool to complete his finishing touches. Perhaps your readers can assist. Yours sincerely, Impatient of Brechin.*'

Not just Dundee, but Dundee in the 1970s – that's power cuts, Cybermen on telly who could flatten the city centre with futuristic weapons, district councillors who did flatten it using, well, who can say, but quite possibly friends and family working in the construction and related industries – I mean, are you in any way surprised that I started inventing alternative realities? I really did eventually dream of running away to Old London Town, where I would become a perky urchin and scamper up and down alleyways. You need very few qualifications for scampering. And then I would take real teeth from poor people to make false teeth for rich people. Because I knew about the past – I was going to live there and so I'd done research. I knew that in the past people made medical appliances out of just anything – George Washington: wooden teeth. Tycho Brahe – sixteenth-century astronomer, I was a precocious child – he had a metal nose. They just loved making things out of metal: metal arms, metal knees, metal elbows.

'How are you liking your metal feet, then?'

'I don't like them. They are heavy and metally and clanky.'

'What about your metal nose, then? We've put a clapper inside, so every time you shake your head it rings like a bell. Two for one!'

'So I cannot even shake my head in sad disgust without sounding like a cat toy . . .'

I knew your average Olde English conversation would have run thus.

'Ho, Sirrah – why liest thou in the street on thy back?'

'Well, my toffee leg melted and then my glass walking stick snapped. I am afraid that I must lie here for ever unless I receive assistance.'

'Alas, good sir, I cannot offer you assistance because of my entire spinal column having been replaced with these strips of gingham.'

Yes, it's nonsense. But where would you be without nonsense? In Dundee.

The imaginary past was one of my happy places. And like all of my other happy places – Gallifrey, Middle Earth, the Land of Green Ginger – it was in here, in my head.

And in here it just got happier and fuller, because my mother taught me to read before I went to school – which was a good thing – until I got to school and worked out that no one else could yet. And so I pretended that I couldn't, and I really couldn't add up and so that made me tense. And when I'm tense I tend to hunch . . . and I'd already got the limp and the whole black look that was working really well for me and . . . basically I went through the whole of my primary education looking like a very tiny Richard the Third.

Now is the playtime of my discontent . . .

My parents, of course, wanted me to be normal. But they were distracted by one of their words – DIVORCE. They got one – which was a good thing, because they didn't like each other, but this meant my mum and me ended up living for a while in a residential caravan in Arbroath. That's basically a big wooden shed with a potentially fatal gas fire. And if you've never stood in a big, damp shed, inhaling just a tiny bit too much carbon monoxide, and stared out through the sleet at an illuminated sign that reads 'Pleasure Land' – then you have a less than full understanding of the cruelty of words.

Not that I understood words then, either. But I did know that I liked them. I remember watching *Three Sisters* on telly. *Three Sisters*, you'll remember, a play by Chekhov in which three sisters spend a lot of their time staring into the middle distance and saying

'*To Moscow, To Moscow . . .*'

And part of you does think, 'You dozy mares, just go to the railway station and tell the man – "To Moscow, To Moscow – day return, please, and we have a family railcard, because of being sisters."'

But part of you does understand – *to* . . . Wanting to go to anywhere else, to be anybody else, to do anything other than what you're doing. *To.* You do understand.

And I got my *to*. I went to university. Where I was a Theatre Studies and Drama student – not English – because I'd already worked out that I was going to be safer saying other people's words, rather than writing my own. Because remember, when you're still a little kid and you have a great story in your head, you're bursting with it – there's a man and he's in a wardrobe and drinking tea and there are snakes – from outer space . . . and the only thing that could make your story better would be if you could somehow put it into someone else's head, cos then it would be bigger, and so you look and you look and you find someone and you tell them your story. And your story makes them happy and that makes you happy, and so everyone is happy. And then you get a little bit older and you've got another story and the man's drinking Tizer with a biscuit and there are more snakes and a lizard that can read your mind . . . and so you look and you look and you find someone and you're going to tell them and then they say . . .

'No. Don't tell lies. Don't make things up, you're too old for that.'

And a little bit of you falls off, turns to dust and blows away.

But then you go to school and – I worked this out really quickly – when you go to school, if you write the story down, teachers *have* to read it. They get paid for that stuff – so you write the story about the man and the biscuits, and the Tizer and the snake, and you hand it in and you wait . . . For minutes, hours, days . . .

And then you get it back . . . and it's all covered in red, as if it's bleeding. And yes, I need you to tell me if my story's no good, so I can make it better, but if you don't tell me the right way, then I'm going to be too young to say – *Hey. I needed that.*

So I was a Theatre Studies and Drama student, thank you very much, and – as such – I got used to doing incredibly stupid things for no good reason at all. But then one day a visiting tutor came to tute us and got each of us – eighteen, I think, always an oversubscribed course, Theatre Studies and Drama has so many applications in the real world – she got all eighteen of us and she gave each one of us one word from the same sentence from a novel – by Dickens. And we stood in a line and – one by one – we each said our words and it sounded dreadful. It was like a little dog coughing – like eighteen different people saying eighteen different words, from eighteen different books from eighteen different non-parallel universes.

And then she said, 'Whatever word you had – that is now *your word*. And for the next three hours you're going to be working with *your word*.'

344

My word was *the*.

Oh, and we worked with our words. We whispered them, we said them to each other, we lay on the floor and whispered them, we yelled them, we had to make a gesture for our word . . .

I was not happy.

But then after the three hours she got us all together again and lined us up and – one by one – we said our words and it sounded beautiful. It was as if the sentence said itself. It was musical and manifest and I thought: *I want that.*

I have no idea what that is – clearly – it had taken me three hours to come to the edge of the beginning or the start of understanding the definite article. I know nothing about nothing. But I do know – *I want that.* That is the beauty of the thing itself, its proper name. I didn't know words gave you that.

And, at about the same time, somebody told me if you're a classical actor and you play large roles, classical parts, Shakespeare – you tend to become a different shape. Because Shakespeare, he's a little bit fussy about when he lets you breathe – so you end up with a torso that is a kind of variation on a theme of opera singer.

Let me recap: this is a man you'll never meet – a dead man – and he can make you a different shape. All of those words in all of those minds, all of those mouths. *I want that.*

But I'd worked out that if I really went for the acting thing, the best I could expect would be to occasionally stumble onstage and say . . .

'Your horse awaits without, my Lord. Thank you.'

Which wasn't going to make me happy. Or anyone else. So I went home. To Dundee. And unemployable. Not that I didn't try. Word of advice – no matter how desperate you are, no matter how low you fall, never become a children's puppeteer. It's a terrible job. Trapped in a hot canvas box while unattended children cut the canvas and try to stab you in the feet, and meanwhile you're unable to defend yourself because of your hands being inserted inside endearing woodland creatures. You can't punch a toddler with your hand up a squirrel, they just don't feel it.

So we'd come home – Mr Fluffy and Mr Squirrelly and me – and we wouldn't ask each other, 'How was your day?' And I couldn't go and sit in bohemian cafés, sipping coffee, flirting with the waiters, trying to knit absinthe. Because of being in Dundee. No, I would sit in bed to keep warm and read books about people who sat in bed to keep warm and wrote books about people who sat in bed to keep warm and wrote books.

And I started thinking and then I started writing.

Now. Who wears shoes in bed? No one. Who, outside of bad pornography, wears socks in bed? No one. So I was barefoot. And if you start writing barefoot, you're going to get used to writing barefoot and then you'll feel comfortable writing barefoot and then you'll be superstitious about writing barefoot and pretty soon you'll feel you can't do anything you care about that has to do with words without being barefoot.

Imagine how convenient that has made the last twenty-five years of what I laughingly call my career. I work a lot on trains. And in universities. At home I could just get frostbite and lose a toe.

But there I am barefoot and reading, and then barefoot and writing and all lit up. I don't even know why, except that I'm no use to anyone, not even myself, but when I write I go to places I've never been to, and I can be people I'll never be and I can do things I've never done. Yet. And that's the beginning of power.

Skip three years of 'No, we don't like your story.'

'No, we hate your story.'

'No, we hate you.'

And then finally, I'm published. I'm really published – in a whole book. And I have to go to London and *do lunch* with my editor – I have an editor – and the restaurant for lunch is so posh that the waiter reads the menu to you because you're going to be far too busy to do your own reading any more. But I like doing my own reading and I'm not posh. I'm currently living on potatoes and cheese my granny sends me because she gets it free from the EU dairy lagoon – in the 1980s if you knew enough pensioners you could live well . . . But, still – I'm published.

I'm so published I've had an author photograph taken . . . In which I must not smile, because then I will look like I've swallowed a circus pony and it's trying to climb back out. I have been advised. I went into my publisher's offices and, yes, everyone there does seem to be called Miffy, or Muffy, or Buffy, and you do feel like enquiring, 'Is there anybody here who isn't one of Santa's little helpers?' But still – I'm published.

And then back in the restaurant – remember the restaurant – it turns out I misheard the soup and when it arrives it is, in fact, cold avocado and bacon – which is, if you think about it, cold, salty, greenish-grey . . . basically like drinking the phlegm of a stranger . . . But, still – I'm published.

Not that I'm making a living – to do that, I lead workshops. That's what you do when you can't write yet: you lead workshops for other people who can't write yet, and hope they can't write yet a little bit more than you can't.

I was just amazed to have a job, but then I was amazed all over again because I worked with people in mental hospitals and prisons and day-care centres and elderly care facilities – like the one that had a sign on the wall that said 'Today is Wednesday' – every day of the week. Over and over, repeating and repeating until I did believe it was true.

The people I worked with didn't even have their proper names: they were wrinklies and dafties and window-lickers – but once you start writing, you get to pick your proper name and the words to say what you need and what you want. And you live in interesting times – because sometimes, if you meet a human being who thinks you're not really a human being at all, then

347

you don't show them that poem you wrote, because a poem is a very human thing and it might disturb them. But sometimes . . . you just go for it – get out of your head, make a bigger happy place.

Like the lady I worked with on a drama project: devising characters and scenes. She was a visually impaired person and she was quite quiet. She would come into rooms and work her way round the walls and not say anything and then she would just sit. She decided she was going to play the part of a nymphomaniac air hostess slash fashion model. And because I lacked faith, I tried to stop her. But she would not be stopped.

And we did the first session and the second session and I was wrapping things up and she interrupted. She said, 'I have a model walk. I want to show you my model walk.' And she stood up – this lady who had never been able to see anything – and she walked right down the middle of the room like a model and then she did a catwalk turn and she walked back. And she was in no way confused about who she was – she knew exactly who she was. And she wanted to be more of the same.

So when people come up to me and say, 'Ah, but language is essentially meaningless. When I say the word *chair*, I mean something completely different to what you mean when you say *chair* . . .'

I don't actually have any time for that.

Point One: what exactly are you using to tell me that language is meaningless?

Point Two: your chair makes you happy and my chair makes me happy, and if we need any more chair-related information it will be in the surrounding sentence, or paragraph, or – heaven help us – chair-based book. And meanwhile I do not believe that if I raced into Wittgenstein's study and yelled, 'Fire!' he'd just say, 'What do you mean, exactly?' . . .

No. He'd be legging it out of the building like everybody else.

And if he didn't, natural selection would render him toasty.

Words are power – it's a cliché, but it's true. Why else would dictators bother to lock up poets – it's not just because poets are often appalling people. Politicians know we are easier to handle when they have our words and we are scared and alone and silent.

But human beings, we're good at words; give us half a chance, a quarter of a chance, any chance at all, and we're all over them. We can manage even very strange and subtle meanings. For example, when you're with someone in a restaurant – table for two – and they reach out and touch your hand and they tell you, 'You know . . . you're a very special person.' You know what that means. We all do know what that means – you're chucked. It's a reverse meaning, it means he's leaving you, changing his number, marrying someone else – but he can't tell you, because of his whole spinal column having been replaced with these strips of gingham.

Advertisers, lawyers, spinners . . . liars – they think we're daft, but we're not. We can work things out. For instance, in 1983 a wordsmith of sorts coined the phrase *repetitive administration of legitimate force*. Which is a fine phrase.

Repetitive – that's a boring, over-and-over sort of word.

Administration – that's boring over-and-over filing, office work.

Of Legitimate – that's legal and fine and dandy, boring filing.

Force – well, that is a bit scary – but in an office, what's it going to involve: paper cuts, a hullabaloo in a quantity surveyor's?

Repetitive administration of legitimate force – a phrase coined in 1983 by a US Army spokesman to describe beating someone in custody and not stopping until they were dead.

We can work it out.

And it's not just the big manipulations – it's those little words, over and over, seeping in.

My mother recently moved to a picturesque, English country village where the local newsagent did not carry the Dundee

Courier & Advertiser. So she took advice and delivery of a popular daily newspaper and she lasted, ladies and gentlemen, one week. Seven days, until her levels of anxiety were so high that she had to stop – she was coming down in the mornings desperately hoping she could open her door and immediately see a black, gay, Gypsy, French, Polish, pre-operative transsexual single mother on benefits, just so that she could do all her hating in one go and still have time for getting to the shops.

All of those words, repeating and repeating: you should hate more, these people – you should fear more, these people – you should be surveilled more, by these people – war is a sad necessity. Over and over until we make them true.

Which is kind of politically incorrect. Then again, I don't know about political correctness. I mean, I don't know about you, but I would quite like my fire-fighters to be able to say they fight fire – because fire is a bad thing, not its fault – but turning up and talking to it roughly will not do the trick. It needs fighting.

I missed my grandfather by half an hour, partly because I couldn't translate 'quite poorly' into 'could die at any moment'.

The truth, that's what I need. That's what gets things done.

Václav Havel, great writer, decided that if enough people in Czechoslovakia told themselves the story that Communism was over in Czechoslovakia, and were in the story that Communism was over in Czechoslovakia, then Communism would be over in Czechoslovakia. And it worked. He called it *The Power of the Powerless*.

Raphael Lemkin – a man of whom very few people have heard. He invented the word genocide. He put it in the dictionary, so he could keep on working to defeat it. He defined it, he found its proper name, so he could make it stop.

Great writers. They're part of why it's a high-status thing to be a writer. And yes, it is a glorious vocation. But if you think about it, a percentage of people who write are just going to be people like me, and if you are people like me, then you can make writing petty and narcissistic in a heartbeat.

Like the time when I was in Sweden and I was thinking, 'I could be big in Sweden – I mean, what ever really happens here? Apart from the Nobel Prize for Literature . . .' And I do an event in Stockholm and it goes really well, and afterwards I have a big queue full of people who want me to put my signature on my books. And there's this woman in the queue and she works her way along and when she reaches me she says, 'Can you write something encouraging.'

And I'm thinking, 'I'm not just going to be big in Sweden. I'm going to be a guru for Swedes everywhere.' And I say, 'Oh, have you been having a dark patch?'

No, no – it's just that I've started the book three times and I just can't seem to get through it.

Which is fair enough. I was there to make her feel better, not the other way around.

The writer's life – arguing with people you made up earlier in deafening and compulsory isolation, in order to please strangers you probably will never, and probably should never, meet.

But that's not a story to tell yourself, because then you'll believe it and you'll have to run – to festivals, readings, the openings of envelopes, just on the road. Where I do want to appear to be witty and friendly and wise, but my entire spinal column has been replaced with a xylophone of pain, and meanwhile I would just like, sometimes, to take advantage of my journeying for flirting. Romance.

Your incredulous silence does you no credit.

I get no help anywhere else.

'Are you A.L. Kennedy?'

Yes.

'Are you a man?'

No.

'You're doing a man's job.'

Well, no, I would like to think the whole typing thing could be attempted by people of all genders, but I do know where this is heading . . .

'Are you a lesbian?'

No. But thanks for asking.

'Well, you're booked in to read in the great, big, out-there gay jamboree tent.'

Which I'm sure will be lovely, if inappropriate, as I have previously mentioned I am not myself a gay person. Very happy to know there is a great big rainbow of sexual orientations and types of love. There is not, in fact – and I know this from bitter personal experience – enough love in the world. But, for me, love would be for the gentlemen.

'We'll have to rewrite the programme.'

Better than me rewriting my life.

And angels and ministers of grace defend me from those festival parties where I have been wrongly described in my absence and then I have to spend those vital first twenty flirting minutes trapped in a corner with some, yes, very nice, earnest young woman with short hair who wants to tell me about how the Outward Bound course she went on has really done wonders for her confidence, because by the time I get clear of her there will be nobody left for me. Except the tweedy men who call me a lady typist – or the one who said, 'Oh, you're so clever, I just want to kiss your brain.'

And how am I expected to travel and to get home after all this fun? – on a plane. What is a plane? Death with snacks. Before you even get aboard, they fingerprint you, they search you, they photograph you, they shout at you – that's pretty much your first day in prison, but without the sex.

And at home, the words are waiting. What is it like: working with words? Well, it's a little bit like taking an infinitely large box containing an infinitely large number of small, possibly furry animals – a bit like hamsters – and then trying to set them out, in order – *stay still* – one after another – *don't do that* – and hoping that you can compel them to say their names in order – *stop it* – in such a way that anyone other than yourself will understand, without your having to *hit them with a hammer*.

And meanwhile you can hear them thinking, 'Found your voice, did you? Maybe next time you'll find some characters and a plot. Oh, and you've won some awards . . . you'll probably never write again. Or better yet – you will – and it'll all be shite.'

I don't even win awards properly. The nicest award I ever got was from the Lannan Foundation – and they're good people, they're American people, they just phone you up and tell you they are giving you a (technical term here) a big wudge of cash. And all you have to do is answer the telephone competently when they call. When I got the call? I'd just had dental surgery and was planning to spend my evening running up and down the corridor, making noises you would associate with putting a puppy in a microwave. And that's when the Lannan Foundation calls.

WHHAgh.

'Hello. Is A.L. Kennedy there? This is the Lannan Foundation. We would like to give you a (technical term) big wudge of cash.'

E-aagh. Thass me.

'O-kay. And are you in perfect medical health at this time?'

I'm taking a lot of drugs.

'I see . . . the bohemian lifestyle . . .'

No. I'm in pain

'Yes, the pain of a sensitive soul, lost in an uncomprehending universe.'

No. I just have a hole in my face.

I mean, I live on caffeine, Complan and crisps – that is, not all the food groups. My life is ridiculous, I get lost, I get tired and bewildered, but I keep on because I get to make stories. I get to be someone I've never been, to go somewhere I can never go, do things I can never do – but I am and I do and I can. I make something out of nothing – that overturns every natural law.

I tell you a story . . . I can tell you a story now . . . about toothache. The way that you have toothache if maybe there's something wrong with a nerve somewhere, and the more you think about it, the more it hurts, throbbing and aching and deeper and stronger and then maybe it gets sharper, really kind of stabs, and it seems to ooze into your other teeth and then the whole jaw and that side of the face, and it's just . . .

It's only words. Airy nothings, colours of breath, and when you breathe in you feel fine and when you breathe out you're better still.

I'll tell you a better story. And this constitutes the audience participation section of the show, about which you were not warned earlier. So I will ask my lovely lighting man to bring up the lights so that I can see you. There. But it's okay. It's audience participation lite. All you have to do is make a magical pointy finger. And all I have to do is stand here and wait until all of you have made a magical pointy finger, or until the end of time, whichever comes sooner. I can see you . . .

And while you wait for the magic to gather in your magical pointy finger, all you have to do is think of someone who makes you smile. Maybe think of the way they smile, the way they sound, or walk, the touch of their hand, the scent of their hair – all the things that mean that when you think of them, you just smile. And in a moment, together, we are going to think of that person who makes us smile and we are going to write together on the air, three little words that should be worn out, that should be tired . . . but we're going to think of that person clearly and strongly and together we're going to write on the air with our magical pointy finger – to them and for them – I LOVE YOU.

354

I write it backwards to help.

But it's only words – they should be able to make you smile. Or feel.

Let me tell you one last story, and this is a story you can be in, as if you were a writer. If you wish. You'll need your magical pointy finger again. It's okay, you're not joining a cult. And in this story you may want to imagine that your whole hand is beginning to fill with golden light – it's a warm and lovely and very fine golden light. And it rises from your wrist, into your palm, into the roots of each finger and on into each joint – warm and very beautiful – and finally your whole hand is full of golden light. It's maybe tingly. It's as if you're gloved in light. And while the golden light builds even more in your hand and your magical pointy finger, you can – if you wish – think of that place (it's usually the solar plexus) where you feel that little spark when you think of someone who makes you smile. And maybe you would like to think that if at any time a part of you had seemed to fall off and turn to dust and blow away, maybe it didn't. Maybe it just hid in that place, where you feel that spark. And maybe – if you wish – you can touch your finger now, full of light, to that place and you can light yourself with thinking, with the way that words wind and bind around each other: light and delight and enlightenment. And maybe you can always do this. Maybe you have whatever you need to make whatever you need to make. If you wish. Your story. You can take it home. It comes free with the pointy finger.

But it's only words – dull little, plain little words like *yes*, *no*, *up*, *the* – but look what they do. I never fell out of love with words. Back in London, when I won the prize, I didn't feel anything, because I don't write for prizes. They are very nice. Pringles and sex are nice. Very nice. But I don't write for Pringles. And because of a slight miscalculation, I don't really write for sex. Which is a good thing, because the only way – I hate to say this – to really do it is for love. Which is a good thing. And a terrible thing – it means people can manipulate me, can not pay me, I'll work every hour God sends, I can have entire relationships with real human beings – beginning, middle, end – and not absolutely notice. But that's just currently my story. I can change that. I can rewrite. And I still get to be barefoot and writing and all lit up. Or barefoot and reading and all lit up – it's the same thing. I love that should I wish to, should I need to, I can have the best possible words for all occasions – like – like, words for love. If I want to, I can tell you . . .

> Sir, I love you more than words can wield the matter;
> Dearer than eyesight, space and liberty:
> Beyond what can be valued, rich or rare:
> No less than life, with grace, health, beauty, honour;
> As much as child e'er loved, or father found;
> A love that makes breath poor and speech unable,
> Beyond all manner of so much, I love you.

Words that I have because somebody wrote them and left them for me to find. And let's not get into that stuff about Shakespeare being a dead white male, so we don't get to play with his stuff – his words aren't male or white, or dead. He's not for everyone, but he does it for me. In the play it's a bit oversold because she's lying – one of the ugly sisters in *King Lear*: Regan, Goneril, Goneril, Regan . . . they're always together . . . you're never sure which is which . . . it's like Ant and Dec . . .

The point is, I get to have those words, I get to have the music of them in me, to make me a different shape, to give to other people and be music in them, and I love that. And words aren't just things to love, they can give you a way of being alive. Being with words, working with words, it's like being in love. It's a way of being wide-eyed, open-mouthed, like a lover . . .

> It adds a precious seeing to the eye;
> A lover's eyes will gaze an eagle blind;
> A lover's ear will hear the lowest sound,
> When the suspicious head of theft is stopp'd:
> Love's feeling is more soft and sensible
> Than are the tender horns of cockled snails . . .

I get to live there. Because of my job. An accident of employment.

I couldn't be like that all the time – I'd get nosebleeds in shops – but to the best of my ability I can visit. And when I first read that, when I first heard that, I knew *I want that* – and I have it. Because someone wrote it and left it for me to find. I have it. You have it. We have it. And the only way I can lose it is if you steal my education, steal my time, steal my quality of life so that it pains me to wake – because that stuff will wake you.

But I don't think you'll let that happen. Because you're here. We've just spent all this time together with nothing but us and words – who knew you could still do that? People ask me why I do this show – you're a writer, you should just write. Well, I do it so I can reach this point and I can say . . . Don't let anyone give you toothache unless you need it – don't let anyone steal your delight, not even yourself. The words are yours – for wishes, dreams, hopes, jokes, news, gossip, poems, stories, swearing – I haven't sworn in all this, but I could. They can be good words. Strong words.

But there's not a word we have that's weak – and every one of them for nothing but our use – without us they fade, without them we are nameless, we are silence, we are the lies and blurs and slogans of other people's minds – when there shouldn't be a beauty we can't sing, there shouldn't be a love we can't declare, there shouldn't be a truth, a hope, a justice, a new reality we can't name and start to make with words. They give us the no and yes of everything, immortality in a mark, a breath. And if you've ever been alone, if you've ever been confined, if you've ever been frightened like a child, then they will hide you. They will save you. And they can, they always can and always will, keep safe your joys and lift you *Up to the Love* of your own life and this world and any other you wish to make. They will light you, no matter where you have to go. If you let them, they will make you shine.

Acknowledgements

'Does That Make Sense?' was first published in *The Cambridge Companion to Creative Writing,* edited by David Morley and Philip Neilsen.

All blogs first appeared at www.guardian.co.uk in the Guardian Online, some have been slightly altered for this edition. All other pieces have appeared on A.L. Kennedy's website www.a-l-kennedy.co.uk and/or have been performed at various festivals nationally and internationally.

INDEX

The following index is in no way exhaustive and may simply provide a sobering commentary on the author's life.